HOME® MAGAZINE'S

How Your House Works

Home® Magazine's
How Your House Works

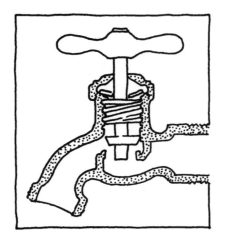

Don Vandervort

BALLANTINE BOOKS

NEW YORK

To Bobbi, Gabe, and Kit

Special kudos to my creative teammates, Marsha Boman and Harry Kerker.
Many thanks to Elizabeth Zack and Joëlle Delbourgo at Ballantine Books; Gale Steves and
Linda Lentz at HOME® Magazine; and Lowenstein Associates. Thanks also to Philip Langdon
for contributing to the section on architectural style and to one of his resources, *Virginia
and Lee McAlester's Field Guide to American Houses*; and architect David Vandervort for his
home plans. In addition, thanks to Kathleen Blease
for her copy editing and Robin Ireland for assisting production.
Last but not least, thank you for buying this book.

— Don Vandervort

Illustrated by Marsha Boman

Designed by Harry Kerker, Kerker Kommunications, Inc.

Copyright © 1995 by Don Vandervort

LIBRARY OF CONGRESS CATALOGING-IN-PUBLICATION DATA

Vandervort, Donald W.
   Home Magazine's how your house works/by Don Vandervort.
      p. cm.
   Includes index.
   ISBN 0-345-38178-5
     1. Dwellings—Maintenance and repair. I. Home magazine.
   II. Title: How your house works.
TH4817.V36 1995   95-995
643'.7—dc20   CIP

MANUFACTURED IN THE UNITED STATES OF AMERICA

First Edition: September 1995

10 9 8 7 6 5 4 3 2 1

TABLE OF CONTENTS

CHAPTER SEVEN:

Architectural Style

CHAPTER EIGHT:

Home Design Basics

CHAPTER NINE:

Home Tools and Materials

Index

A House Revealed

If a pipe were to burst, would you be able to find the shutoff valve before you were ankle-deep in water? Do you know how electricity is routed from the utility pole to the toaster in your kitchen? Can you make intelligent choices about home materials, such as lighting, roofing, and flooring? Can you identify the architectural style of your home?

If you answer no to any of these questions, *How Your House Works* will be an invaluable resource for you. This book lifts the roof and strips the walls to reveal the inner workings of a house, demystifying the many parts, materials and systems one by one.

A house can be bewildering—a complex assemblage of parts designed to address specific needs. Its chief purpose is to provide shelter, but we also expect our homes today to be energy efficient, to be easy to maintain, and to be comfortable. In addition, we want our houses to represent our style favorably to our friends and neighbors and to return solid value when sold.

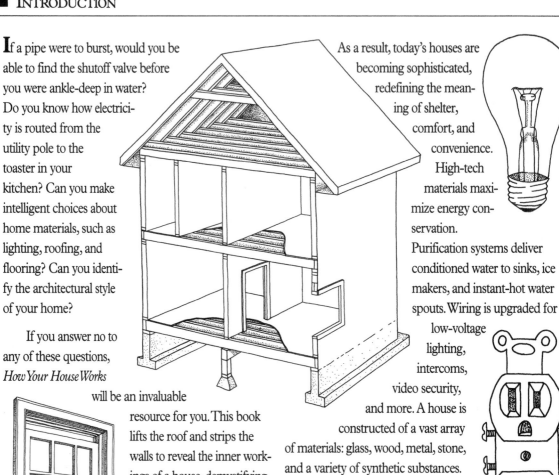

As a result, today's houses are becoming sophisticated, redefining the meaning of shelter, comfort, and convenience. High-tech materials maximize energy conservation. Purification systems deliver conditioned water to sinks, ice makers, and instant-hot water spouts. Wiring is upgraded for low-voltage lighting, intercoms, video security, and more. A house is constructed of a vast array of materials: glass, wood, metal, stone, and a variety of synthetic substances.

Because your house is probably your largest single investment—and because it's where you spend a great deal of your time—it makes sense to be familiar with it and comfortable with basic building terminology. By understanding the inner workings of your home, you can make informed decisions when hiring repair people, handling basic maintenance chores, and buying home improvement products. Knowing how walls and ceilings are constructed, for example, will help

The planning that goes into a house is also discussed. Beginning on page 180, you can trace the roots of your house's overall design. If you're looking to do some remodeling, you will find information on how to read architectural plans and an overview of other basic home-planning information. Toward the end of the book, you'll find helpful hints on basic household tools and a resource guide for purchasing building products and materials.

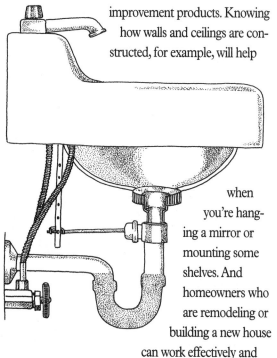

when you're hanging a mirror or mounting some shelves. And homeowners who are remodeling or building a new house can work effectively and intelligently with architects, designers, and builders once they have a clear understanding of trade jargon and your house's makeup.

How Your House Works begins with chapters on the major mechanical systems: electrical, heating/air conditioning/ventilation, and plumbing. Starting on page 104, it deals with the structure: first the framing, then the roof, walls, windows, doors, and other elements that make up the shell. On page 158, you'll find a discussion of a home's interiors, a look at the various surfaces and details, from walls to countertops.

If you're a homeowner, let this book be your primer. If you're an architect, designer, or contractor, use it as a visual glossary and reference for material choices—from types of energy-saving glazing to the working parts of faucets. But if you simply have an inquiring mind, let it take you on a journey into the walls, beneath the floors, and through the systems of houses, showing you how your house works.

Electrical Systems

Electricity is a wonder. Little more than a century ago, Alexander Graham Bell, Guglielmo Marconi, and Thomas Edison captured this force that is present in all matter and put it to work. Now electricity zings through wires to power the many conveniences that make our lives comfortable. It warms and lights our homes and enables phones, faxes, radios, televisions, stereos, security systems, and more.

This chapter explains how electricity is delivered, measured, routed, and controlled, and points out the basic components of today's electrical systems.

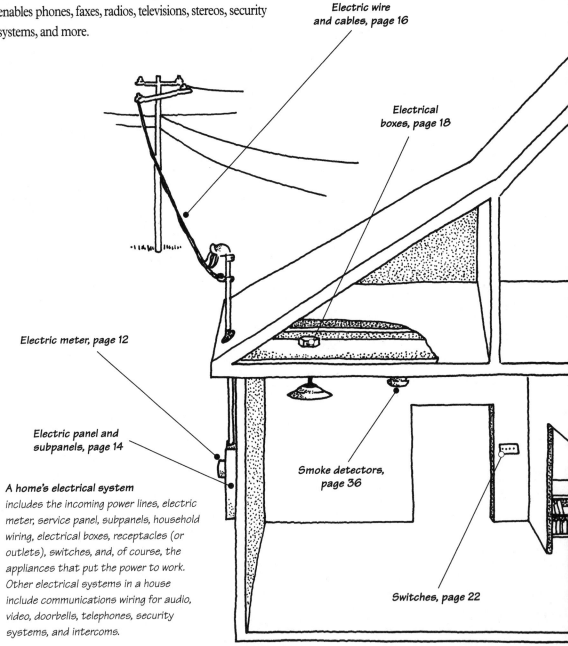

Electric wire
and cables, page 16

Electrical
boxes, page 18

Electric meter, page 12

Electric panel and
subpanels, page 14

Smoke detectors,
page 36

Switches, page 22

A home's electrical system
includes the incoming power lines, electric meter, service panel, subpanels, household wiring, electrical boxes, receptacles (or outlets), switches, and, of course, the appliances that put the power to work. Other electrical systems in a house include communications wiring for audio, video, doorbells, telephones, security systems, and intercoms.

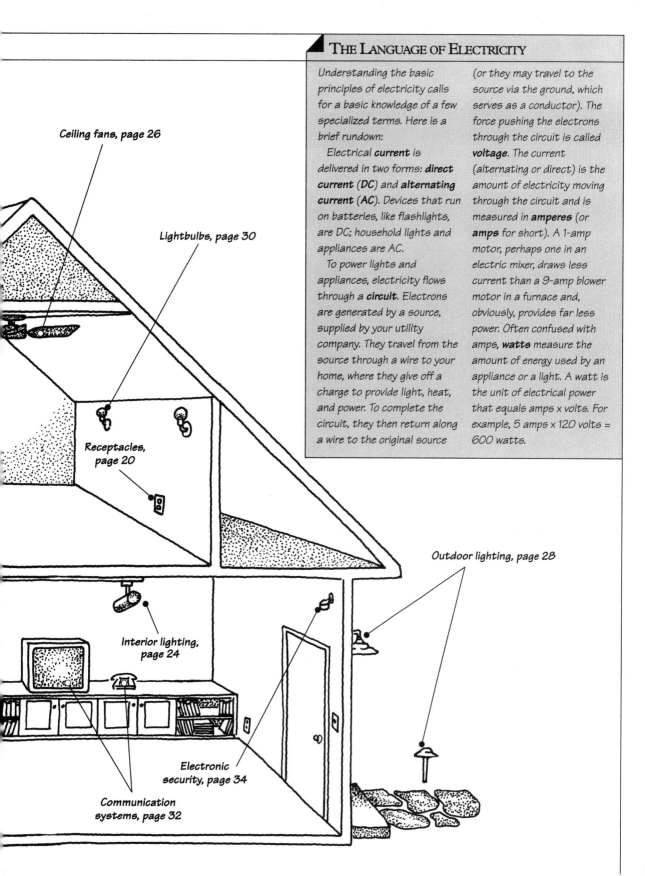

Ceiling fans, page 26

Lightbulbs, page 30

Receptacles, page 20

Outdoor lighting, page 28

Interior lighting, page 24

Electronic security, page 34

Communication systems, page 32

THE LANGUAGE OF ELECTRICITY

Understanding the basic principles of electricity calls for a basic knowledge of a few specialized terms. Here is a brief rundown:

Electrical **current** is delivered in two forms: **direct current (DC)** and **alternating current (AC)**. Devices that run on batteries, like flashlights, are DC; household lights and appliances are AC.

To power lights and appliances, electricity flows through a **circuit**. Electrons are generated by a source, supplied by your utility company. They travel from the source through a wire to your home, where they give off a charge to provide light, heat, and power. To complete the circuit, they then return along a wire to the original source (or they may travel to the source via the ground, which serves as a conductor). The force pushing the electrons through the circuit is called **voltage**. The current (alternating or direct) is the amount of electricity moving through the circuit and is measured in **amperes** (or **amps** for short). A 1-amp motor, perhaps one in an electric mixer, draws less current than a 9-amp blower motor in a furnace and, obviously, provides far less power. Often confused with amps, **watts** measure the amount of energy used by an appliance or a light. A watt is the unit of electrical power that equals amps x volts. For example, 5 amps x 120 volts = 600 watts.

The utility company's electrical lines may enter a house overhead from a power pole or underground from a buried pipe called a *conduit*. Normally, where these lines enter your house, you'll find an electric meter mounted on the wall. This meter looks like a large glass jar with wheels and dials inside. It's one part of your house you don't own; the power company owns it and uses it to measure your family's electrical consumption each month.

Inside the electric meter is a small motor that drives a series of four or five dials when electricity is consumed at your home. These dials measure *kilowatt hours*, the units of electricity for which you're billed.

A kilowatt hour—1,000 watt hours—is the amount of energy required to light ten 100 watt lightbulbs for one hour.

Each month, a utility company representative records the dial readings. The previous month's reading is subtracted from the current month's to come up with the usage that appears on your bill. If you know how to read an electric meter, you can subtract the previous month's reading from the current month's to track actual energy usage and the accuracy of your bills.

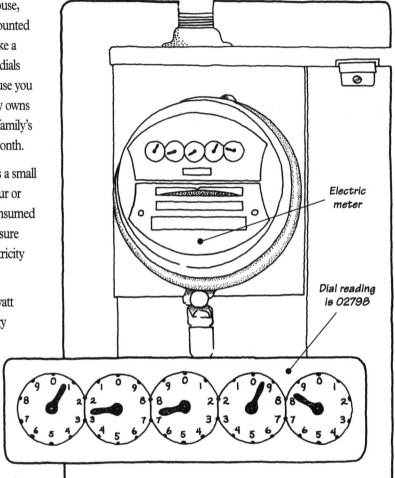

Electric meter

Dial reading is 02798

Read an electric meter *from right to left, jotting down the number each pointer has passed or is pointing to. Note that the numbers circle the dials alternately clockwise and counterclockwise. If the dial hasn't quite reached a certain number, record the next lowest digit. If you're not sure whether or not the dial has passed a certain number, study the one to its right to see if it has passed zero. Write the numbers down in the same order that you take them—from right to left— but read the result from left to right. The meter shown would read 02798.*

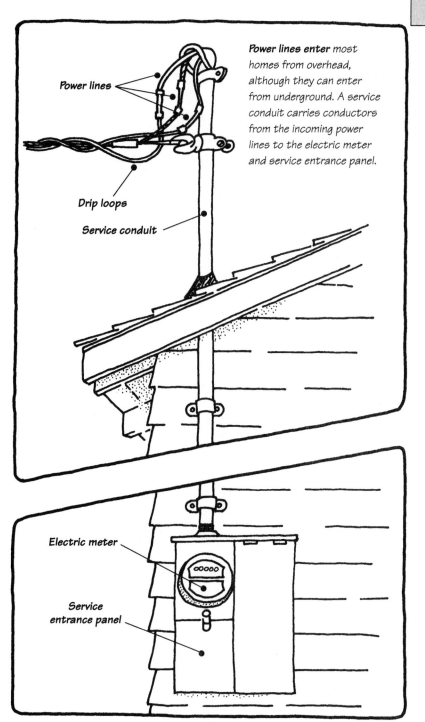

Power lines

Drip loops

Service conduit

Power lines enter most homes from overhead, although they can enter from underground. A service conduit carries conductors from the incoming power lines to the electric meter and service entrance panel.

Electric meter

Service entrance panel

Once electricity is carried beyond the meter, it is distributed to lights, receptacles, and appliances throughout the house by several circuits. The incoming power line enters the house at the service entrance panel, or *main panel*, where it is sectioned off into main dual circuits that service outlets and appliances.

Main panels come in many sizes and configurations. A panel can be mounted on the outside of the house, separate from or combined with the meter, or on an inside wall behind or next to the meter.

The main panel includes a mechanical device for disconnecting the house's electrical circuits from the incoming power. In most contemporary systems, this device is a *circuit breaker*. (Older types of disconnect systems utilize levers and fuses—you pull down on a lever or pull out a fuse block to shut off the power to the house circuits.) A circuit breaker is a switch that may be shut off manually or tripped automatically by a failure in the electrical system, usually an overload that could cause the wires to heat up or even catch fire.

The maximum amperage the main panel can deliver at one time is marked on the main breaker. Although a 100-amp main may be sufficient to handle all of a small home's electrical needs, most new homes feature a 150- to 200-amp capacity. Main panels that deliver 60 amps or less are undersized for contemporary needs.

Every circuit breaker is rated for the type of wire and amount of current required by its circuit. The most typical capacities for lights and receptacles are 20 and 15-amps, respectively. Standard circuit breakers for 120-amp circuits take one slot; breakers for 240-amp circuits take two. Some manufacturers make extra-thin circuit breakers that take only half the space of standard breakers but handle the same circuit loads.

Larger-capacity circuit breakers are used for electric stoves, water heaters, clothes dryers, air conditioners, and similar appliances that draw a lot of power. Larger breakers may also connect secondary panels, called *subpanels*, that have their own set of circuit breakers leading to household circuits. Subpanels may be located in a completely different part of the house.

Outdoor, kitchen, and bathroom receptacles should be protected by a special *ground-fault circuit interrupter* (GFCI) circuit breaker to guard against electrocution. Because it is highly sensitive to any short, this type of breaker may need resetting more frequently than standard breakers and should be tested periodically by the homeowner by turning the circuit breaker off, then on.

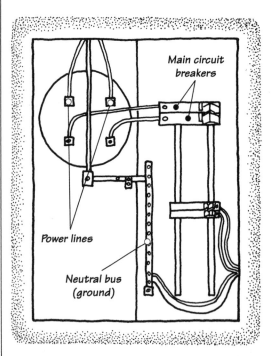

Main circuit breakers

Power lines

Neutral bus (ground)

Behind the cover of the main panel, power lines connect to the two top lugs of the meter mount. Electricity runs from the top lugs through the meter to the bottom lugs to which the main circuit breaker is connected. The main circuit breakers then deliver electricity to the two bus bars, which, in turn, pass it along to the secondary circuit breakers. All circuits are connected to a ground (a conductor that is driven into the earth). Danger: Do not remove cover of main panel.

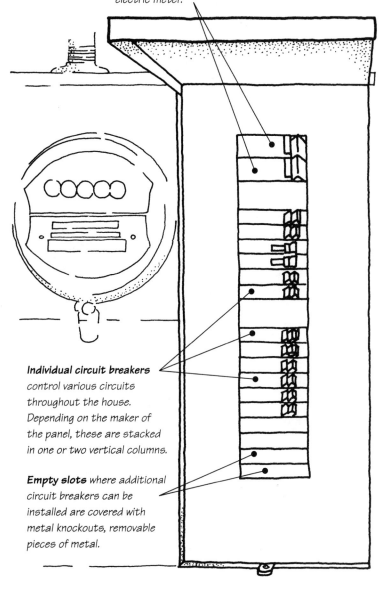

The main circuit breakers are usually at the top of the main panel. These breakers shut off all the electricity to the house, but they do not shut off the electricity that runs to the breakers from the electric meter.

Individual circuit breakers control various circuits throughout the house. Depending on the maker of the panel, these are stacked in one or two vertical columns.

Empty slots where additional circuit breakers can be installed are covered with metal knockouts, removable pieces of metal.

Nearly everyone has experienced a power failure. When this happens, first determine if the problem lies in your house's system or if it is a utility company outage. If the whole house is out and it looks like your neighbors have lost power too, call the utility company. If any of your home's electrical power is working—the lights are on in another room, for example—the problem is with your home's own electrical system.

Generally, the problem is caused by an overloaded circuit, a short circuit, or loose wiring. If the outage occurs when a hair dryer, electric heater, or some other device that draws a lot of current is being used, it is probably the result of a simple overload. If the circuit is overloaded, a circuit breaker should trip or a fuse should blow. Check the subpanel or main panel that serves the circuit. Reset any breaker that is off, or replace any expired fuse.

If the problem isn't that simple, turn off or unplug everything from the troubled circuit, then reset the breaker or replace the fuse. If the circuit blows immediately, there is probably a charred wire or defective device in the circuit that will require replacement by an electrician. If it doesn't blow, turn lights back on and plug in appliances one by one to check for the overload or short circuit. If the lights or receptacles still don't work, there is probably a short circuit caused by a loose wire somewhere; in this case, too, call an electrician.

Electrical Systems

Wires and cables of various sizes bring electricity to a house and route it to all the lights, switches, receptacles, and electrical appliances. Generally speaking, large cables deliver electricity to the house and smaller cables and wires distribute it throughout.

Nearly all household wire is copper. A rubber, plastic, or paperlike coating, called *insulation*, serves as a barrier to keep the electrical charge (and heat) where it belongs—in the wire.

"Wire" is a comprehensive term commonly used to refer to all types of cable and wire. Technically, an individual wire is called a *single conductor*; several single conductors twisted together or combined together in a sheath make a *cable*.

Just as highways can handle more cars than small streets, large conductors can handle more electricity than small ones. The diameter of a metal conductor is indicated by an AWG (American Wire Gauge) number: the smaller the number, the larger the wire. Most household lighting and receptacle circuits are wired with AWG 14 or AWG 12 conductors.

In addition to standard electrical wire, a house has several other types of wire needed for the telephone, cable television, stereo speakers, and so on. Most of these wires do not carry a dangerous electrical current because they operate on very low voltage or carry only sound or picture signals, not electrical power.

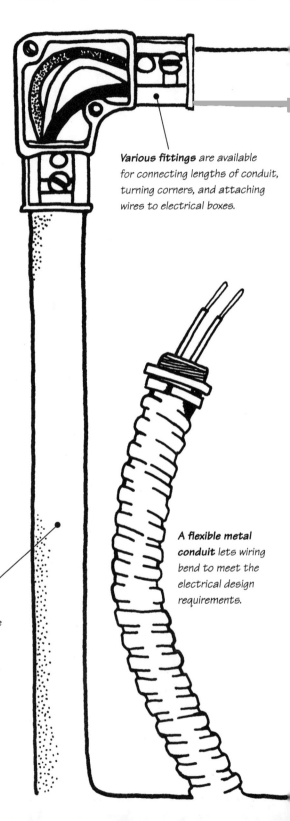

Various fittings are available for connecting lengths of conduit, turning corners, and attaching wires to electrical boxes.

A flexible metal conduit lets wiring bend to meet the electrical design requirements.

A rigid conduit protects wire from damage or, if outdoors, weather conditions. Where wiring is exposed, such as in a basement area, conductors run through this steel or plastic (PVC) tube. If you need to add wire, you can pull it through the conduit that provides a sort of raceway through a house. For home use, ½-inch and ¾-inch-diameter are the most common sizes.

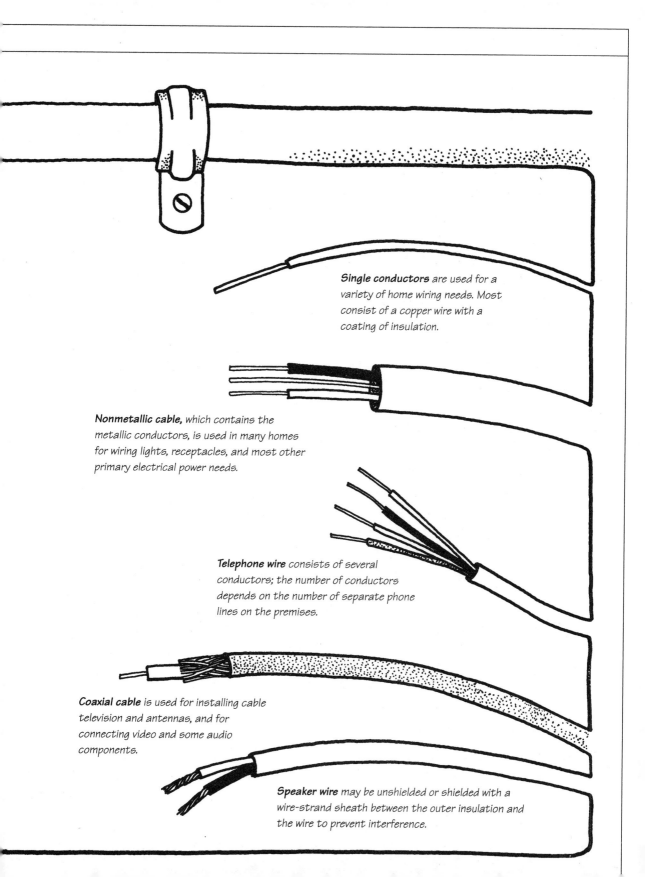

Single conductors are used for a variety of home wiring needs. Most consist of a copper wire with a coating of insulation.

Nonmetallic cable, which contains the metallic conductors, is used in many homes for wiring lights, receptacles, and most other primary electrical power needs.

Telephone wire consists of several conductors; the number of conductors depends on the number of separate phone lines on the premises.

Coaxial cable is used for installing cable television and antennas, and for connecting video and some audio components.

Speaker wire may be unshielded or shielded with a wire-strand sheath between the outer insulation and the wire to prevent interference.

Every permanent light fixture, switch, and receptacle mounts inside an electrical box that's usually set into the wall, the ceiling, or, in some cases, the floor. These boxes provide support for the fixture or switch and a safe container for electrical connections.

Electrical boxes are made of plastic or galvanized steel. Only metal boxes are used in metal conduit systems since their bodies are part of the electrical grounding that is essential to a safe system. But either steel or plastic varieties may be used with systems that use non-metallic cable, if allowed by electrical regulations.

In the building trade, boxes are termed *utility, outlet,* or *switch boxes,* depending on their size and shape. A variety of faceplates, adapters, and extension rings make them easy to modify for any of these uses.

A *nail-on box* is made to be nailed onto wall studs during construction; generally it includes a pair of nails that protrude from one side. A *cut-in* box has special flanges that allow it to be retrofitted into an existing wall. A *pancake* box, almost as flat as its name implies, may be mounted directly onto a ceiling or wall or attached to a hanger bar.

Boxes are also referred to by the number of receptacles or switches they can receive. A *two-gang* box is designed for two side-by-side devices, a *three-gang* box for three, and so on.

Nail-on round box

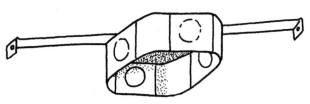

Metal ceiling box with hanger

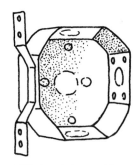

Side bracket round box

Pancake box

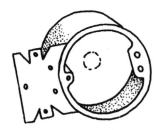

Front bracket round box

Cut-in ceiling box with spring ears

Ceiling, junction, or utility boxes, typically round or octagonal, can be used at wire junctions or for mounting light fixtures. Because they're often used for light fixtures, some types come with adjustable mounting hangers that are nailed to ceiling joists.

Front bracket two-gang box

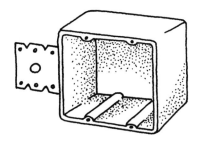

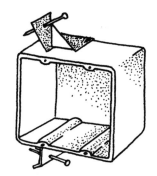

Side bracket two-gang box

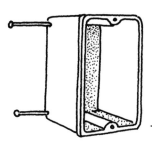

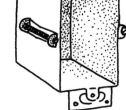

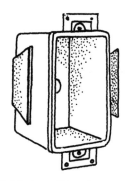

Nail-on single gang box   **Cut-in box with side clamps**   **Cut-in box with spring ears**

Wall, switch, or handy boxes, usually square or rectangular, hold light switches and receptacles. They are referred to as single, two-gang, three-gang, and so on, depending upon how many switches or receptacles they can hold. Some have nail-on brackets; cut-in types are made for retrofitting in existing walls.

Weatherproof switch box

Weatherproof receptical box

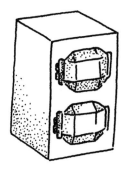

Outdoor boxes are watertight and are meant to be used with special receptacle or switch covers that keep out moisture. A rubber or foam gasket is used to seal the joint between the cover and the box.

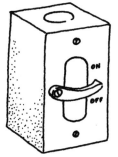

Electrical Systems

Receptacles, sometimes called outlets, provide a place to plug in lamps, toasters, and other electrical appliances that are not "hard wired"—that is, permanently wired to the electrical system.

In the United States, most standard home electrical circuits are on a 120-volt line. Conventional receptacles have two places to plug in devices and so are called *duplex receptacles*. As shown in the illustration at right, contemporary receptacles include a half-round hole that receives the grounding plug on an electrical cord. A wire leads from this hole to the system's ground to provide protection against shock when an appliance is plugged into it.

Some receptacles in older homes don't have grounding plugs; they have only the paired slots. If your home's receptacles are like these, you've probably discovered grounding adapters, those little plugs that convert the end of a three-pronged plug to two-pronged. If you use one of these, be sure to attach the adapter's grounding metal flange to the wall receptacle's center screw, which must be grounded. Otherwise, you'll defeat your electrical system's safety grounding.

Outdoor receptacles are mounted with special covers that seal out the weather. (Standard types are not safe for outdoor use.)

Air conditioner

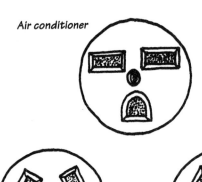

Dryer

Range

Receptacles for 240-volt appliances, such as clothes dryers, air conditioners, and electric ranges, use receptacles with plug configurations that are different from those on standard receptacles. (Never try to force an electrical cord's plug into a receptacle that doesn't match.)

Reset button

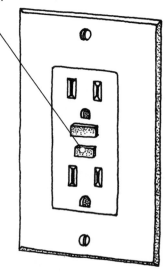

A ground-fault circuit interrupter, also called a GFI or GFCI, shuts off a circuit instantly if it senses a hazardous short or overload. The receptacle type looks like a regular receptacle except it has a reset button in the middle. In new construction, these are usually required in bathrooms, in kitchens, and outdoors. Often a GFCI is the first receptacle mounted along a circuit—between the electrical panel and other receptacles on the same circuit—so it will automatically protect the others on the same line.

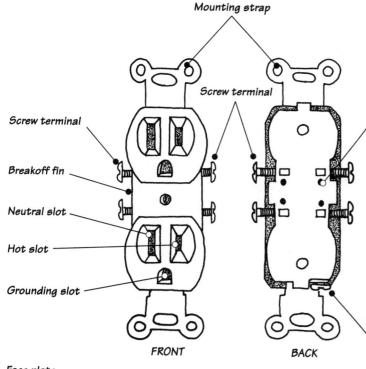

Mounting strap

Screw terminal

Push-in terminal

Screw terminal

Breakoff fin

Neutral slot

Hot slot

Grounding slot

Green grounding terminal

FRONT

BACK

A conventional duplex receptacle offers two places for plugging in appliances. For 120-volt circuits, duplex receptacles mount into electrical boxes recessed into walls. Receptacles have a green grounding screw that should be connected to the house ground—a metal conduit or a green wire.

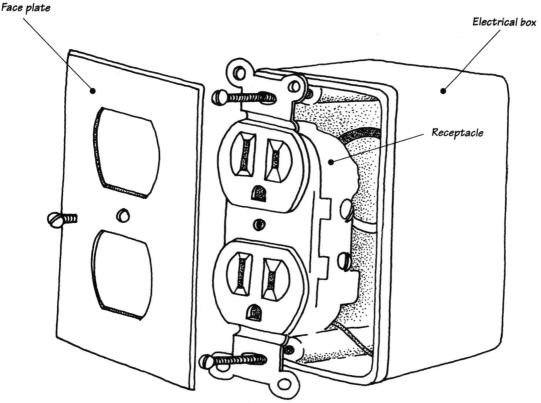

Face plate

Electrical box

Receptacle

Electrical Systems

Switches open and close electrical circuits, allowing power to flow through lights and appliances or cutting it off. The most familiar of these, the common light switch, is referred to by hardware dealers and electricians as a *single-pole switch*. A switch that operates lights from two locations—the ends of a hallway, for example—is called a *three-way switch*.

In recent years, there has been something of a design renaissance in light switches. New switches offer a wide range of features, such as full-range dimming, a delayed fade from on to off, dimmers that remember a range of different settings, switches that automatically turn on lights when a person enters a room, central lighting controls that operate lights anywhere in the house, and even hand-held infrared remotes.

Some switches are operated with keys, timers, or photoelectric eyes that sense daylight. Some switches are paired up with receptacles (a *combination switch*) and others have their own indicator that lights when the switch is on. Outdoor switches are mounted in a special box, and operated with a lever. Special dimmers are needed for fluorescent and neon lights and loads greater than 1,000 watts.

Switches should match the amp and voltage ratings for the circuit. If your home has aluminum wiring, the switches should be designated CU-AL for compatibility.

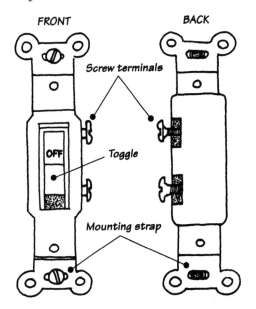

FRONT   BACK

Screw terminals

Toggle

Mounting strap

A single-pole light switch is the simplest and most common type. Flipping up this lever completes the circuit, turning on lights or appliances, while flipping it down breaks the circuit, turning them off. A single-pole switch has two brass terminal screws on the side. (The number of terminal screws identifies the type of switch.)

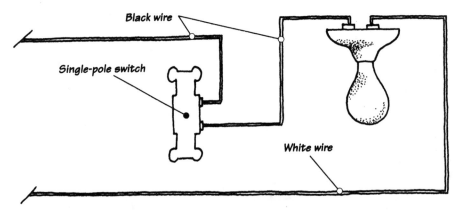

Black wire

Single-pole switch

White wire

A switch opens and closes a circuit, allowing current to flow through lights and electrical appliances.

A dimmer controls the amount of electricity that flows to a fixture. You can buy types operated with a toggle, a dial, a slide, or electronic buttons.

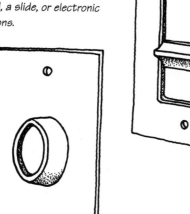

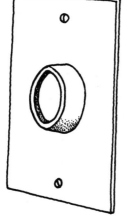

A four-way switch is combined with three-way switches to control lights from three or more different locations. It has four terminal screws, may have a green grounding screw, and has no markings on the toggle.

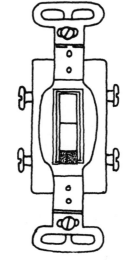

Two three-way switches are used to control a light from two locations, such as at each end of a hallway or stairwell. A three-way switch has three terminal screws, may have a green grounding screw, and has no "on" or "off" markings on the toggle.

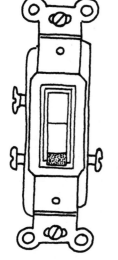

Three-way switches

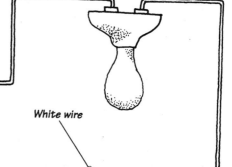

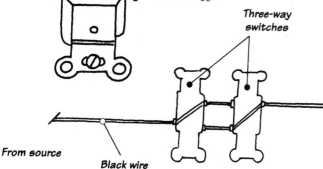

White wire

From source

Black wire

Electrical Systems

Electric lighting is a twentieth-century convenience that's easy to take for granted—until the power goes out. There is nothing like the pitch dark to bring home just how much we rely on light. Thanks to lighting, we can carry on work, reading, eating, and the many other activities of home life long after the sun has set.

Although some older homes still have single light fixtures plunked squarely in the center of each room's ceiling, many of today's houses employ a much more sophisticated lighting scheme. A variety of fixtures, thoughtfully placed, add to the function, comfort, beauty, and drama of a house.

Experts group lighting types into three categories: general, task, and accent. General, or *ambient*, lighting provides overall illumination by way of ceiling or wall-mounted fixtures, chandeliers, recessed lights, or track lights. Task lighting is more specific, supplying direct light for reading, sewing, and cooking. Accent lighting can add drama by spotlighting objects or highlighting interesting aspects of a house.

Some of the main types of lighting fixtures are shown here. Depending on the particular varieties, they may use standard incandescent bulbs, fluorescents, or low-voltage lamps. See page 30 for more information about bulbs.

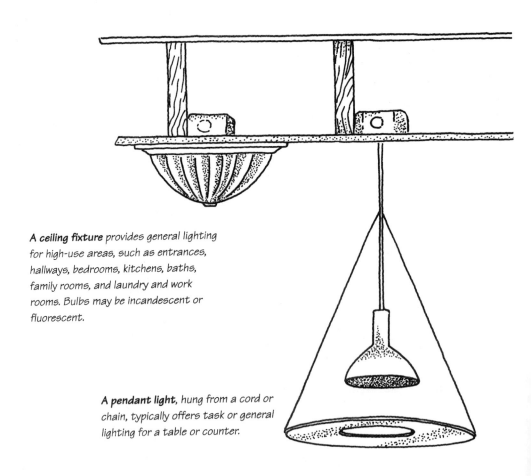

A **ceiling fixture** provides general lighting
for high-use areas, such as entrances,
hallways, bedrooms, kitchens, baths,
family rooms, and laundry and work
rooms. Bulbs may be incandescent or
fluorescent.

A **pendant light**, hung from a cord or
chain, typically offers task or general
lighting for a table or counter.

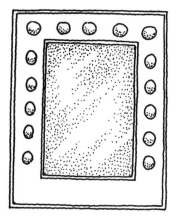

Strip lighting provides task lighting in the bathroom or at a vanity.

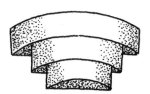

Wall-mounted fixtures can supply general lighting, provide dramatic accents, or serve as task lighting.

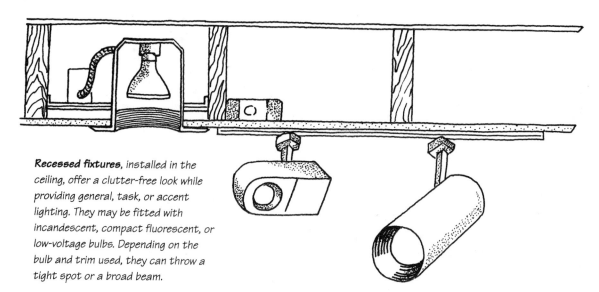

Recessed fixtures, installed in the ceiling, offer a clutter-free look while providing general, task, or accent lighting. They may be fitted with incandescent, compact fluorescent, or low-voltage bulbs. Depending on the bulb and trim used, they can throw a tight spot or a broad beam.

Track lighting is very flexible. Individual fixtures are fitted onto a surface-mounted or suspended track and may be adjusted to throw light in any direction. For accent lighting, a tight beam can be directed at an object. For indirect, ambient lighting, beams can be bounced off walls or ceilings.

Electrical Systems

One of the most sensible solutions to home comfort has been helping to heat and cool residences for more than a hundred years: the ceiling fan. By stirring up breezes in the summer and forcing warm air downward in the winter, ceiling fans effectively reduce the demand on conventional heating and cooling systems. And they do it with charm.

Because of the slight breeze it creates, a fan makes a room more comfortable at higher temperatures during the summer; the room's thermostat can be set five to seven degrees higher. And in the winter, a fan recirculates rising warm air that would otherwise collect—and be wasted—at the ceiling.

The amount of air a fan moves depends on its construction and placement. The number, length, and pitch of the blades are important, as is the fan's distance from the ceiling and the revolutions per minute (rpm) delivered by the fan's motor.

Most fans have three to five blades made from solid wood, plywood, or veneered composite board and given any one of several finishes. Fans typically are from 30 to 60 inches in diameter.

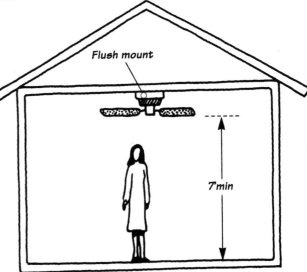

A fan's location is usually in the center of a room, where it will have the greatest effect. Blade tips must be at least 2 feet from walls or sloped ceilings. They may be mounted flush or suspended from a droprod. They should never be mounted lower than 7 feet from the floor.

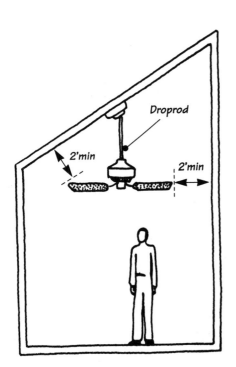

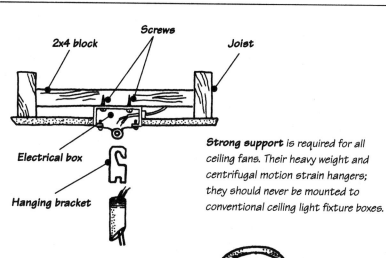

2x4 block **Screws** **Joist**

Electrical box

Hanging bracket

Strong support is required for all ceiling fans. Their heavy weight and centrifugal motion strain hangers; they should never be mounted to conventional ceiling light fixture boxes.

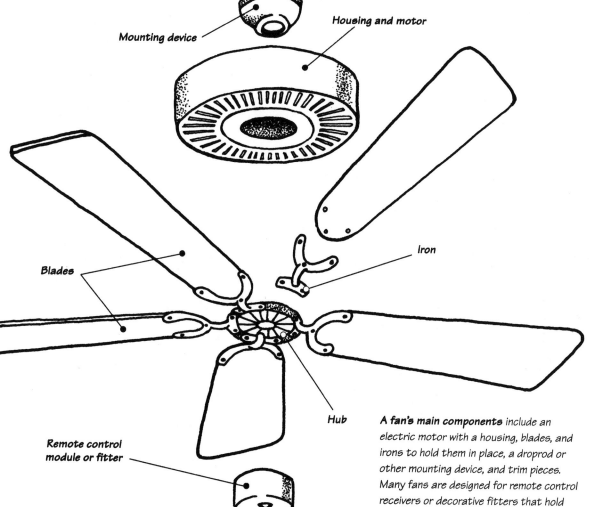

Mounting device

Housing and motor

Iron

Blades

Hub

Remote control module or fitter

A fan's main components include an electric motor with a housing, blades, and irons to hold them in place, a droprod or other mounting device, and trim pieces. Many fans are designed for remote control receivers or decorative fitters that hold lamps beneath the blades. Some fans feature a wall-mounted or remote control.

Electrical Systems

Outdoor lighting beautifies gardens, lengthens the hours outdoor areas may be used, and provides safety and security. It is used to provide general illumination, to light walkways, house numbers, and the like, and to create dramatic accents.

There are several types of outdoor fixtures, each with specific purposes. Spots and floods highlight trees and walls. Spread fixtures spill low-level light over plants and walkways. Short, decorative post lights, called *bollards*, provide ambient light. Deck and patio lights tuck under railings, steps, or benches. Waterproof fixtures highlight pools and fountains.

Although house lights, post lights, and some spots and floods are powered by standard 120-volt electrical current, most decorative outdoor lighting systems are low-voltage. With these, a transformer steps down the household current to a much safer 12-volt system. (Standard 120-volt electrical current is especially dangerous to work with where it may come in contact with the ground.) *Always shut off the power or unplug any outdoor lighting system before doing any work on it.*

Low-voltage wiring, lamps, and holders are smaller than incandescent ones and throw brighter, more energy-efficient light. And because low-voltage wiring is relatively safe, it's much easier for do-it-yourselfers to install. Transformers are rated from about 25 to 300 watts; the total number of lights they power must not exceed their maximum wattage rating.

Programmable timers automatically turn lights on and off at preset times. Other controls use a daylight-sensing photoelectric eye to switch on lights at dusk; motion sensors turn on lights when they detect movement within a certain range.

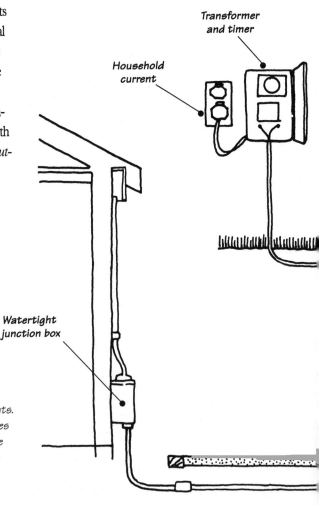

Transformer and timer

Household current

Watertight junction box

Standard 120-volt household current may power some outdoor lights. Watertight junction boxes and conduits isolate the wires from contact with the ground or with moisture.

Typical outdoor fixtures offer general, ambient, accent, and task lighting. Many of these fixtures can serve multiple roles.

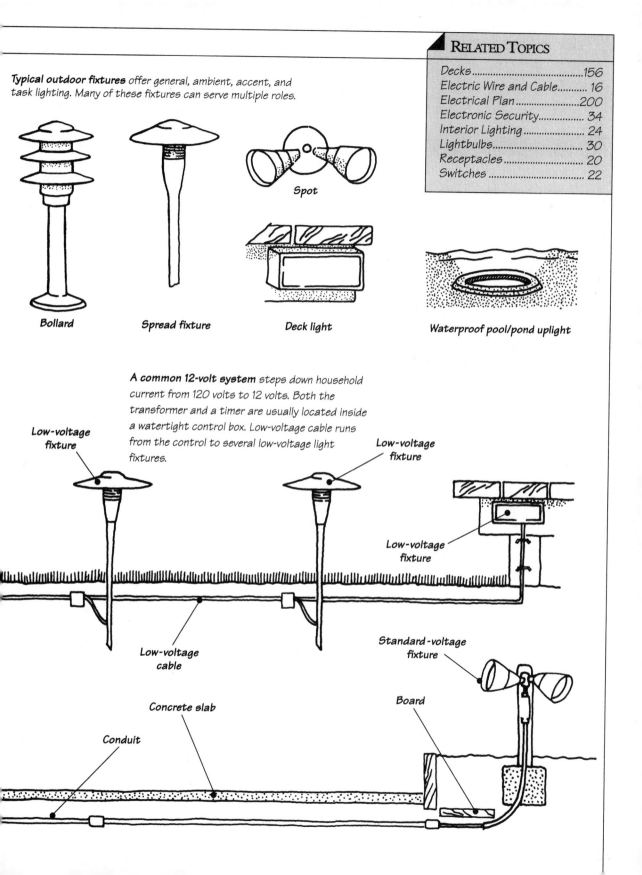

Bollard

Spread fixture

Spot

Deck light

Waterproof pool/pond uplight

A common 12-volt system steps down household current from 120 volts to 12 volts. Both the transformer and a timer are usually located inside a watertight control box. Low-voltage cable runs from the control to several low-voltage light fixtures.

Low-voltage fixture

Low-voltage fixture

Low-voltage fixture

Low-voltage cable

Standard-voltage fixture

Board

Concrete slab

Conduit

Electrical Systems

In 1879 Thomas Edison discovered that running electricity through a thin wire would cause it to glow enough to produce light—and the incandescent lightbulb was born. That thin wire, called a *filament*, soon became the focus of thousands of tests to produce a material that would burn white hot without vaporizing. The earliest bulbs solved the problem with a tiny carbon wire; modern bulbs run electricity through a tungsten filament. To help keep the filament cool, it's placed in a vacuum inside a glass globe and surrounded by inert gases.

Today, several types of bulbs (also called lamps) are available. Energy-efficient models have specialized filaments, as do long-life bulbs. Quartz halogen lamps, most often used in low-voltage fixtures, burn hotter and brighter than do conventional incandescents.

Fluorescents, which have been around since the late 1930s, employ a different technology: they send a spark through a tube coated with phosphors and filled with mercury vapor. Compact fluorescents, a relatively recent development, apply new refinements in fluorescent technology to a bulb type that will fit into conventional incandescent fixtures. Highly efficient, fluorescents produce about four times as much light as do incandescent bulbs of comparable wattage and usually last about twenty times longer.

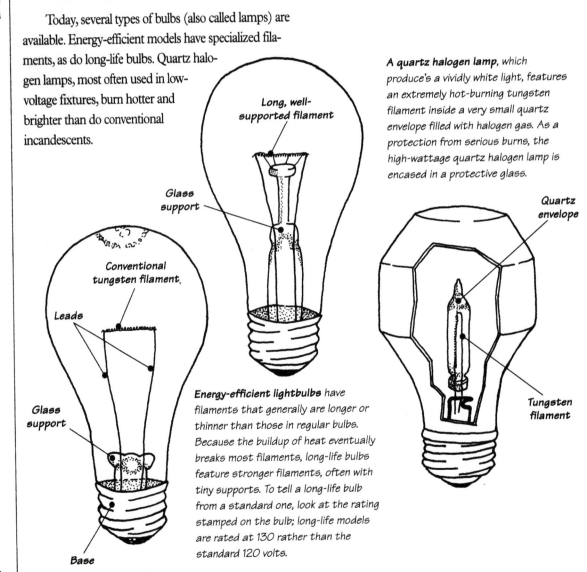

A quartz halogen lamp, which produce's a vividly white light, features an extremely hot-burning tungsten filament inside a very small quartz envelope filled with halogen gas. As a protection from serious burns, the high-wattage quartz halogen lamp is encased in a protective glass.

Long, well-supported filament

Glass support

Conventional tungsten filament

Leads

Glass support

Base

Quartz envelope

Tungsten filament

Energy-efficient lightbulbs have filaments that generally are longer or thinner than those in regular bulbs. Because the buildup of heat eventually breaks most filaments, long-life bulbs feature stronger filaments, often with tiny supports. To tell a long-life bulb from a standard one, look at the rating stamped on the bulb; long-life models are rated at 130 rather than the standard 120 volts.

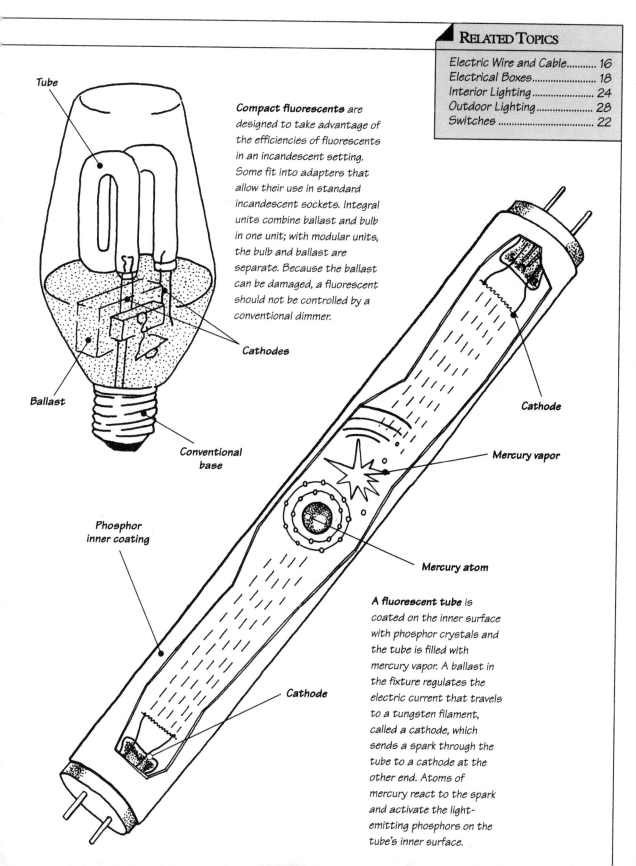

Tube

Compact fluorescents are designed to take advantage of the efficiencies of fluorescents in an incandescent setting. Some fit into adapters that allow their use in standard incandescent sockets. Integral units combine ballast and bulb in one unit; with modular units, the bulb and ballast are separate. Because the ballast can be damaged, a fluorescent should not be controlled by a conventional dimmer.

Cathodes

Ballast

Conventional base

Cathode

Mercury vapor

Phosphor inner coating

Mercury atom

Cathode

A fluorescent tube is coated on the inner surface with phosphor crystals and the tube is filled with mercury vapor. A ballast in the fixture regulates the electric current that travels to a tungsten filament, called a cathode, which sends a spark through the tube to a cathode at the other end. Atoms of mercury react to the spark and activate the light-emitting phosphors on the tube's inner surface.

Electrical Systems

Cable television, multiple phone and fax lines, intercoms, video security, and built-in audio speakers: the world of household communication systems has grown immensely since the basic doorbells and telephone lines of yesteryear.

Most of these systems are quite simple and utilize low-voltage wiring that is ordinarily easy to work with and relatively safe to handle. They are based on the principle that sound and video images may be converted to an electrical current that travels through a wire and converted back to sound or picture at the other end.

A microphone converts sound to electrical impulses, for example, and a speaker turns the impulses back into sound. A television camera changes an image into impulses that are then returned to their image format by a picture tube.

Signals may originate from outside the house, as is the case with the telephone and television. Or communications may take place entirely within the house: intercoms, doorbells, and video monitors, for instance. Regardless, they all work similarly.

An intercom is basically an in-house telephone. A transformer drops standard 120-volt household current to low-voltage power for the system. From the master speaker or control unit, pairs of wires route to each of the substations which, like telephone handsets, contain microphones and speakers.

With a video intercom, both sound and picture are carried over the doorbell-style wire to the master monitor. Image and sound are converted to electrical impulses by the video camera and microphone and sent to the master monitor, where they are then returned to picture and sound.

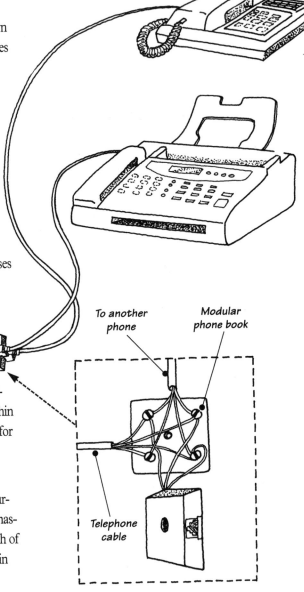

Splitter

To another phone

Modular phone book

Telephone cable

Telephone cable, or bell wire, runs along or through the walls and floors of most homes to connect the phones. This cable contains four color-coded conductors: red, green, yellow, and black. (Newer homes may feature eight-conductor wire.) In a home with only one phone line, all telephones are connected at various outlet boxes, or blocks, to two of these wires, normally the red and green. The remaining wires are reserved for a second telephone, fax, or modem line. In some cases, one may be used to light a dial.

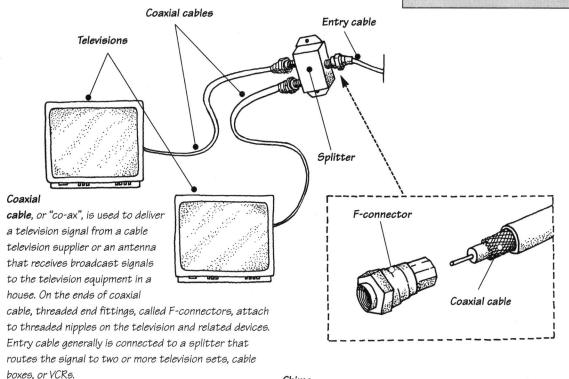

Televisions

Coaxial cables

Entry cable

Splitter

F-connector

Coaxial cable

Coaxial cable, or "co-ax", is used to deliver a television signal from a cable television supplier or an antenna that receives broadcast signals to the television equipment in a house. On the ends of coaxial cable, threaded end fittings, called F-connectors, attach to threaded nipples on the television and related devices. Entry cable generally is connected to a splitter that routes the signal to two or more television sets, cable boxes, or VCRs.

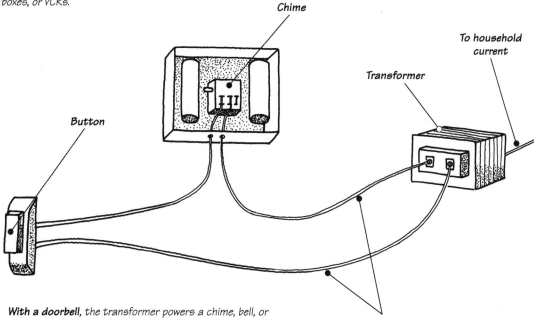

Chime

To household current

Transformer

Button

Low-voltage wires

With a doorbell, the transformer powers a chime, bell, or buzzer; the button completes a circuit that lets the electricity through to sound the bell or buzzer.

With the growing concern over crime, home security systems have come into greater demand. Statistics show that houses protected by such systems are only a third as likely as unprotected houses to be burglarized, and those broken into tend to have much smaller losses.

There are two main types of systems: wired and wireless. All systems consist of sensors placed at strategic locations throughout the house that communicate with a central control unit. The control unit, in turn, is linked to an alarm and, in some cases, to an automatic telephone dialer that can summon help by phone.

A wired system is connected by small, low-voltage wires; because such a system requires routing wire discreetly throughout the house, it's usually installed by an alarm company, although some do-it-yourself models are available.

A wireless model employs tiny radio transmitters that can signal the central control unit when activated. Although it's a bit less reliable than a wired model, it's much easier to install.

All control units have batteries that kick in if there is a power failure or if the wires are cut. Some even have batteries that automatically recharge when the unit is on-line with the household power.

Electronic security systems that connect to automatic dialers are offered by telephone monitoring services that respond to calls. These services can track not only burglaries but medical emergencies and fires.

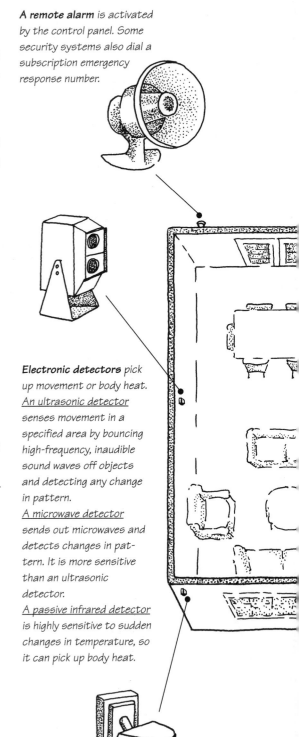

A remote alarm *is activated by the control panel. Some security systems also dial a subscription emergency response number.*

Electronic detectors *pick up movement or body heat.* <u>*An ultrasonic detector*</u> *senses movement in a specified area by bouncing high-frequency, inaudible sound waves off objects and detecting any change in pattern.* <u>*A microwave detector*</u> *sends out microwaves and detects changes in pattern. It is more sensitive than an ultrasonic detector.* <u>*A passive infrared detector*</u> *is highly sensitive to sudden changes in temperature, so it can pick up body heat.*

A glass-breakage detector mounts on a window and is set off by vibration or breakage. A wired window screen, when cut or removed, sets off the alarm.

A mechanical plunger switch is used primarily on steel doors and windows, where a magnetic switch won't work. When the door or window is opened, the plunger pops up and activates the alarm.

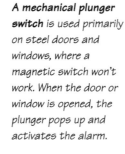

A wired control panel divides a house into zones and is mounted out of sight. It can be disarmed with a keypad or a remote control.

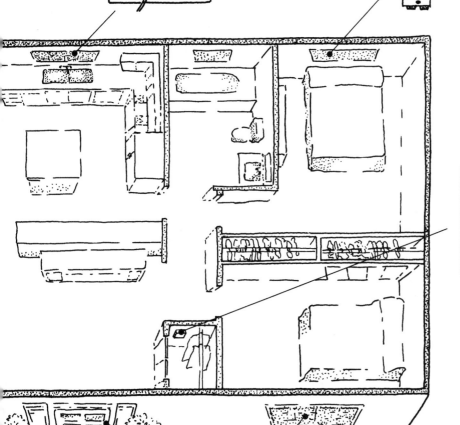

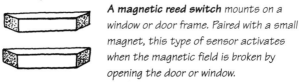

A magnetic reed switch mounts on a window or door frame. Paired with a small magnet, this type of sensor activates when the magnetic field is broken by opening the door or window.

Electrical Systems

A properly working smoke detector doubles the odds of surviving a home fire. A detector stands guard around the clock and when it first senses smoke, sounds a shrill alarm. Because most fatal fires occur during the night, this early warning often buys a family the precious time it takes to escape.

Most smoke detectors are battery powered, but some, particularly those installed during house construction, are wired into a home's electrical system. Most of the ones that run on line voltage (household current) have a battery backup in case a fire knocks out the house's electrical power.

The main problem with battery-powered smoke detectors is that they're often neglected. It's estimated that a third of all smoke detectors have missing or dead batteries. To combat this, all battery-operated detectors are supposed to signal a low battery; newer models won't close if the battery is removed.

Standard smoke detectors work by ionization; some use a photoelectric cell. With ionization, a tiny amount of radioactive material conducts electricity through the air between two electrodes. When smoke upsets the current, the alarm sounds. Photoelectric models use a small beam of light. When smoke causes the light to disperse, the alarm begins to bleat its warning.

Smoke detectors should be located on each level of a house and outside each sleeping area (one hallway detector can serve several bedrooms). Some models sound false alarms when they detect high bathroom humidity or normal levels of smoke from cooking; it's best not to install them within 20 feet of a kitchen, garage, furnace, hot water heater, or within 10 feet of a bathroom. Also avoid drafty locations.

Bedroom

Bedroom | Hall | Bedroom

Living room | Kitchen | Garage

Basement

Mount a detector according to the manufacturer's directions; on the wall or ceiling but not within 4 inches of a corner, where smoke may not collect.

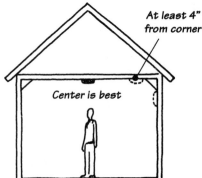

At least 4" from corner

Center is best

A smoke detector's workings include a sensing chamber, an alarm, and a battery or other power source. A test button lets you know if the battery, sensor, and alarm are working properly. Batteries should be replaced at least once a year.

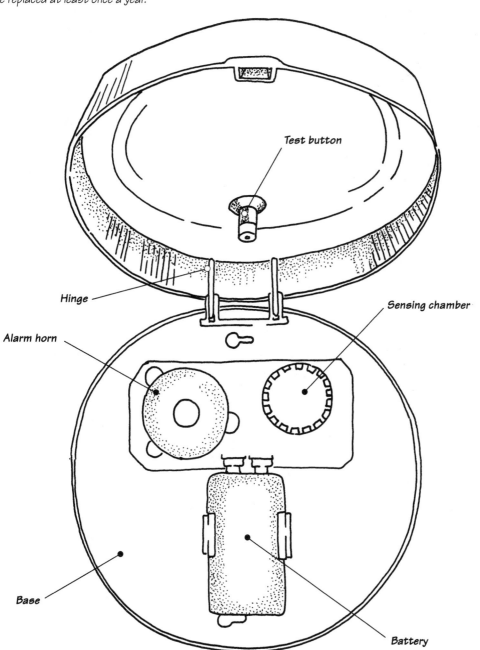

Test button

Hinge

Alarm horn

Sensing chamber

Base

Battery

Comfort Systems

Thanks to modern technology, today's houses have evolved beyond their basic role of providing shelter. They have become total environments that sustain, refresh, and provide us with a high level of healthful comfort. From air conditioners to zone heating systems, a wide variety of devices and systems equip today's homes for these responsibilities.

Before we begin our overview of comfort systems, there are two important facts you should know about air movement. First, air seeks a balance. This means that warm air always moves from a warm place to a colder one, and vice versa; the greater the difference, the faster the air moves. This is how drafts are created indoors. Second, heated air rises. The air in a room tends to stratify unless it's stirred up; warm air gathers near the ceiling, cool air moves toward the floor.

Radiant heat from the sun or from a radiant heater travels in a straight line to warm cooler objects—such as roofs, walls, even people—rather than the air. Those objects absorb the heat and may reradiate it to other cooler surfaces. Although the air temperature may be chilly, you can still feel warm with radiant heating.

Convection carries heat through the air, particularly through large, enclosed spaces where air moves freely. As warm air rises, it gives off heat to the surfaces around it, causing it to cool, sink, and be replaced by warmer rising air.

Conduction carries heat through a solid material, such as a wall. Generally speaking, the denser the material, the more easily it conducts heat; foam board insulation, which is not dense at all, slows heat conduction through the house walls and roof.

Radiation

Convection

Conduction

Heat travels by radiation, convection, and conduction. The sun's radiant heat travels in a straight line, warming exterior walls and roofs and—through windows—interior walls, floors, and furnishings. Heat is also conducted through walls and roofs. Convection is the movement of heat as it rises, cools, and sinks.

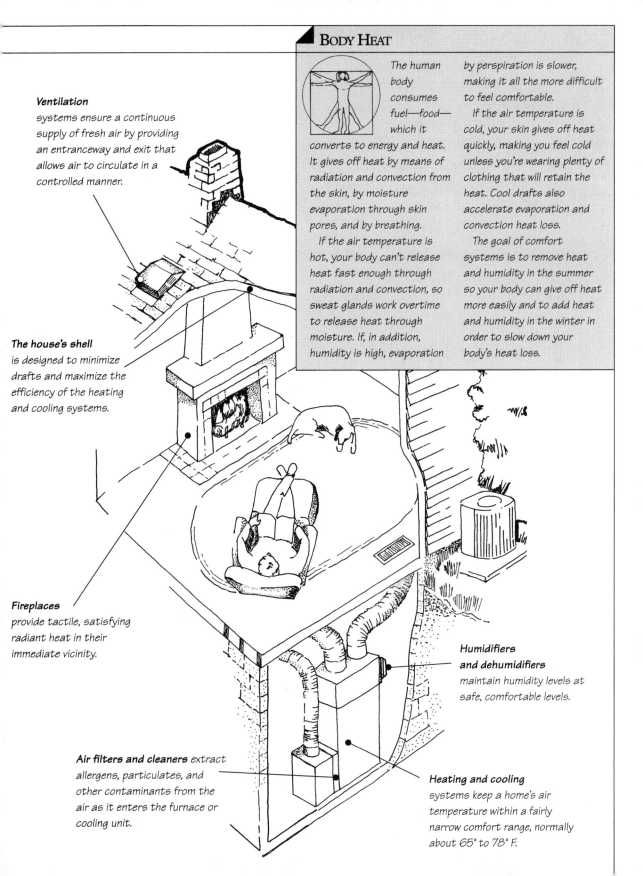

Ventilation
systems ensure a continuous supply of fresh air by providing an entranceway and exit that allows air to circulate in a controlled manner.

The house's shell
is designed to minimize drafts and maximize the efficiency of the heating and cooling systems.

Fireplaces
provide tactile, satisfying radiant heat in their immediate vicinity.

Air filters and cleaners extract allergens, particulates, and other contaminants from the air as it enters the furnace or cooling unit.

Humidifiers and dehumidifiers
maintain humidity levels at safe, comfortable levels.

Heating and cooling
systems keep a home's air temperature within a fairly narrow comfort range, normally about 65° to 78° F.

BODY HEAT

The human body consumes fuel—food—which it converts to energy and heat. It gives off heat by means of radiation and convection from the skin, by moisture evaporation through skin pores, and by breathing.

If the air temperature is hot, your body can't release heat fast enough through radiation and convection, so sweat glands work overtime to release heat through moisture. If, in addition, humidity is high, evaporation by perspiration is slower, making it all the more difficult to feel comfortable.

If the air temperature is cold, your skin gives off heat quickly, making you feel cold unless you're wearing plenty of clothing that will retain the heat. Cool drafts also accelerate evaporation and convection heat loss.

The goal of comfort systems is to remove heat and humidity in the summer so your body can give off heat more easily and to add heat and humidity in the winter in order to slow down your body's heat loss.

Comfort Systems

Furnaces, air conditioners, heat pumps, air cleaners, humidifiers, and the many other devices that make a home comfortable have one thing in common: they all require a source of energy, a fuel, to operate. Many types of fuel are used for energy, including natural gas, fuel oil, electricity, liquid propane gas (lpg), kerosene, wood, coal, and solar heat.

Availability, cost, and convenience are the criteria used in choosing a particular energy source. Also important is the effect consuming a given fuel may have on the environment.

Electricity is the most widely available source of energy. Although it's the only viable power source for lighting, air conditioning, heat pumps, and motor-driven appliances, it is a prohibitively expensive fuel for resistance-type heating in all but a few areas of the country.

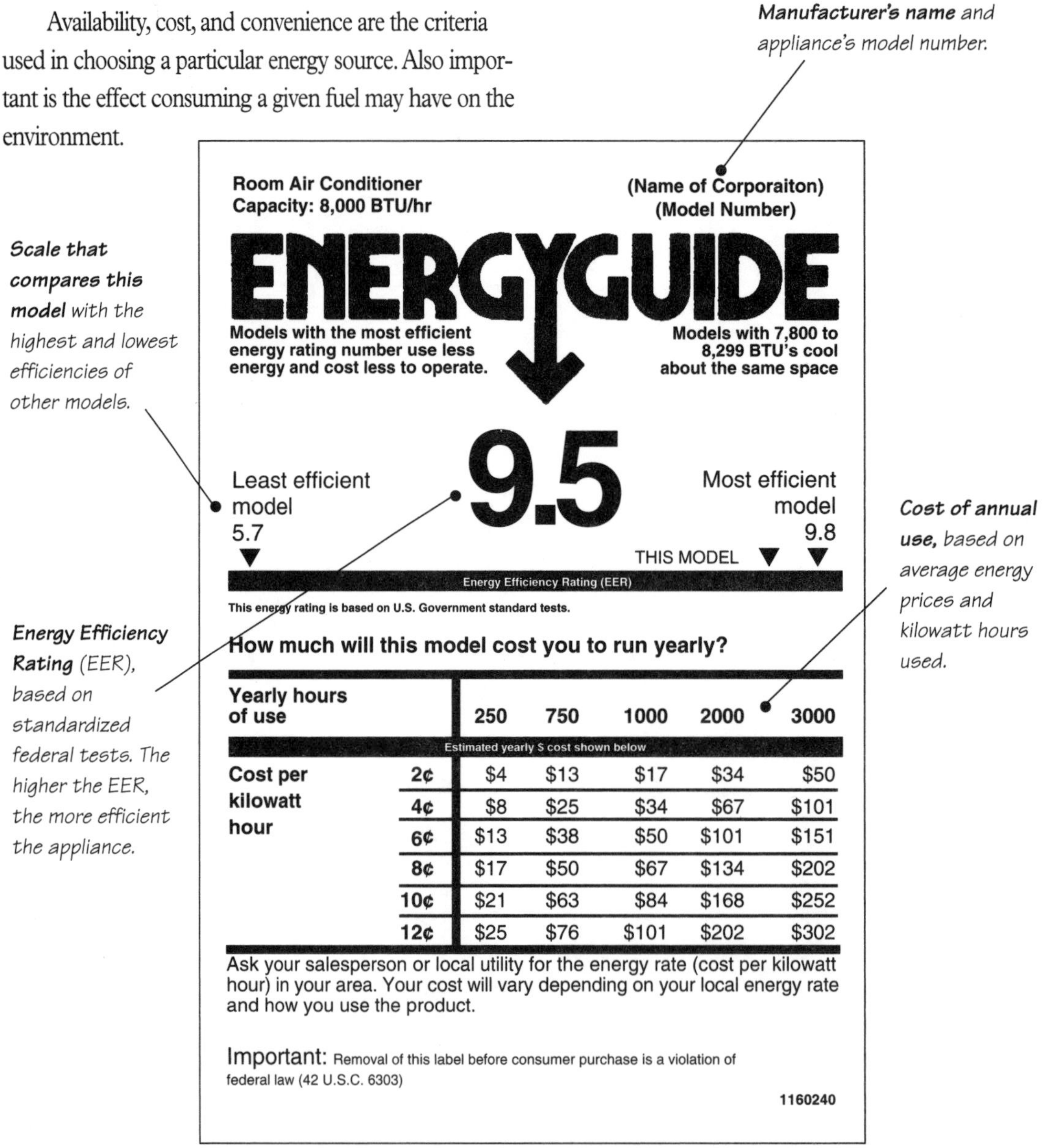

Manufacturer's name and appliance's model number.

Scale that compares this model with the highest and lowest efficiencies of other models.

Energy Efficiency Rating (EER), based on standardized federal tests. The higher the EER, the more efficient the appliance.

Cost of annual use, based on average energy prices and kilowatt hours used.

Room Air Conditioner
Capacity: 8,000 BTU/hr

(Name of Corporaiton)
(Model Number)

ENERGYGUIDE

Models with the most efficient energy rating number use less energy and cost less to operate.

Models with 7,800 to 8,299 BTU's cool about the same space

9.5

Least efficient model
5.7
▼

Most efficient model
9.8

THIS MODEL ▼ ▼

Energy Efficiency Rating (EER)

This energy rating is based on U.S. Government standard tests.

How much will this model cost you to run yearly?

Yearly hours of use		250	750	1000	2000	3000
Estimated yearly $ cost shown below						
Cost per kilowatt hour	2¢	$4	$13	$17	$34	$50
	4¢	$8	$25	$34	$67	$101
	6¢	$13	$38	$50	$101	$151
	8¢	$17	$50	$67	$134	$202
	10¢	$21	$63	$84	$168	$252
	12¢	$25	$76	$101	$202	$302

Ask your salesperson or local utility for the energy rate (cost per kilowatt hour) in your area. Your cost will vary depending on your local energy rate and how you use the product.

Important: Removal of this label before consumer purchase is a violation of federal law (42 U.S.C. 6303)

1160240

Natural gas, the most popular fuel for heating, is relatively affordable, clean burning, convenient, stable in price, and widely available. It's also very versatile; it fires furnaces, ovens and stoves, fireplaces, water heaters, clothes dryers, barbecues, and more.

In remote areas, liquid propane gas is a popular alternative. It offers the same benefits as natural gas but, because it's sold in portable cylinders or delivered by truck to larger pressurized storage tanks, it isn't as convenient as piped-in natural gas.

Solar energy is also a favorite alternative heating source in today's homes, and often serves as a supplement to conventional systems. For more about solar heating, see page 64.

Oil is also a popular fuel. Although oil is clean burning and suitable for furnaces, boilers, water heaters, and more, oil prices fluctuate widely. And, because oil must be delivered by truck and stored in a large tank, it isn't as convenient as gas.

Wood and other solid fuels, such as coal and fuel pellets, are used in some areas, particularly where these fuels are readily available and other energy sources are not. They are used for fueling furnaces, fireplaces, stoves, boilers, and water heaters. Because of particulate emissions in smoke and soot, new solid-fuel-burning appliances must meet strict federal emissions standards.

From refrigerators to water heaters, all major household appliances meant for heating and cooling are posted with a federal "Energy Guide" label that rates their energy efficiency. These labels convey a wealth of information about the energy requirements of the appliance, its yearly operating costs, and how it compares to other models. Some labels use numbers to illustrate the yearly cost of operation, and some use dollar amounts.

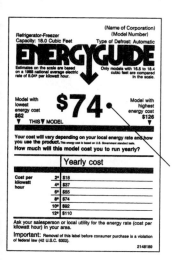

Estimated annual operating cost for this model, based on national averages of energy rates.

Although central heating—that is, a heating system employing a heat source located outside a room—is considered a modern convenience, it actually dates back to ancient Greece. It is believed that in 350 B.C. the Great Temple of Ephesus was warmed by heated air that was circulated through flues laid in the floor. Today, with electricity to drive blowers, forced-air systems heat nearly 35 million American homes.

A forced-air heating system draws the room air through ductwork to a furnace, where the air is filtered and heated. The warmed air is then blown back into the rooms through other ductwork. With older "gravity" furnaces, the heated air is delivered by natural convection, not by a blower; the warmed air simply rises through the ducts to heat the rooms above.

Most furnaces are gas-fired, but some are fueled by oil, coal, wood, or electricity. With a conventional furnace, natural gas is piped to a burner that's located inside a combustion chamber. There, the gas is mixed with air, then ignited by a pilot light, a spark, or a similar device controlled by a thermostat. The flame warms a metal box—the *heat exchanger*— where the air is heated as it flows through. The exhaust gases that are given off by the burners are vented outside through a flue that runs through the roof or, with newer high-efficiency models, through a wall. An electric forced-air furnace uses an electric heating element rather than a flame to warm the heat exchanger.

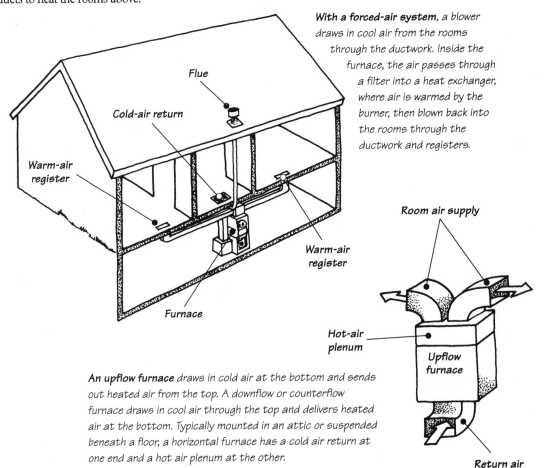

With a forced-air system, a blower draws in cool air from the rooms through the ductwork. Inside the furnace, the air passes through a filter into a heat exchanger, where air is warmed by the burner, then blown back into the rooms through the ductwork and registers.

Flue

Cold-air return

Warm-air register

Warm-air register

Furnace

An upflow furnace draws in cold air at the bottom and sends out heated air from the top. A downflow or counterflow furnace draws in cool air through the top and delivers heated air at the bottom. Typically mounted in an attic or suspended beneath a floor, a horizontal furnace has a cold air return at one end and a hot air plenum at the other.

Room air supply

Hot-air plenum

Upflow furnace

Return air

A forced-air system can be combined with an air-conditioning unit, a humidifier, and an air filter. The system's ductwork is usually metal wrapped in insulation to help keep in heat. In some cases, flexible ductwork is preferred. Note: asbestos-wrapped ductwork should not be disturbed by homeowners since the asbestos fibers are dangerous to breathe.

A furnace turns on when the room temperature dips below a set level signaled by the thermostat. When this happens, a gas valve regulates and delivers fuel to the burner. The burner is ignited in the combustion chamber, creating heat that is transferred to the heat exchanger. The warm air then moves to the hot-air plenum, then to the ductwork that runs throughout the house. The combustion fumes are vented through a flue that runs through the roof or, with high-efficiency models, through the wall.

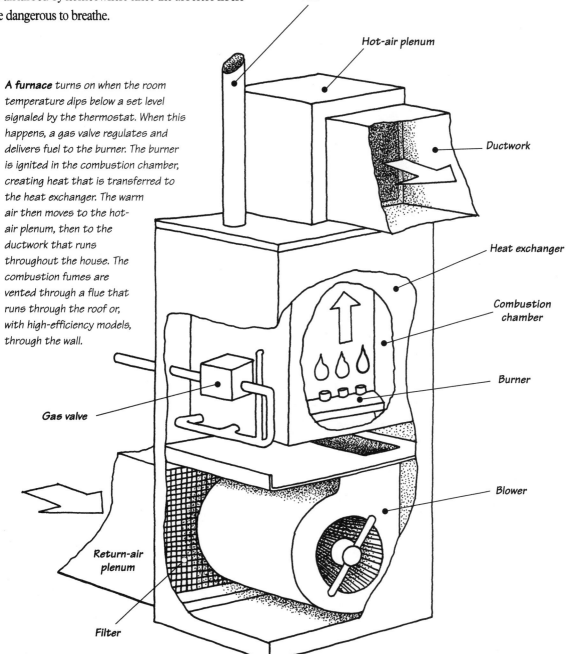

Flue

Hot-air plenum

Ductwork

Heat exchanger

Combustion chamber

Burner

Gas valve

Blower

Return-air plenum

Filter

Radiant hydronic heating employs hot water or, in older buildings, steam to deliver heat throughout the house. A boiler heats the water and circulates it through a system of pipes or tubing to the registers, radiators, or circuits of pipes that radiate the warmth to each room.

Although hydronic heating has long been popular in Europe, American residential systems installed in the 1950s proved unreliable and difficult to maintain, stalling their acceptance by most homeowners. In recent years, however, a new generation of in-floor hydronic heating has employed corrosion-proof hot water tubing, making it more reliable and, therefore, more popular. With this type of system, the heat is evenly distributed and the house's floors are warm underfoot.

Hydronic heating offers quiet, constant heat and doesn't stir up allergens or dust. Because the system warms people and objects rather than just air, a room feels warm even if a door is opened or the room is somewhat drafty or slightly cooler than normal. On the downside, a radiant system cannot be combined with a cooling system, a humidifier, or an air filter unit the way a forced-air system can.

A variety of equipment may heat the water: a natural gas or propane water heater or boiler, an electric boiler, a wood boiler, an electric heat pump, a solar collector, or a geothermal energy system.

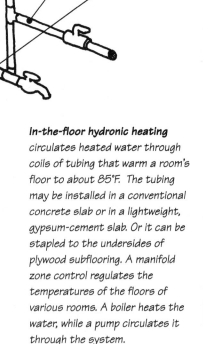

Manifold zone control

Water supply

Expansion tank

Boiler

Pump

Drain

In-the-floor hydronic heating circulates heated water through coils of tubing that warm a room's floor to about 85°F. The tubing may be installed in a conventional concrete slab or in a lightweight, gypsum-cement slab. Or it can be stapled to the undersides of plywood subflooring. A manifold zone control regulates the temperatures of the floors of various rooms. A boiler heats the water, while a pump circulates it through the system.

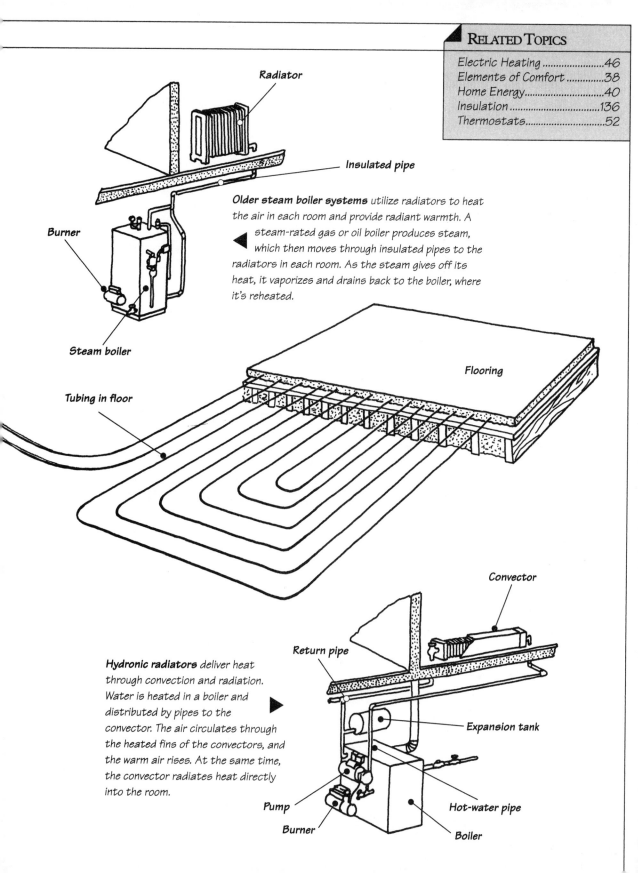

Radiator

Insulated pipe

Older steam boiler systems utilize radiators to heat the air in each room and provide radiant warmth. A steam-rated gas or oil boiler produces steam, which then moves through insulated pipes to the radiators in each room. As the steam gives off its heat, it vaporizes and drains back to the boiler, where it's reheated.

Burner

Steam boiler

Flooring

Tubing in floor

Convector

Return pipe

Hydronic radiators deliver heat through convection and radiation. Water is heated in a boiler and distributed by pipes to the convector. The air circulates through the heated fins of the convectors, and the warm air rises. At the same time, the convector radiates heat directly into the room.

Expansion tank

Hot-water pipe

Pump

Burner

Boiler

Electricity is a clean, easily-accessed form of energy that's readily available to power appliances, illuminate lightbulbs, and so on. And because electric heating equipment is generally more affordable than other types, electric heaters are often preferred by home builders. Unfortunately, though, electricity is a relatively expensive heating fuel. (For more information on heating fuels, see "Home Energy" on page 40.) In most areas, electric heat is best reserved for specialized applications, such as heating an added-on room, temporarily warming a bathroom, or heating a home where other more affordable fuels are not available.

Although electricity is used for indirect heating—to heat air in the heat exchangers of some forced-air furnaces and to power heat pumps, for example—here we look at how it is used to produce *direct heat*— that is, the heat released directly within the room being heated.

How does electricity create heat without burning anything? An electrical current travels through resistance wires, cables, or foils, causing these elements to heat up as they resist the electrical flow. These heating elements may be enclosed in tubes, sheaths, cabinets, or panels.

Baseboard heaters, one of the most common types of electrical heating appliances, draw room air off the floor, pass it over heating elements, and send it back into the room. Some have fans to assist the air movement, while some work solely by convection.

Radiant panels and radiant heating cables and foils generate heat that warms objects rather than the air that surrounds them.

Electric radiant heating systems *are installed in floors and ceilings. Radiant heating cables wind back and forth inside a concrete slab floor or under a standard framed floor, while flexible radiant heat foils or strips are laid or fastened between floor or ceiling joists.*

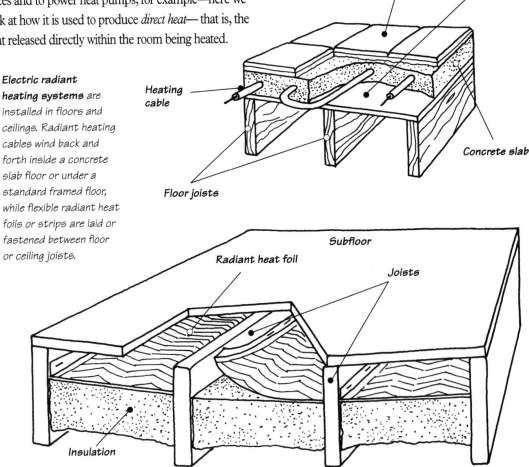

Tile

Subfloor

Heating cable

Concrete slab

Floor joists

Subfloor

Radiant heat foil

Joists

Insulation

Electric forced-air heaters fit into the wall and blow out warm air. A small fan and a row of heating elements inside the unit are controlled by a thermostat.

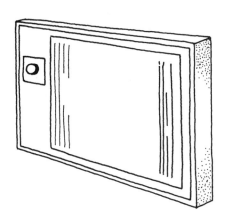

Baseboard heaters are simply screwed to the base of the wall. The air is drawn in through the bottom and heated by electric elements; the warmed air then rises into the room. The electric elements are often shaped like metal fins, and some are filled with fluid to maximize their heat retention.

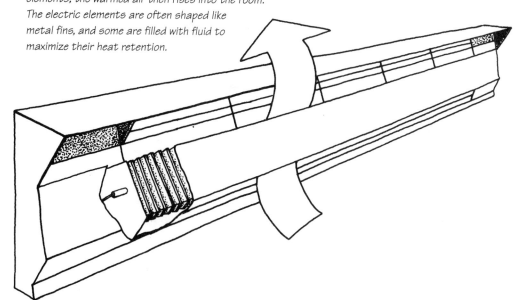

Comfort Systems

Air conditioners cool, filter, and dehumidify the air. There are two basic types: central air conditioners cool an entire house and room air conditioners cool single rooms and small areas. Hybrids—*split ductless systems*—cool different zones of a house, each controlled separately.

Air conditioners are powered by electricity, and a considerable amount of energy is needed to run them. They also use a refrigerant to transfer heat from indoors to outdoors. This refrigerant circulates through a closed-circuit loop of copper tubing that runs between an outdoor coil, called a *condenser*, and an indoor coil, called an *evaporator*. The refrigerant raises and drops in temperature as it absorbs and gives off heat, and it changes from liquid to gas and back to liquid again as its temperature and pressure change.

When cold refrigerant circulates through the indoor evaporator, it absorbs the heat from the room air that is blown across it. As the refrigerant absorbs the heat, it vaporizes and travels through the tubing to the condenser coil and compressor unit that are outdoors. As it moves through the unit, it emits heat that dissipates into the outdoor air; an electric fan that blows across the coil assists the process. As a result, the refrigerant cools and becomes a high-pressure liquid. An expansion valve further reduces the temperature and pressure, then returns the refrigerant to the evaporator, completing the cycle.

A central air conditioner usually is combined with a forced-air furnace, utilizing the furnace's blower to draw room air into the unit through the return-air ductwork that runs throughout the house. The furnace's air filter is used to remove dust, hair, and lint. When the room air moves past a chilled indoor coil—the evaporator coil—it releases heat. The resulting cold air travels on to the plenum, usually a large metal box at the top of the furnace, where it's channeled to the air supply ductwork and returned to the rooms. A condensate drain carries away moisture that's created when warm air cools and condenses.

Condenser fan

Case

Blower

Evaporator coil

Condenser coil

Compressor

Front cover

A room air conditioner, mounted in a window or built into an exterior wall, contains a condenser coil, a compressor, an evaporator coil, and a blower, just like its larger cousin, the central air conditioner.

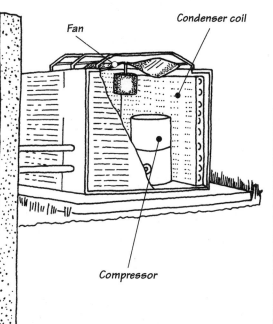

Air supply
duct to rooms

Refrigerant
filled tubing

Fan

Condenser coil

Evaporator coil

Compressor

Return air duct
from rooms

Furnace or
air-handling unit

Filter

Blower

A split-system central air conditioner's primary components are separated: an evaporator coil is installed indoors with the furnace and a condenser coil and compressor unit are placed outdoors.

Comfort Systems

A heat pump uses air-conditioning principles to extract heat from one place and deliver it to another, with one big difference: the system is reversible. In addition to expelling heat from indoors, like an air conditioner, the system can be reversed to add heat like a furnace.

Most heat pumps circulate refrigerant in tubing that runs between an outdoor coil and an indoor coil. In the heating cycle, the outdoor coil serves as the condenser to collect heat, while the indoor coil serves as the evaporator to give off heat. In the cooling cycle, the coils switch roles. (For more information on condensor and evaporator coils, see "Air Conditioners," on page 48.)

Most heat pumps are *air-source*; that is, they extract heat from the air, even at incredibly low temperatures. A split air-source system has an outdoor unit that's composed of a compressor, a coil, a fan, and a reversing

A split air-source heat pump has an indoor and an outdoor unit connected by refrigerant-filled tubing. A blower in the indoor unit delivers warmed or cooled air through ductwork.

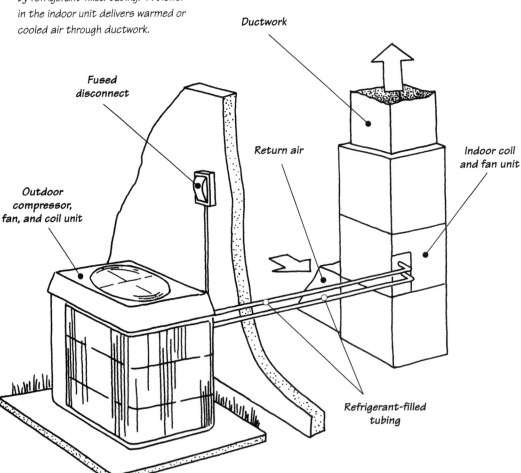

Fused disconnect

Ductwork

Return air

Indoor coil and fan unit

Outdoor compressor, fan, and coil unit

Refrigerant-filled tubing

valve, connected with refrigerant-filled tubing to an indoor unit that contains a fan, an indoor coil, and a supplemental resistance heating element. A blower draws in the room air through a filter and passes it across the indoor coil. The air passing the indoor coil either gathers or gives off heat, depending on whether the system is set to warm or cool. Ductwork and registers deliver warmed or cooled air to the rooms. Electrical power is supplied through the fused disconnect and a thermostat turns the heat pump off and on in concert with changes in the indoor air temperature.

Other types of heat pumps take heat from the earth or from groundwater. These types are quite involved and expensive to install, but they are very efficient heat sources. They circulate a solution of water and antifreeze, or just plain water, through a system of buried tubing. The circulated water/antifreeze gathers heat from the earth or from groundwater where the temperature normally is warmer than outside air in the winter and cooler in the summer, making heat transfer much more effective than with air-source systems.

A package heat pump combines a condenser and evaporator in a single unit that's typically placed on the roof. Ductwork delivers warmed or cooled air to and from the rooms below.

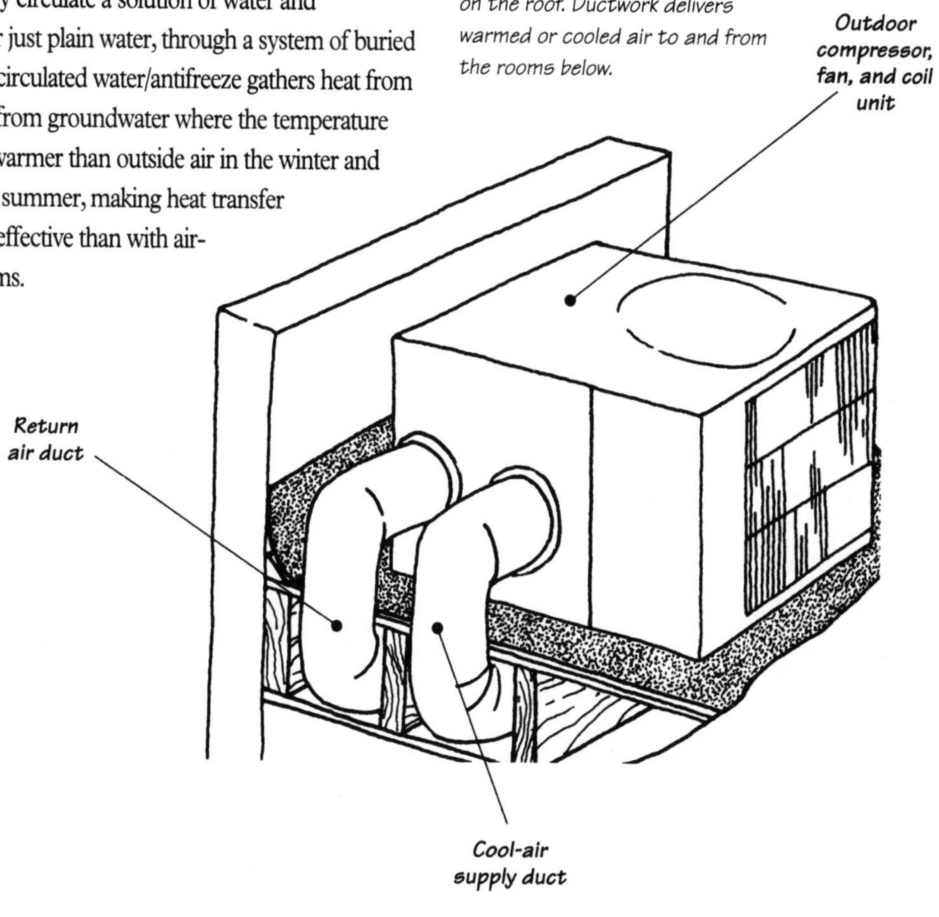

Outdoor compressor, fan, and coil unit

Return air duct

Cool-air supply duct

Comfort Systems

In the early seventeenth century, Dutchman Cornelis Drebbel invented the thermostat. Placing a float in a mercury thermometer, he rigged levers and pivots so that dampers would adjust a furnace's draft as the temperature rose. Although today's thermostats are far more sophisticated, they draw from the principles of that early invention.

Thermostats control nearly all types of heating and cooling equipment, keeping room temperatures within a set range. By doing so, they ensure comfort, cut energy waste, and offer considerable convenience.

A thermostat has a temperature sensor and an activating switch. Some are mechanical, others electronic. Not all thermostats work with all types of furnaces and heaters; a forced-air thermostat, for example, won't necessarily work with a heat pump.

Programmable, electronic thermostats couple sensors with circuitry to do the job. Typical programmable thermostats can handle both heat-only systems—such as forced-air, steam, hot water, and, in some cases electric—and complete air-conditioning systems. Most are like minicomputers that can automatically align heating and cooling to changing daily needs, eliminating unnecessary energy usage and reducing energy costs.

The most sophisticated thermostats operate zone systems that split a house into two or more zones, each controlled by separate thermostatic settings. These thermostats open and close dampers that are set in ductwork, sending warmed or cooled air to the areas where it's wanted.

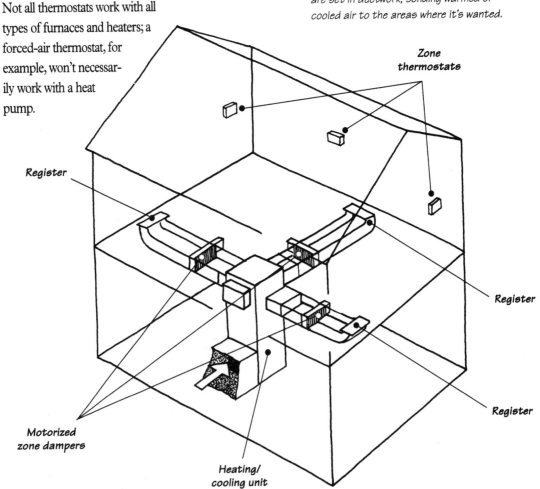

Zone thermostats

Register

Register

Register

Motorized zone dampers

Heating/ cooling unit

If you haven't already done so, maybe it's time to consider switching from a manual thermostat to an electronic, programmable model. Electronic thermostats have become very affordable and can repay their cost quickly through energy savings. Every degree of heat you reduce will cut about 3 percent from your heating bill. If you lower the temperature from 68° to 59°F for an eight-hour period every night, for example, you'll save about 9 percent. Here's what to look for in a programmable thermostat:

• **Daily Cycles.** Some thermostats allow up to four cycles per twenty-four-hour period; others allow only one. It's important to have at least two cycles per day—one for night and one for midday.

• **Weekly Schedules.** Some thermostats treat each day of the week identically. Others allow one schedule for five days (normally weekdays) and a separate schedule for two days (weekends). The most flexible thermostat can program each day of the week separately.

• **Overrides.** Be sure you can control the thermostat and the fan manually so you can use any setting you want, instead of the factory default settings.

• **Ease of Use.** To simplify programming, many thermostats have default settings that you can opt to use. These settings will also kick in if, for some reason, power is interrupted and your programmed settings are erased. Most models, however, have backup batteries that save your programmed settings in the event of power loss.

A programmable thermostat can be set to raise the room temperature a half hour before you get up, then lower it when you head off to work. Before you arrive home, it can readjust the temperature to a comfortable level once again. It can be set to any schedule you desire.

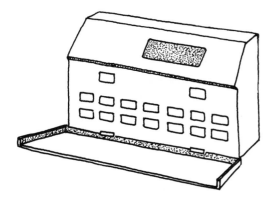

Inside a conventional electro-mechanical thermostat, a bimetal coil contracts when cold and expands when warm. The sensor's movement trips a switch on or off. The switch may be simply an open contact that closes, or it may be a mercury-activated switch, in which case mercury in a small glass vial completes or breaks an electrical circuit when the vial is tilted by the bimetal coil.

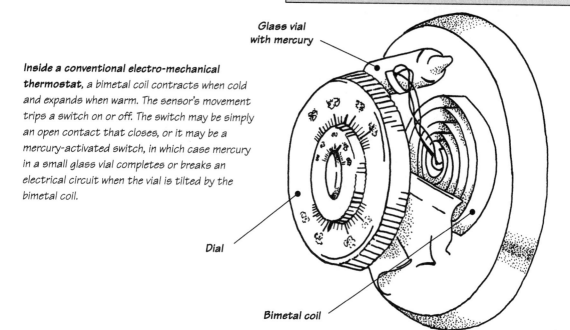

Glass vial with mercury

Dial

Bimetal coil

Balanced humidity inside a house is important not only for comfort but for the upkeep of the house itself. When the humidity level—the amount of water vapor in the air— drops too low or rises too high, a variety of problems can develop.

Dry air draws moisture out of everything, from your eyes, lips, and skin to your home's carpets and furniture. Bothersome static electricity increases. Wall studs, drywall, plaster, and other building materials can shrink or crack and furniture joinery can come apart.

High humidity in the summer is uncomfortable. During the winter, the first signs of overly humid air usually appear when vapor hits the cold inner surfaces of windows and condenses there. Although this normally isn't a serious problem, the same condensation can collect on the inner surfaces of exterior walls, unless walls are fitted with a proper vapor retardant; otherwise, the buildup of condensation can rot the structure and ruin insulation. Peeling, blistering, or cracking paint on the exterior wall indicates that moisture is working from inside to outside. In addition to condensation problems, humid air encourages mold, mildew, and bacterial growth indoors.

New, highly insulated, energy-efficient houses tend to accumulate humidity generated inside the house because they reduce the rate of air exchange with the outdoors. Older, "leaky" houses tend to have a dryness problem, particularly in the winter. Cold outdoor air, which carries very little moisture, infiltrates a house through cracks and openings and is warmed by the heating system, which makes it even drier.

What levels are comfortable? The normal range of comfort is considered to be from 30 percent to 50 percent relative humidity in the winter, 40 percent to 50 percent in the summer.

The most obvious way to reduce humidity is to use an air conditioner or, in a house that doesn't have central air conditioning, a dehumidifier. Sometimes humidity can be reduced to an acceptable level simply by using kitchen and bathroom exhaust fans. Other methods include venting the clothes dryer outdoors, taking shorter showers, and running only full loads in clothes washers and dishwashers. It is also important to eliminate sources of leaks or standing water in the basement or crawl space.

If you need to increase the humidity in your home, you may be able to bring it to a comfortable level simply by turning off the ventilation fans when you shower or cook and by sealing up your house with weather stripping and caulking. To add a significant level of humidity to your home, install a humidifier.

Tabletop and console humidifiers are relatively inexpensive and portable. Both are filled manually, usually on a daily basis. Tabletop units output 2 to 4 gallons of water per 24 hours; consoles output 8 to 14 gallons. Some disperse steam or a cool mist; others blow air through a damp evaporative filter. Central evaporative humidifiers are installed on forced-air furnace plenums, as shown here.

A humidistat turns the humidifier off and on when humidity levels stray from a set range. Although a humidistat allows the system to work more or less automatically, it must be adjusted when the room temperature changes in order to maintain fairly constant indoor relative humidity levels.

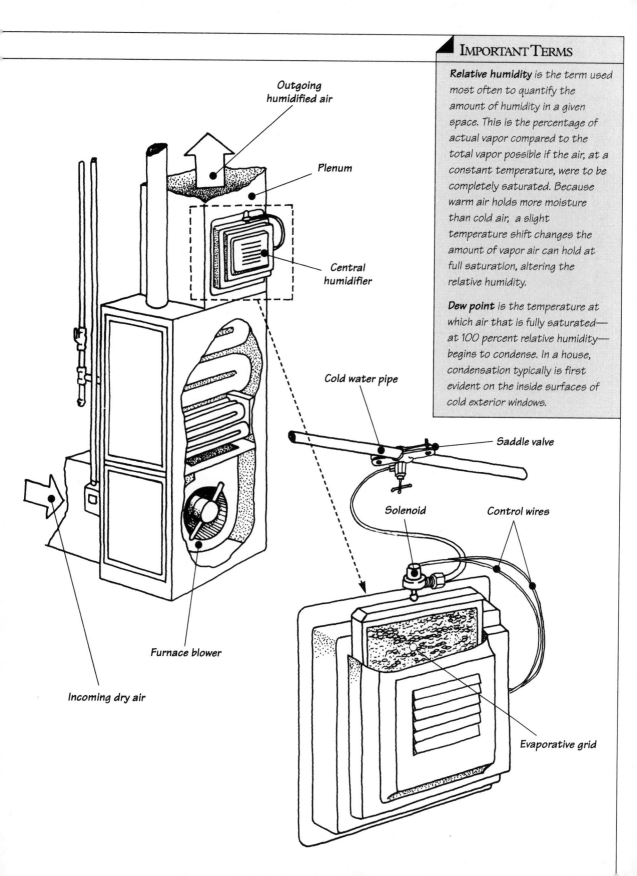

Outgoing
humidified air

Plenum

Central
humidifier

Cold water pipe

Saddle valve

Solenoid

Control wires

Furnace blower

Incoming dry air

Evaporative grid

Although dust is most noticeable where it settles and collects, the average house has about 3 million dust particles suspended in every cubic foot of air. For allergy sufferers, asthmatics, people with bronchial problems, and those who are hypersensitive to airborne particulates, this can be a serious problem that air cleaners and filters are designed to solve.

Dust is the minute residue sloughed off by a house and its occupants. It comes from fireplace, cigarette, and cooking smoke; skin and pet dander; molds, mildew, and fungi; pollen and plant spores; and a variety of other sources. Visible dust is about 10 microns in diameter; respirable dust—the type that can lodge in your lungs—is more commonly about 0.3 micron. In comparison, a sharp pencil dot is about 200 microns in diameter.

Air cleaners and filters are designed to remove dust from the air. They are made as self-contained, tabletop or console appliances that serve small areas or single rooms. There are also whole-house filters that attach to a house's forced-air furnace. They work by mechanical filtration, electrical attraction, or a combination of the two methods.

Mechanical or *media* filters strain dust from the air as a fan propels the air through the unit's filter membrane. Most are good at catching the large particles of dust, but only high-grade filters, such as HEPA filters, eliminate most of the microscopic dust.

Tabletop and room units *send the air through a series of filters to clean it: a foam prefilter to screen out large particles, the primary filter or electrical-attraction device to catch smaller particles, a carbon filter to remove odors and some gases, and a postfilter for any remaining particles.*

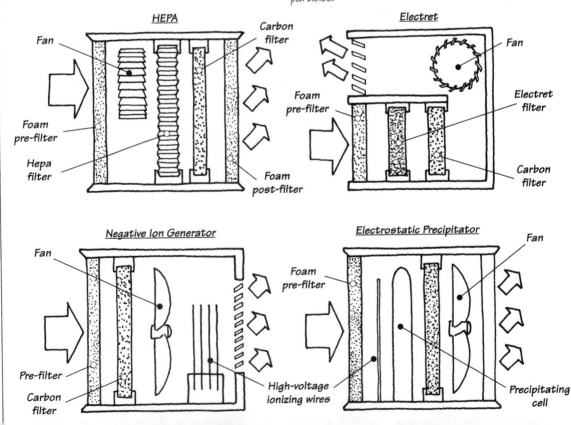

Electrical-attraction cleaners use a principle similar to "static cling"; they charge particles in the air or a collection device in the filter (or both) to create a magnetic attraction between particles and filter. One version, *electret* or *electrostatic* filters, have polyester fibers that create their own charge. *Electrostatic precipitating* filters have high-voltage wires that charge the air and plates that attract the dust.

Somewhat different, the *negative-ion generator* uses tiny, charged wires or needles to create ions—gas molecules with a negative charge—that latch onto airborne particles, which are then attracted to the unit's filter. A fan in the unit distributes the ions back into the room, where they stick to walls, floors, and other surfaces.

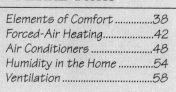

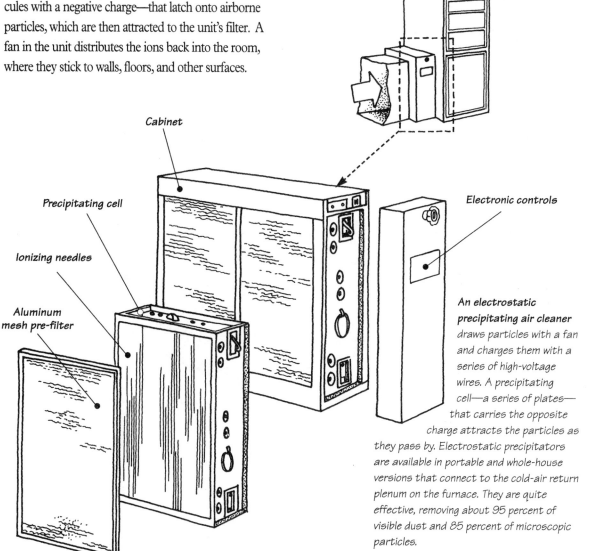

Cabinet

Precipitating cell

Ionizing needles

Aluminum
mesh pre-filter

Electronic controls

An electrostatic precipitating air cleaner draws particles with a fan and charges them with a series of high-voltage wires. A precipitating cell—a series of plates—that carries the opposite charge attracts the particles as they pass by. Electrostatic precipitators are available in portable and whole-house versions that connect to the cold-air return plenum on the furnace. They are quite effective, removing about 95 percent of visible dust and 85 percent of microscopic particles.

Comfort Systems

A little humidity is important to a home's comfort, particularly in the winter. But too much vapor, combined with fumes from synthetic materials, pesticides, cleansers, and household chemicals can make a house's air not only uncomfortable but downright toxic. The answer? Ventilation.

While a house should not be drafty, it also should not be airtight; it should breathe, drawing in fresh air and exhaling stale and toxic air. In fact, some experts recommend that half of a home's air volume should be exchanged every hour. You can do this, of course, by opening the doors and windows, but that is not a feasible, economical solution. The trick is to provide needed ventilation without sending costly heated or cooled air out the window.

A house can be well ventilated with the proper combination of vents and fans in the attic and crawl space, for example, coupled with vents in specific areas of the interior.

Attic ventilation is critical to exhausting unwanted heat and moisture. By circulating fresh air through an attic, heated, moisture-filled air is carried away. A ridge vent, coupled with adequate soffit vents, can provide effective attic ventilation in most houses. Houses that need a ventilation boost often require fans or turbine vents.

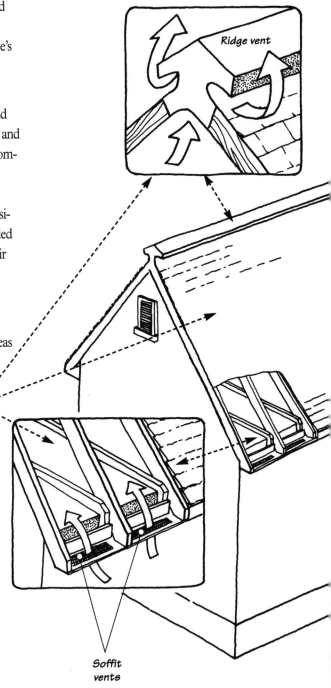

Ridge vent

Soffit vents

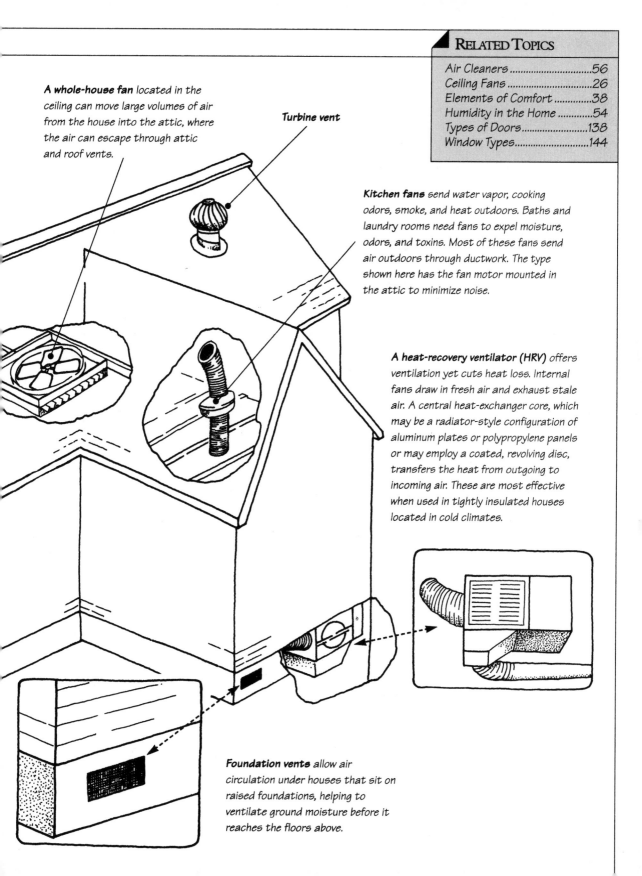

A whole-house fan located in the ceiling can move large volumes of air from the house into the attic, where the air can escape through attic and roof vents.

Turbine vent

Kitchen fans send water vapor, cooking odors, smoke, and heat outdoors. Baths and laundry rooms need fans to expel moisture, odors, and toxins. Most of these fans send air outdoors through ductwork. The type shown here has the fan motor mounted in the attic to minimize noise.

A heat-recovery ventilator (HRV) offers ventilation yet cuts heat loss. Internal fans draw in fresh air and exhaust stale air. A central heat-exchanger core, which may be a radiator-style configuration of aluminum plates or polypropylene panels or may employ a coated, revolving disc, transfers the heat from outgoing to incoming air. These are most effective when used in tightly insulated houses located in cold climates.

Foundation vents allow air circulation under houses that sit on raised foundations, helping to ventilate ground moisture before it reaches the floors above.

Comfort Systems

Flickering flames, glowing embers, the essence of wood smoke: nothing is quite as cozy as a fire on a cold winter's day. Of course, for a fire, a house needs a fireplace that will safely contain it, encourage the fuel to burn, exhaust smoke, and deliver warmth to the room.

A traditional fireplace heats by radiation. Radiant heat from the fire warms objects in a room, not the air. Heat is retained by the walls of the fireplace, too, and released slowly into the room.

Unfortunately, most traditional fireplaces are notoriously inefficient at heating. They may actually increase drafts in a house by drawing room air through the mouth of the fireplace and sending it up the chimney along with as much as 90 percent of the heat generated by the fire. Some contemporary fireplaces have glass doors to cut heat loss and drafts; in addition, they draw combustion air directly from outdoors so the fire doesn't take warmed air from the room. Some efficient models also

have vents that pipe room air past the firebox so it can be heated then returned to the room. And some fireplaces are specially designed to maximize radiant heat delivery and retention.

Although classic fireplaces are built in place on a solid foundation of brick and other masonry materials, many newer fireplaces are prefabricated from metal and installed in wood-frame walls. They generally have a metal shell and a brick-lined firebox. Prefabricated fireplaces, also known as *zero-clearance* fireplaces, are highly insulated, so they can be installed within an inch of combustible materials, such as wall framing. They are preferred in new construction because they're much lighter in weight, are faster and easier to install than standard masonry units, and are energy efficient.

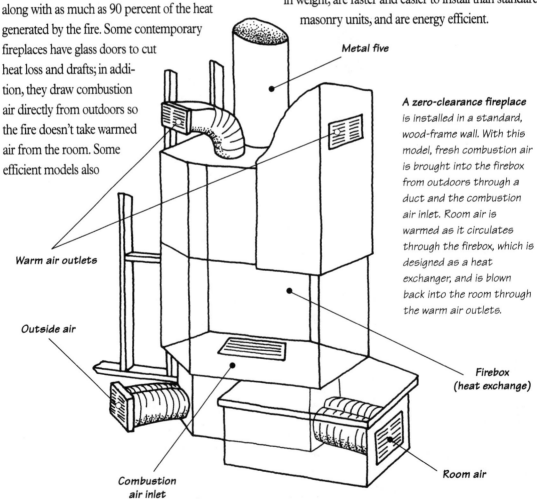

Metal five

A zero-clearance fireplace is installed in a standard, wood-frame wall. With this model, fresh combustion air is brought into the firebox from outdoors through a duct and the combustion air inlet. Room air is warmed as it circulates through the firebox, which is designed as a heat exchanger, and is blown back into the room through the warm air outlets.

Warm air outlets

Outside air

Firebox (heat exchange)

Combustion air inlet

Room air

Fundamentally, this is how a fireplace works: the fuel is placed in a combustion chamber, called the firebox, and ignited. To supply the flame, the firebox draws oxygen either from the room or from outdoors. The flame produces radiant heat, which warms the room. The combustion gases, the smoke, are expelled through a flue and chimney. As heated air and smoke rise up the chimney, they create a self-perpetuating current that continues to draw upward. As the wood burns, it creates ash, which is collected in an ash pit and should be emptied out periodically.

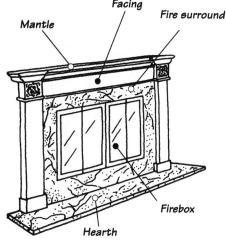

Mantle

Facing

Fire surround

Firebox

Hearth

A fireplace's hearth and facade may be made of brick, rock, concrete, marble, granite, tile, or other noncombustible materials. Codes and common sense restrict how close to the opening combustible materials—such as wood paneling, wood flooring, or wallboard—may be located.

A chimney cap keeps objects from falling into the chimney and, with a spark arrester, keeps sparks from escaping.

The chimney flue, made from insulated metal or terracotta, safely carries combustion gases up the chimney.

The smoke dome and wind shelf are designed to work together to funnel smoke and gases out the chimney.

The damper, a door made of cast iron or steel, regulates the draft up the chimney.

The firebox contains the fire and sends smoke upward. It also maximizes heat radiation into the room.

The ash pit is a fireproof storage area for ash. It's accessed through a cleanout, a small metal door outside.

The foundation supports the weight of the fireplace and chimney, distributing it evenly to the ground.

A wood stove essentially is a metal container for a fire. Made from cast iron or brick-lined, welded plate steel, a wood stove has an inlet for combustion air and an outlet for combustion gases, the smoke. Most modern stoves are airtight and allow the amount of combustion air that feeds the flame to be controlled. This control allows a wood stove to burn far more efficiently than a traditional open fireplace.

Wood stoves built during the 1970s and early 1980s offer efficiencies of from 50 percent to 60 percent; those built since new governmental requirements were put in place in 1988 offer 75 percent to 90 percent overall efficiency—that is, they convert up to 90 percent of their fuel to heat.

Concern about particulate emissions—the dangerous gases and toxins carried by wood smoke—have forced changes in design, too. Although old wood stoves gave off up to 50 grams of particulates per hour in smoke, new certified stoves give off about 5 grams.

Three types of stoves meet the new standards: catalytic, noncatalytic, and pellet-fired. Built as both freestanding stoves and fireplace inserts, they burn cleanly because they are built to generate secondary combustion, which burns excess gases; in doing this, they turn more fuel into heat.

A catalytic stove uses a catalytic combustor to reburn combustion gases at low temperatures. Noncatalytic stoves burn cleanly and efficiently by preheating the incoming combustion air and circulating combustion gases. Pellet stoves are sophisticated combustion appliances that burn pellets made from recycled sawdust and similar biomass wastes. Pellets produce a very hot fire, burning more efficiently than cord wood. Pellet stoves utilize electronically controlled combustion systems, blowers, and heat exchangers to produce heat very efficiently.

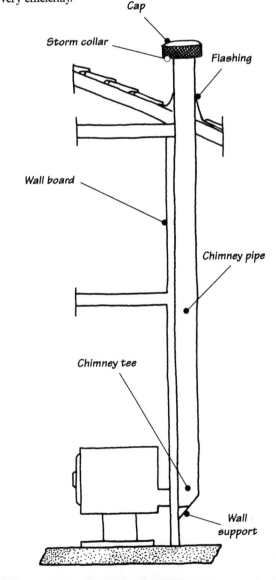

Wood and pellet stove chimneys *vary, depending on the type of unit and where it's situated in the house. One common type utilizes double-wall metal chimney flue pipe, locked together in sections. Storm collar and flashing prevent leaking at the roof. A chimney cap arrests sparks.*

Stove pipe location

Masonry airflow baffle

Secondary combustion chamber

Noncatalytic stoves send interior air through a system of airflow baffles that are heated by the combustion in the firebox to maximize efficiency, using convection and radiation to transmit warmth.

In a pellet stove, pellets are loaded into a hopper at the top or front of the stove and delivered to the combustion chamber at a controlled rate by an auger. Combustion air, blown into the chamber, encourages a superheated flame. The room air is drawn across the heat exchanger by a fan, heated, then returned to the room. Residual combustion gases are vented outside, normally through a 3-inch flue that exits out the unit's back or top.

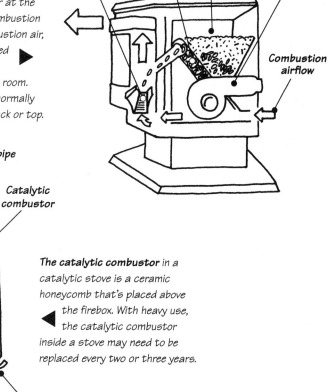

Combustion chamber and burn pot

Feed auger

Hopper

Combustion fan

Combustion airflow

Heat grill

Stovepipe

Catalytic combustor

The catalytic combustor in a catalytic stove is a ceramic honeycomb that's placed above the firebox. With heavy use, the catalytic combustor inside a stove may need to be replaced every two or three years.

Fresh air intake

Comfort Systems

When the oil embargo of the 1970s spurred an interest in alternative energy sources, many home builders began to take a serious look at solar energy. And although homes heated solely by the sun have proven to be expensive to build, a number of solar heating principles have been adopted to partner conventional heating systems.

There are two types of solar heating systems: *active* and *passive*. An active system employs mechanical devices, such as solar panels and circulation fans. A passive system, the more common of the two, relies on construction design and techniques to collect, store, and distribute the sun's warmth in the winter.

To make the most of the sun's energy, a solar house is "tight"—that is, designed to minimize heat loss and outside air infiltration. It is heavily insulated; windows are dual- or triple-glazed, windows and doors are weather-stripped, and all potential points of air leakage in walls are caulked.

Common methods of collecting and releasing passive solar heat include *direct solar gain*, *sunspaces*, and *thermal mass storage*. The house's orientation to the sun is key. The south-facing elevation collects the sun's heat through windows, sunspaces, such as greenhouse rooms, and heat-absorbing walls and floors. Wall and floor materials are often made of masonry so they will be slow to heat up with the sun's midday intensity, then release heat slowly into rooms through the night.

North, east, and west walls generally have only a few windows because the north and east walls receive very little sun in winter and a west wall receives too much in the summer.

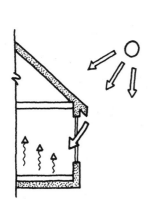

A *sunspace*—often a greenhouse room—uses direct gain principles but can be opened or closed off from adjoining rooms to control the heat flow.

With direct-gain solar heating, sunlight enters through a house's windows and warms the floors inside. The floors, particularly if they're masonry, slowly release the warmth into the rooms.

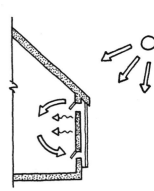

In thermal mass storage, heavy masonry walls can collect the sun's warmth during the day and gradually release it to interior rooms. A trombe wall has an exterior layer of glass or plastic that helps to build up heat.

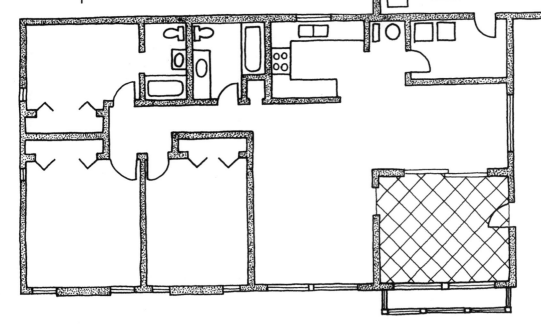

N

All walls and ceilings are well insulated and sealed against heat loss and air infiltration. North, east, and west windows are small and few in number to further prevent heat loss.

Some type of backup heat source usually is provided to augment solar heat.

South-facing walls offer direct solar gain through windows and collect heat in the mass of walls. Floors just inside south-facing windows are often covered with tile or other masonry that can retain heat. Roof overhangs protect windows from the hot, high-angle summer sun.

Sunspaces offer efficient heat collection. Many are used as small greenhouses, day rooms, or air-lock entries. The sunspace area shown has plenty of glazing for solar heat gain and masonry floors for storage and gradual release of heat. Interior doors control release of heat to a house's interior areas.

If you've ever lived without plumbing, even for a weekend camping trip, you can appreciate how important it has become to modern living. Drinking water, baths, showers, toilets, dishwashers, clothes washers, gardens—none of these are possible, or at least practical, without plumbing systems.

A house has several plumbing systems. Water supply piping brings water to the house and distributes it to fixtures and appliances, including outdoor sprinklers and irrigation. Drain and waste plumbing disposes used water and waste. Vent piping exhausts sewer gases and provides proper pressure for the drainpipes. Gas piping delivers fuel to gas-fired appliances. Some homes have pipe systems that serve specialty needs—swimming pool plumbing and built-in vacuum piping, for example.

In this chapter, we'll explore the various plumbing systems and fixtures of a house. But first, let's take a look at the basic components of any plumbing system: the pipes and fittings.

Outdoor plumbing systems *include hose bibbs, sprinkler systems, and drip irrigation. All of these are usually connected directly to the incoming cold water pipe.*

Water supply plumbing *delivers fresh water to all fixtures and appliances that require it; inside the house, the supply is split into two runs at the water heater. In some homes, the hot water line is connected to a water softener. Cold water typically is piped directly to all appliances and fixtures.*

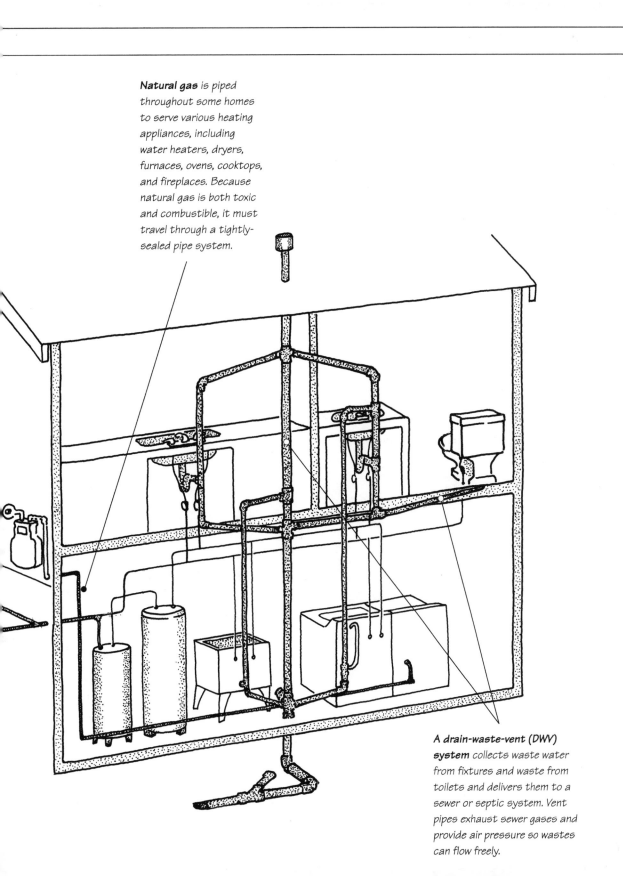

Natural gas is piped throughout some homes to serve various heating appliances, including water heaters, dryers, furnaces, ovens, cooktops, and fireplaces. Because natural gas is both toxic and combustible, it must travel through a tightly-sealed pipe system.

A drain-waste-vent (DWV) system collects waste water from fixtures and waste from toilets and delivers them to a sewer or septic system. Vent pipes exhaust sewer gases and provide air pressure so wastes can flow freely.

Pipe Schemes

Plumbing systems are composed of pipes and fittings. Metal or plastic pipes are joined by a variety of fittings designed to couple lengths in a straight line, turn corners, branch in two directions, reduce or enlarge pipe size, or connect to some type of fixture.

Pipes are made from several different metals and plastics. You often can identify a pipe's purpose by its size and makeup: indoor water supply pipes generally are copper or galvanized iron pipe in diameters of ½ inch, ¾ inch, or 1 inch; some water supplies in these diameters are made of plastic pipe. Gas piping is also this size, but is usually made of black (uncoated) or galvanized iron pipe.

Smaller-diameter, flexible copper or plastic tubing is used for water supplies that feed ice makers, hot water dispensers, water filters, and the like. Fittings may be brass or plastic. You'll also find flexible (sometimes ribbed) pipes serving from a small wall valve to toilets and faucets and flexible piping rated for delivering gas from valves to water heaters, dryers, cooktops, and other gas appliances.

Larger-diameter pipes, from 1 ½ inches to 4 inches, handle drain, waste, and vent (DWV) piping. A 4-inch or larger plastic or cast-iron pipe usually serves the main *soil stack*, the waste and vent line that serves toilets and other bathroom fixtures. Pipes that are 1 ½ inches or larger in diameter generally serve other waste and vent lines; light-gauge plastic pipe from 1 ¼-inch to 1 ½-inch diameter is sometimes used for built-in vacuum cleaning systems.

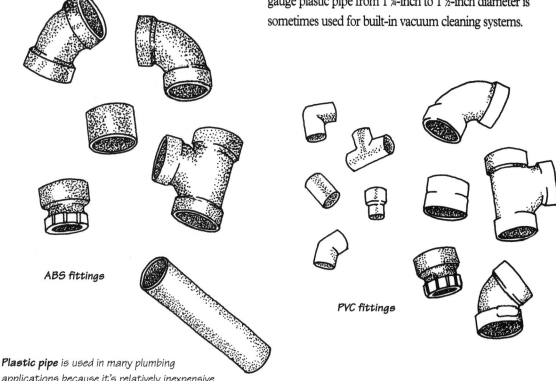

ABS fittings

PVC fittings

Plastic pipe is used in many plumbing applications because it's relatively inexpensive, easy to install, and impervious to corrosion. In some locations, plastic pipe is not allowed by codes for supply piping. Rigid pipe may be PVC (polyvinyl chloride) for cold water or DWV plumbing, CPVC (chlorinated polyvinyl chloride) for hot and cold water, and ABS (acrylonitrile-butadiene-styrene) for DWV piping. Flexible plastic tubing is made from PB (polybutylene) and PE (polyethylene). Plastic pipe is rated for the pressure it can handle; this rating is stamped on the pipe.

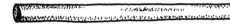

Galvanized iron pipe and fittings were standard for water supply plumbing before 1960 and are still common. The galvanized zinc coating on the outside of this pipe resists rust and corrosion, but inside the pipe clogs with mineral deposits and corrodes over time. Watertight connections are made with threaded fittings. Larger-diameter galvanized iron pipe is used for vent plumbing in some houses.

Rigid copper pipe is widely preferred for water supply piping. It's sturdy and durable, resists mineral buildup, and can handle both cold and hot water. Hard supply pipe is sold in three thicknesses: Type M (thin wall), Type L (medium wall), and Type K (thick wall). Most above-ground plumbing is Type M.

Soft copper supply pipe is more expensive than hard copper pipe, but it's flexible enough to be routed without as many fittings. Type L (medium wall) is more often used than Type K (thick wall) for aboveground applications.

Cast-iron pipe is a strong, durable material used for drain, waste, and vent (DWV) plumbing. Two types are common: the older hub or "bell-and-spigot," type that is joined with lead and oakum, and the newer hubless fitting that is connected with special rubber gaskets and stainless steel band clamps.

Copper pipe may be joined with soldered fittings or flare/compression fittings that can be disassembled.

A dielectric union should be used anywhere copper is connected to an iron pipe. This prevents corrosion from electrolysis that occurs when two dissimilar metals are joined together.

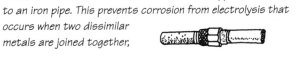

Pipe Schemes

Water travels under pressure through a system of pipes to your home. On these two pages, you can trace the route of municipal water from the street to your house.

The water company uses a meter to measure how much water you use, unless you use a well and your water use isn't tracked. This meter is often buried in a housing with a removable lid, located in front of the house near the street. In cold-winter areas, it may be inside the basement or crawl space, often placed where the meter reader can check it monthly without disturbing you. The water service delivers water to the meter through a large pipe called a main, which is often parallel to the street.

Once it passes through the main and meter, the water is controlled at different locations in your home with various types of valves, including the gate valve, the globe valve, and the hose bibb.

The water meter measures the amount of water that is used in your house. The meter uses dials or a digital readout to record how many cubic feet of water travel through it. The service's meter reader records the numbers each month and the company computes the difference between last month's and this month's readings to figure your bill. Reading a digital meter is easy—just like reading a car's odometer. To read a dial-type meter, record the smallest of the two numbers near the tip of each needle.

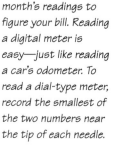

A main shutoff valve, a gate valve, is often located on each side of the water meter. The one on the street side is the water company's valve, which shuts off the system when work is being done on it or your meter is being changed. The other valve controls water that flows to your house. This is the main shutoff. Turn it completely clockwise to stop all water from flowing through your water supply system—both indoors and outdoors.

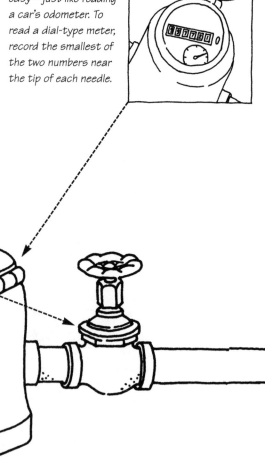

The hose bibb, an outdoor faucet, is simply a specialized valve that is threaded to receive a garden hose. The type with a wall-attachment flange is called a _sillcock_. Water flow is controlled by a seat washer, which, when worn, causes the faucet to drip.

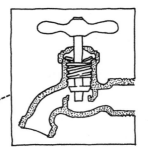

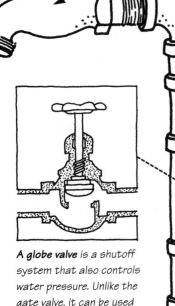

A _globe valve_ is a shutoff system that also controls water pressure. Unlike the gate valve, it can be used partially opened. Angled varieties are also available.

Two separate networks deliver water throughout a house—cold water and hot water pipes. They usually run in tandem, branching off to serve faucets, fixtures, and appliances. The cold water pipes carry water from the water service to all fixtures and appliances, including the water heater. In some cases, outdoor faucets and irrigation systems are fed by the cold water pipe before it reaches the house. Hot water pipes, which originate at the hot water heater, serve only those fixtures and appliances that require hot water; they don't, for example, go to the toilet.

The water in the pipes is under relatively high pressure. The pipes must be strong enough to handle the pressure, and their fittings and connections must be secure enough not to leak.

As discussed on page 68, supply pipes are generally copper with soldered fittings, or galvanized iron with threaded fittings. Plastic is used in some cases and is often the material of choice for outdoor piping.

Horizontal lines are called *runs* and vertical lines are called *risers*. A *stop valve* is often installed at the wall or floor below a faucet or fixture. A short, flexible *supply tube* runs from that valve to the fixture. The valve allows you to shut off the supply to the specific faucet or fixture in the event of an emergency or when repairs are needed, without shutting off water to the rest of the house.

Supply pipes are attached to the house's framing members with pipe straps; they may be fitted into drilled holes or notches. At the framing, the steel straps protect the pipes from nail punctures. Hot water pipes are often wrapped with insulation for energy efficiency.

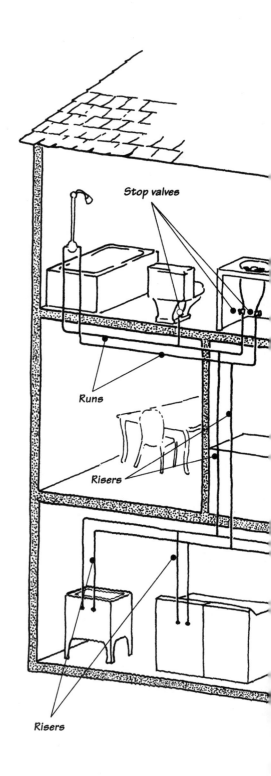

Stop valves

Runs

Risers

Risers

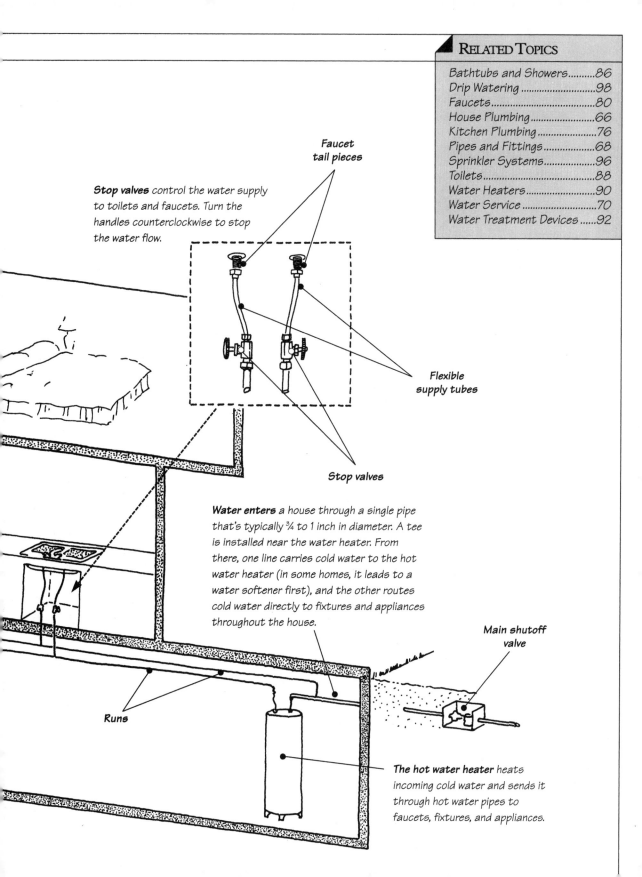

Faucet tail pieces

Stop valves control the water supply to toilets and faucets. Turn the handles counterclockwise to stop the water flow.

Flexible supply tubes

Stop valves

Water enters a house through a single pipe that's typically ¾ to 1 inch in diameter. A tee is installed near the water heater. From there, one line carries cold water to the hot water heater (in some homes, it leads to a water softener first), and the other routes cold water directly to fixtures and appliances throughout the house.

Main shutoff valve

Runs

The hot water heater heats incoming cold water and sends it through hot water pipes to faucets, fixtures, and appliances.

Pipe Schemes

The drain, waste, and vent (DWV) system is made of large-diameter pipes that carry water and wastes to the sewer line or septic tank. As its name implies, this system has three important components: drain lines collect water from sinks, showers, and tubs; waste lines carry wastes from toilets; and vent lines exhaust sewer gases and provide the necessary air pressure to allow wastes to flow freely.

All drain and waste lines slope slightly downward from the fixture toward the sewer or septic system, and the water and wastes move by simple gravity. The pipes are large in diameter—typically 1 ¼ inches to 4 inches—to prevent blockages. The main soil stack for toilets is normally a 4-inch pipe; showers usually have 2-inch pipe drains. Sinks, lavatories, bathtubs, and laundry tubs may be served by 1 ¼-inch to 2-inch pipes.

Most drain piping today is cast iron, plastic, or in some houses, copper. Some vent pipes are made of galvanized iron.

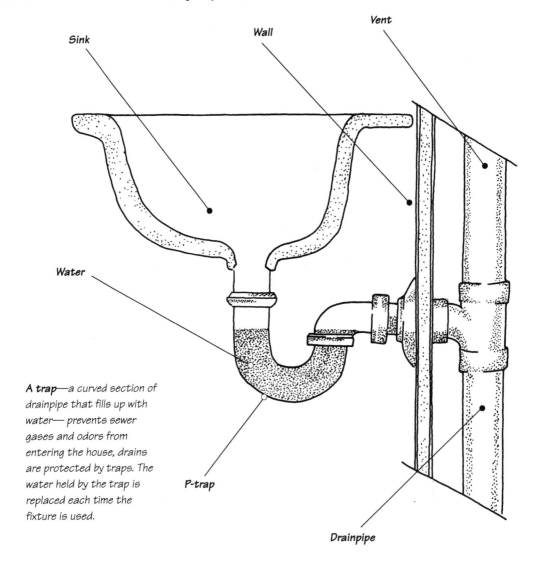

Sink

Wall

Vent

Water

A trap—a curved section of drainpipe that fills up with water— prevents sewer gases and odors from entering the house, drains are protected by traps. The water held by the trap is replaced each time the fixture is used.

P-trap

Drainpipe

A vent line carries sewer gases through the home's roof. Several vents may be connected and joined to the soil stack, as shown here, as long as there is no drain above the last connection point. Or vents may pass through the roof individually.

Drainpipes carry water and wastes to the soil stack.

The soil stack is the main thoroughfare for waste. At the roof, it is a vent; at the base, it leads to the sewer or septic system.

A cleanout should be located in all waste lines at easily accessible locations. A cleanout is simply a Y-shaped fitting that is capped off. If a blockage occurs, this is the easiest place for a plumber to clear, or "snake out," the line.

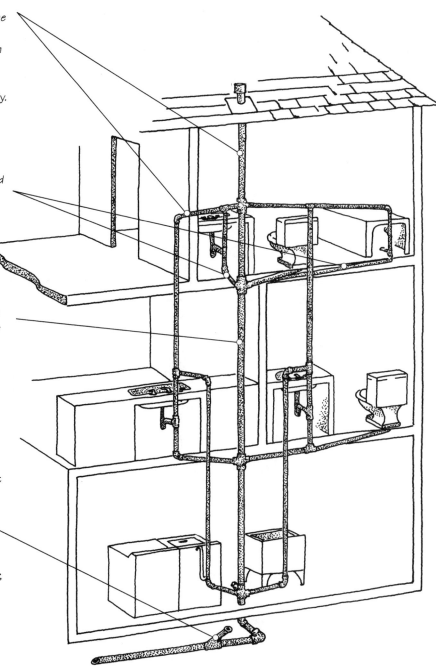

Most kitchens have a simple plumbing setup that includes hot and cold water supply lines, a waste line for the sink and, for kitchens with a gas range, a gas supply pipe. Many kitchens also have hookups for a dishwasher, a disposer, an ice maker, a water treatment system, and an instant hot water dispenser, but these generally are tied into the sink's plumbing.

Beneath the sink, there are two small valves: one for the hot water supply, the other for the cold. Turning these valves clockwise stops the flow of water through the flexible supply tubes that route water to the faucet.

On the cold water shutoff valve, there may be other water connections—sometimes by way of a *saddle valve*. This is where connections are made with flexible copper or plastic tubing to serve a water treatment device, an ice maker, a water chiller, or an instant hot water dispenser.

Shutoff valves serve the hot and cold water supplies to the faucet. Flexible supply tubes connect the valves to the threaded tailpieces of the faucet. Faucets with a separate or integral sprayer have a sprayer hose that connects onto another tailpiece at the center of the faucet body.

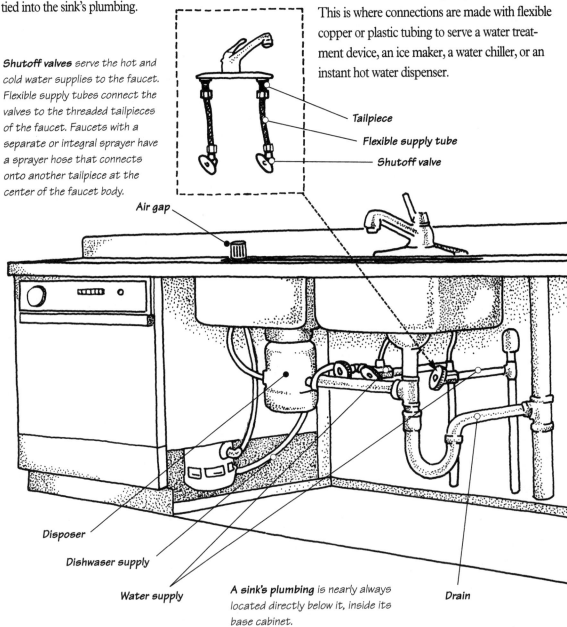

Tailpiece

Flexible supply tube

Shutoff valve

Air gap

Disposer

Dishwaser supply

Water supply

A sink's plumbing is nearly always located directly below it, inside its base cabinet.

Drain

The dishwasher may or may not have its own dedicated supply pipes and shutoff valves. Most drain by way of a hose that connects to an air gap fixture that's mounted at the sink top and prevents tainted water from siphoning back into the dishwasher. (The hose may just loop up under the countertop instead.) From the air gap, the dishwasher hose connects with the sink trap or the disposer.

Gas supply for a gas range usually is controlled by a shutoff valve beneath the range. A flexible supply line delivers the gas to the appliance.

A *gas range* is served by a flexible gas connector, controlled by a gas valve located on the wall or the floor behind it.

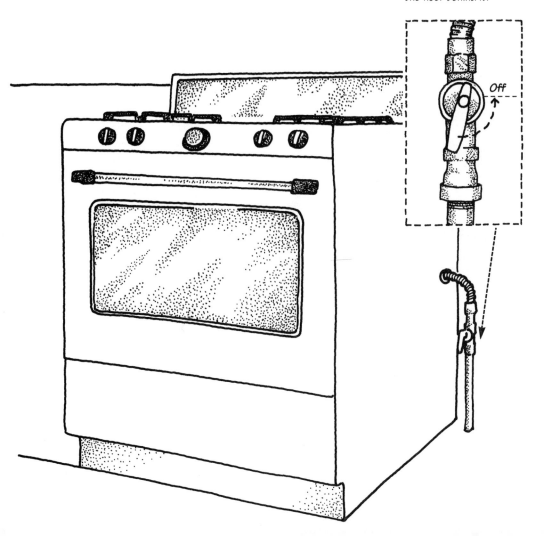

Off

Pipe Schemes

The kitchen sink is the central fixture in the most active room of the house. Day in and day out, it is the focal point of food preparation and cleanup. Accordingly, kitchen sinks are made to be both attractive and extremely durable.

Modern sinks no longer consist of a simple faucet and bowl. They have multiple bowls of various sizes and shapes and are designed with integral drainers, cutting boards, soap dispensers, instant hot water dispensers, purified water taps, sprayers, and more. They are available in stainless steel, enameled metal, solid surfacing (countertop-type) materials, and quartz composites.

Stainless steel sinks are available in many sizes and several thicknesses, measured by gauge. The lower the gauge number, the thicker the material. For durability and resistance to denting, scratching, and staining, 18-gauge or thicker is best.

Enamel sinks have cast iron or pressed steel under their surfaces; cast iron is preferred. Although they are easy to keep clean and come in a variety of colors, their weight calls for strong countertops.

Some solid-surface countertop materials may be formed to include rimless, seamless sinks that are a perfect match. Because the color and pattern goes through the material, scratches can be buffed out.

Quartz composite sinks come in a variety of colors and patterns. These are attractive, stylish alternatives to more conventional materials.

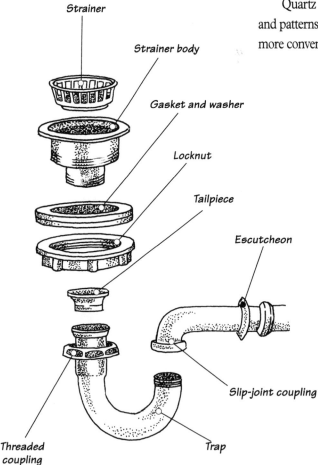

Strainer

Strainer body

Gasket and washer

Locknut

Tailpiece

Escutcheon

Slip-joint coupling

Threaded coupling

Trap

A kitchen sink drains by way of several components. The strainer fits into a strainer body that's inserted through the sink's hole and sealed with a bead of plumber's putty. Underneath are a rubber gasket and metal washer, and a large locknut or retainer tightens the body in place. The trap, always filled with water, seals the pipe so sewer gases won't enter the house. Waste water exits through the trap, down the vented drainpipe to the main stack. A garbage disposer mounts directly to a special strainer body. The trap then connects to an outlet on the disposer.

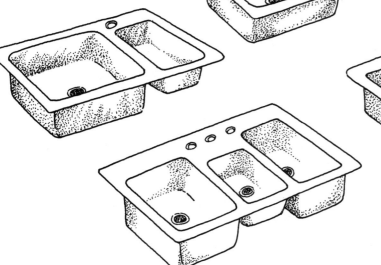

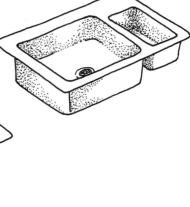

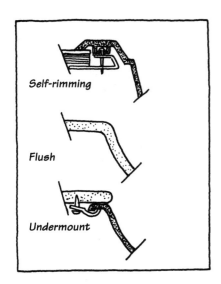

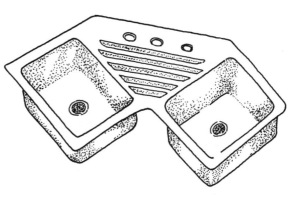

Kitchen sinks may have single or multiple bowls in a variety of shapes and sizes. They mount in three different ways: self rimming, flush, or undermounted. Self-rimming sinks have a molded edge that overhangs the countertop. Flush sinks are supported by metal strips around the perimeter or are an integral part of the countertop material. Rimless or undermount sinks are fastened or fused to the underside of the countertop.

Although there are hundreds of different styles, colors, and shapes of faucets, the working mechanisms of nearly all can be grouped into four types: cartridge, compression, ball, and disc. These names refer to the parts that actually control the flow of water through a faucet.

Three of these—cartridge, ball, and disc faucets—are mixing faucets. They normally have a single handle or control, although cartridge and disc types are also made with two handles. The compression faucet has two controls, one for hot, the other for cold water.

Compression faucets have washers or seals that restrict water flow by closing against a valve seat when the handle is turned. The other types don't use washers for the off-and-on action, although they do have O-rings and neoprene seals to prevent leaking. They're referred to as "washerless."

Because washers and seals wear out with use, resulting in the familiar drip, washerless faucets are generally favored over the washer type.

The drawings here show the workings of the four main types of faucets. Note where the washers, seals, and O-rings are located. If your faucet leaks or drips, chances are these parts have become worn and simply need to be replaced. If you do the work yourself, be sure to turn off the water to the faucet first, using the shutoff valves beneath the sink.

*A **disc faucet** has two discs: a movable upper disc, and a fixed lower disc. When the upper disc is turned or lifted and lowered against the lower disc, it regulates the flow of water through inlet and outlet holes. If this type of faucet leaks, the culprits are usually the inlet and outlet seals or sediment buildup in the inlets.*

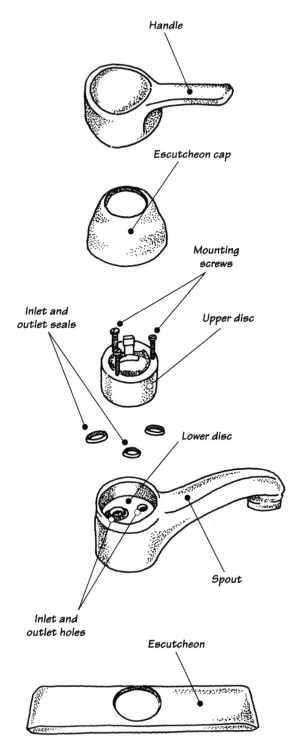

Handle

Escutcheon cap

Mounting screws

Inlet and outlet seals

Upper disc

Lower disc

Inlet and outlet holes

Spout

Escutcheon

A **cartridge faucet** has a hollow metal or plastic cartridge insert that seals the spout or faucet body. Depending on how holes in the cartridge align with the stem, water is mixed and controlled. Leaks generally are caused by worn or broken O-rings; drips usually mean the cartridge should be replaced.

A **compression faucet** has two separate handles. When a handle is turned, it raises or lowers the washer or seal at the base of the stem, controlling the water flow through the faucet. ▼

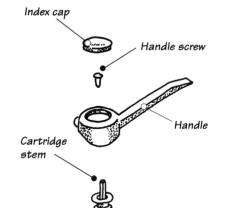

Index cap

Handle screw

Handle

Cartridge stem

Retaining ring

Spout

Faucet body

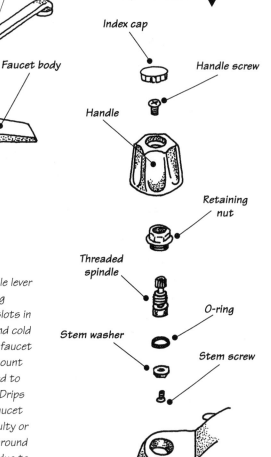

Index cap

Handle screw

Handle

Retaining nut

Threaded spindle

O-ring

Stem washer

Stem screw

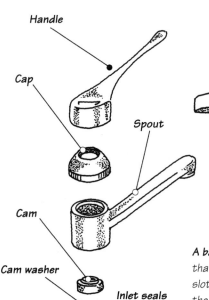

Handle

Cap

Spout

Cam

Cam washer

Ball

Inlet seals and springs

Faucet body

A **ball faucet** has a single lever that operates a rotating slotted metal ball. The slots in the ball align with hot and cold water inlet seats in the faucet body to regulate the amount of incoming water allowed to reach the mixing spout. Drips ◀ with this type of faucet usually indicate faulty or worn inlet seals. Leaks around the spout generally are due to worn or broken O-rings.

Bathrooms require water supply and drain-waste-vent systems for toilet, lavatory, tub, and shower fixtures. The supply lines normally run in tandem, then split off to serve the hot and cold inputs of each fixture. Drains typically run under the floor, culminating in the soil stack; vents are often interconnected.

Showers and bathtubs are supplied by a valve that is attached permanently to supply pipes. The most popular type of valve is called a *diverter valve*. A diverter valve will send water through the tub spout or the shower head.

Fluctuations in water pressure can cause scalding or cold temperature shocks in the shower. This normally happens when a toilet is flushed, causing the water pressure in the cold water pipes to dip. This problem is exacerbated in plumbing that's clogged with mineral deposits, in relatively small supply piping (½-inch), and in showers with low-flow showerheads. (Even so, low-flow showerheads are highly recommended for conserving water. Low-flow showerheads reduce water usage from an average 5 to 8 gallons per minute to about 2.5 gallons per minute.)

A *pressure-balance* tub or shower valve is designed to compensate for changes in water pressure. For additional scald protection, most antiscald valves have a stop that prevents the handle from rotating beyond a set position, limiting the amount of hot water the valve can deliver.

Drain and waste pipes
carry away waste water from sinks, tubs, showers, and toilets.

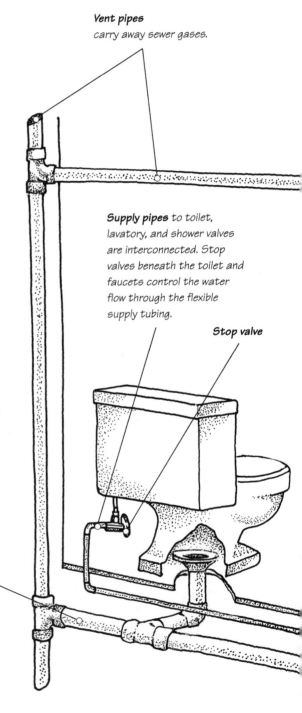

Vent pipes
carry away sewer gases.

Supply pipes to toilet, lavatory, and shower valves are interconnected. Stop valves beneath the toilet and faucets control the water flow through the flexible supply tubing.

Stop valve

A pressure-balance valve has a special diaphragm or piston mechanism that moves when the water pressure changes to maintain a balance between the hot and cold water inputs. Most pressure-balance valves reduce water flow to a trickle if the cold water supply fails.

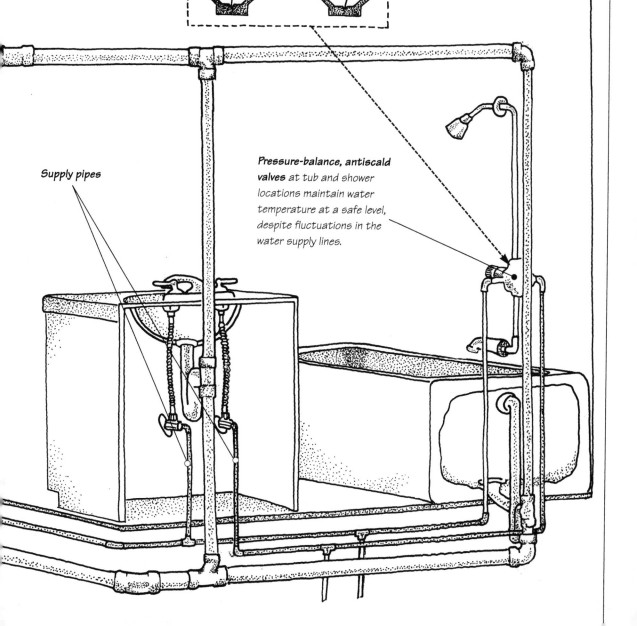

Supply pipes

Pressure-balance, antiscald valves at tub and shower locations maintain water temperature at a safe level, despite fluctuations in the water supply lines.

Bath sinks, or lavatories, are similar to kitchen sinks (see page 78) with a few notable differences. First, although bath sinks are made from the same variety of metals and other materials as kitchen sinks, many are made from vitreous china. Although china would be prone to chipping or cracking with the heavy use a kitchen sink receives, it is sufficiently durable for the bath. Because of this, beautifully-finished bath sinks are available in nearly every color of the rainbow.

Of course, most bath sinks are smaller than kitchen sinks. In addition, they come in many different shapes, including oval, round, angular, and curved. Although bath sinks are often set into counters,

they're also available freestanding. Pedestal sinks have beautiful lines but offer no storage. Some older bath sinks are wall-mounted.

A bath sink typically has two fixture holes on either 4-, 6-, or 8-inch centers. The wider types are meant to receive a split-set faucet, with faucet handles separate from the spout. The 4- or 6-inch holes may receive a center set or single-lever faucet. (See page 80 for more information on faucets.)

The drainpipe in a bath sink usually is fitted with a pop-up stopper that raises and lowers to control the flow of water down the drain.

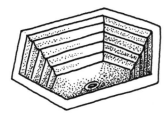

Bathroom sinks are available in a variety of shapes and styles. Sink bowls may have molded, self-rimming edges that overhang the countertop; may be rimless; may be mounted to the countertop's underside; or may be an integral part of the countertop.

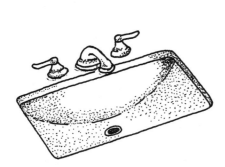

The sink drain has a flange that is sealed to the sink hole with a bead of plumber's putty. This flange is screwed into the drain body, which is tightened to the underside of the sink bowl with a locknut. The tailpiece, which may contain a pop-up stopper, attaches with slip-joint couplings.

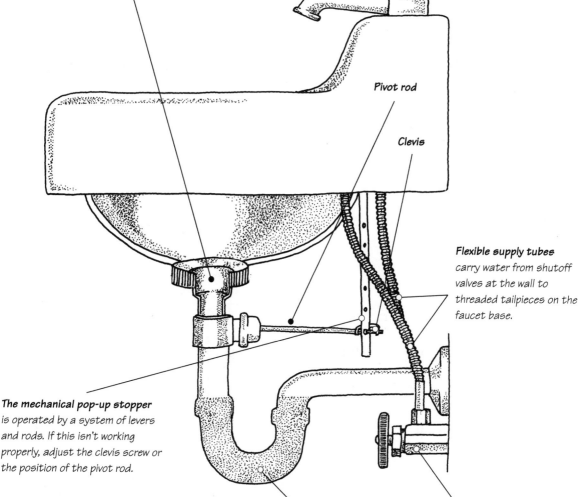

Pivot rod

Clevis

Flexible supply tubes carry water from shutoff valves at the wall to threaded tailpieces on the faucet base.

The mechanical pop-up stopper is operated by a system of levers and rods. If this isn't working properly, adjust the clevis screw or the position of the pivot rod.

The sink trap remains filled with water so sewer gases won't enter. It's connected to a threaded nipple inserted in a tee in the drain line.

Shutoff valve

Bathtubs and showers fundamentally are very simple appliances designed to contain water and to drain spent water into the sewer system. Of course, from those basics, developed a world of possibilities. Bathtubs and showers come in different types, sizes, shapes, colors, and configurations.

Bathtubs may be either built-in or freestanding. Built-in tubs range from familiar tub/shower combinations to ultramodern computerized whirlpool tubs that maintain a given water temperature. Freestanding tubs come in many styles, too, from classic claw-footed tubs to elegant jet models.

The best bathtubs are made from enameled cast iron. Although they're incredibly heavy, particularly in large sizes, cast-iron tubs have deep, durable finishes. Tubs made from acrylic reinforced with fiberglass are also good and, because they're lighter and more easily molded, they come in more styles than cast iron. Some tubs are also made of fiberglass, but this tends to fade in direct sunlight and scratch a little too easily.

Showers may be built-in or prefabricated. Built-in showers are essentially small rooms with walls of tile, stone, or some other waterproof material and a glass door that slides or swings open. The floor may be a one-piece unit made of plastic or some type of solid-surfacing material. Or it may be tile or a similar material with a pan that's flashed and hot-mopped using methods similar to those for a flat roof (page 125).

Prefabricated showers, like bathtubs, are made from fiberglass or acrylic that is reinforced with fiberglass; they come in a wide range of colors and styles. Some are made as single, one-piece units that are installed during construction, while others are modular units consisting of a base and three walls.

*A **shower** may be a built-in compartment, a modular set, or a single unit.*

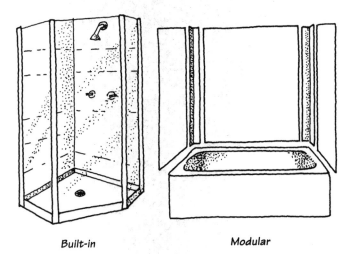

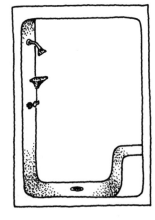

Built-in   Modular   Single unit

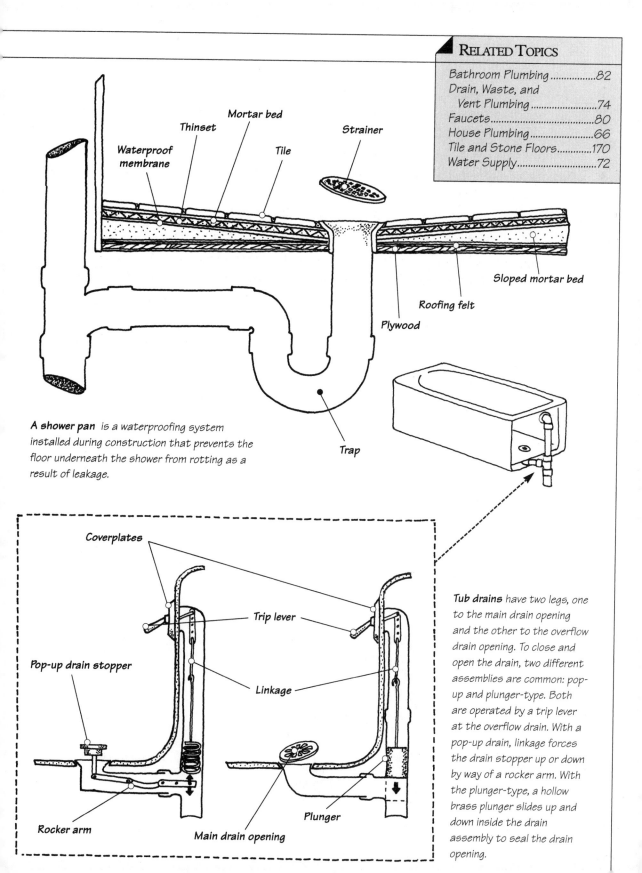

Waterproof membrane

Thinset

Mortar bed

Tile

Strainer

Sloped mortar bed

Roofing felt

Plywood

Trap

A shower pan is a waterproofing system installed during construction that prevents the floor underneath the shower from rotting as a result of leakage.

Coverplates

Trip lever

Pop-up drain stopper

Linkage

Rocker arm

Main drain opening

Plunger

Tub drains have two legs, one to the main drain opening and the other to the overflow drain opening. To close and open the drain, two different assemblies are common: pop-up and plunger-type. Both are operated by a trip lever at the overflow drain. With a pop-up drain, linkage forces the drain stopper up or down by way of a rocker arm. With the plunger-type, a hollow brass plunger slides up and down inside the drain assembly to seal the drain opening.

Pipe Schemes

The simple but ingenious mechanics of the toilet have changed very little since the earliest "water closet" was invented by Thomas Crapper in the nineteenth century. The toilet, although not one of the more glamorous of home fixtures, is designed to do a very specific job: to carry away waste and prevent sewer gases from entering the house. And unless something goes wrong with a toilet, it handles its role adroitly.

Opening the back lid, it's easy to be intimidated by all of those strange-looking parts. But a toilet actually operates quite simply. As shown in the drawing, a toilet has two main parts made from vitreous china: a tank and a bowl. Some toilets are cast as a single piece; others are made in two separate parts that are joined together.

When a toilet is ready for use, both tank and bowl are partly filled with water. Passages between the bowl and the *closet bend* (the top of the waste pipe) form a trap that remains filled with water at all times, blocking the rise of sewer gases.

When the toilet is flushed, the trip lever lifts a stopper between the tank and bowl, called a *flush valve*, letting the water in the tank flow into it. The pressure of the cascading water forces the bowl's water and waste down the waste pipe. The water flowing into the bowl also cleans the bowl. The bowl's water is replenished from the tank through a *refill tube*.

As the tank of a conventional toilet empties, a *float ball* drops, activating the *ball cock* (simply a water valve), which releases water into the tank. Some ball cocks operate on water pressure, without a float ball. The water is delivered to the ball cock through a supply tube that's connected to a valve at the wall or floor. When turned clockwise, this valve will shut off the flow of water to the tank. To prevent overflow and flooding, the top of the overflow opens and acts as a drain if the tank's water level rises too high.

A minimum-flush mechanism seals the flush valve seat when the tank is still partially full, keeping full pressure on the flush with less water. Although older toilets use 5 to 7 gallons of water to complete the flushing action, all new toilets are made to use a maximum of 1.6 gallons or less per flush.

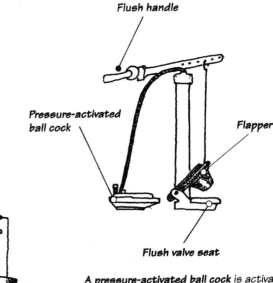

Flush handle

Pressure-activated ball cock

Flapper

Flush valve seat

A pressure-activated ball cock is activated by a drop in the tank's water pressure. This type, easily adjusted to deliver various amounts of water to the tank, eliminates the need for a float.

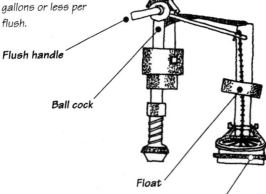

Flush handle

Ball cock

Float

Flush valve seat

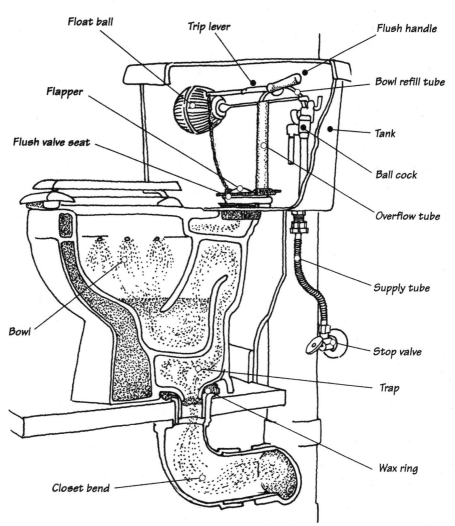

Trip lever

Bowl refill tube

Flush handle

Float ball

Ball cock

Tank-fill tube

Overflow tube

Flapper or seat ball

Flush valve seat

A conventional float ball, lift wire, and seat ball or flapper mechanism has been the standard flushing device for many years.

This cut-away view shows the relationship of the tank to the bowl and how the toilet's base forms a trap to block sewer gases. The flush handle raises the trip lever, which raises the flush valve flapper or seat ball from the flush valve seat and lets water rush into the bowl. The stop valve at the wall delivers water through a supply tube to the ball cock. When the float ball drops, the ball cock opens, filling the tank until the ball floats back to its upper position. An overflow tube sends excess tank water into the bowl. The refill tube replenishes water in the tank through the overflow tube.

Float ball

Trip lever

Flush handle

Flapper

Bowl refill tube

Flush valve seat

Tank

Ball cock

Overflow tube

Supply tube

Bowl

Stop valve

Trap

Wax ring

Closet bend

Pipe Schemes

A water heater converts energy to heat and transfers that warmth to water. It's connected to a cold water supply pipe and has an outgoing hot water pipe, or system of pipes, that supplies heated water to one or more taps and appliances. A conventional water heater stores heated water in its tank. The less common tankless water heater doesn't store water; instead, it routes heated water straight to taps or appliances.

The majority of water heaters are fueled by natural gas, although propane and electric water heaters are not unusual. Where natural gas is available, it is a much less expensive fuel than electricity.

Small instant hot water dispensers are simply miniature electric water heaters that serve only one faucet. They have a small, under-sink tank that heats and holds nearly boiling water, at about 190° F, and delivers it under low pressure through a separate sink-top spout.

A gas-fueled water heater warms water via a burner beneath its tank. Natural gas or, in some cases, propane or kerosene is piped to a gas valve. A thermostat that detects the water temperature in the tank regulates the fuel delivery to the burner, which is ignited by a pilot light or spark ignition. A vent or flue collects the toxic emissions from the burner and pipes them through the tank. At the top of the tank, this connects to a vent pipe that exhausts the gases out through the house's roof. Some newer, high-efficiency water heaters have fan-assisted vents that can be piped out through a wall.

Electric cable

Heating elements with thermostats

In an electric water heater, a heavy electric cable delivers energy to heating elements. An electric water heater doesn't create combustion gases, so no vent is required. A typical heater has one 5,500-watt or, for faster heating, two 4,500-watt elements. Separate thermostats control each element, cycling on as needed.

A tankless water heater circulates water through a series of burners or electric coils when a hot water faucet or appliance is turned on. Because the water heater doesn't store hot water, it costs less to operate and doesn't run out of hot water unless the flow exceeds its heating ability.

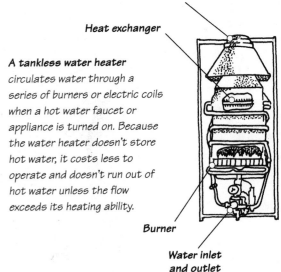

Flue

Heat exchanger

Burner

Water inlet and outlet

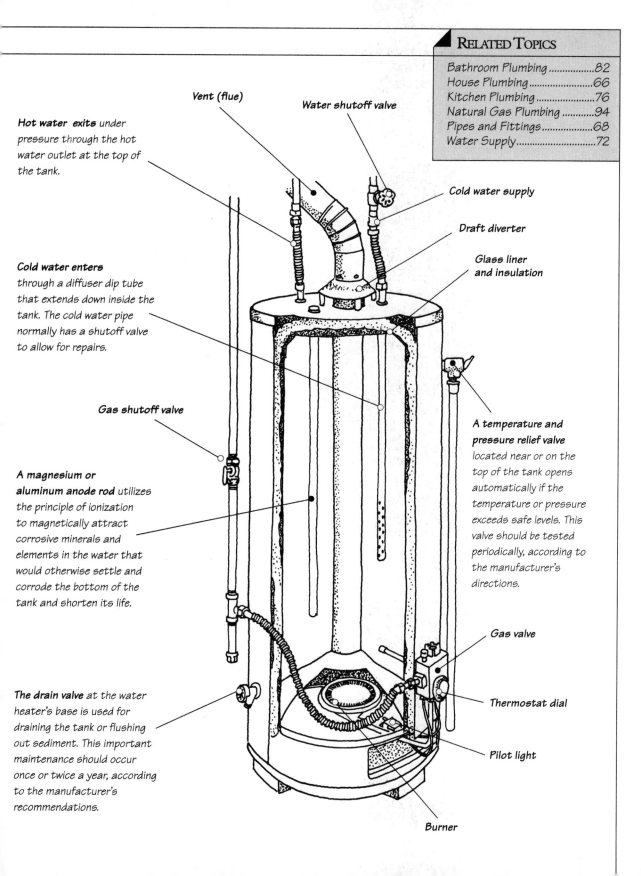

Vent (flue)

Water shutoff valve

Hot water exits under pressure through the hot water outlet at the top of the tank.

Cold water supply

Draft diverter

Glass liner and insulation

Cold water enters through a diffuser dip tube that extends down inside the tank. The cold water pipe normally has a shutoff valve to allow for repairs.

Gas shutoff valve

A magnesium or aluminum anode rod utilizes the principle of ionization to magnetically attract corrosive minerals and elements in the water that would otherwise settle and corrode the bottom of the tank and shorten its life.

A temperature and pressure relief valve located near or on the top of the tank opens automatically if the temperature or pressure exceeds safe levels. This valve should be tested periodically, according to the manufacturer's directions.

Gas valve

Thermostat dial

The drain valve at the water heater's base is used for draining the tank or flushing out sediment. This important maintenance should occur once or twice a year, according to the manufacturer's recommendations.

Pilot light

Burner

In recent years, some home drinking water has been found to contain a host of hazards that standard municipal water treatment procedures don't remove. To eradicate some of the chemicals and toxins that can find their way into drinking water, some homeowners install water treatment devices.

Built-in water filters utilize several different technologies to clean water. Some filters use only one of these methods, while others take advantage of two or more in order to combat a wide range of contaminants.

Most water problems occur with small water utilities or wells, since small suppliers don't administer quality tests frequently. The right filter for your home depends on the contaminants that need to be removed, which must be determined by testing.

Water softeners reduce the mineral content of hard water, substituting sodium (salt) for minerals, such as calcium, magnesium, and iron. This also reduces mineral buildup in pipes and appliances. But because they add sodium—a potential health hazard—to water, it's smart to install a softener only on the hot water side of a water supply system so it won't affect the drinking water.

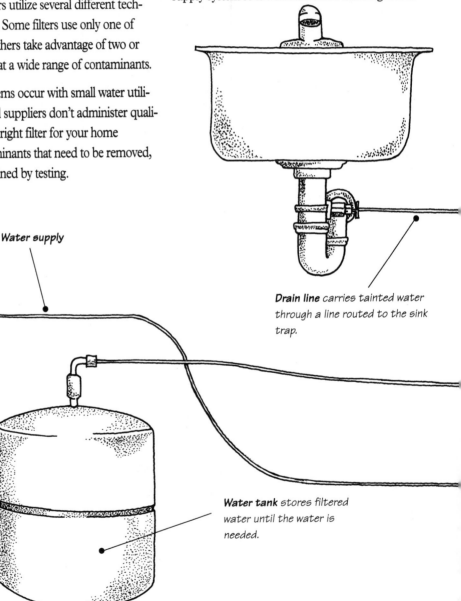

Water supply

Drain line carries tainted water through a line routed to the sink trap.

Water tank stores filtered water until the water is needed.

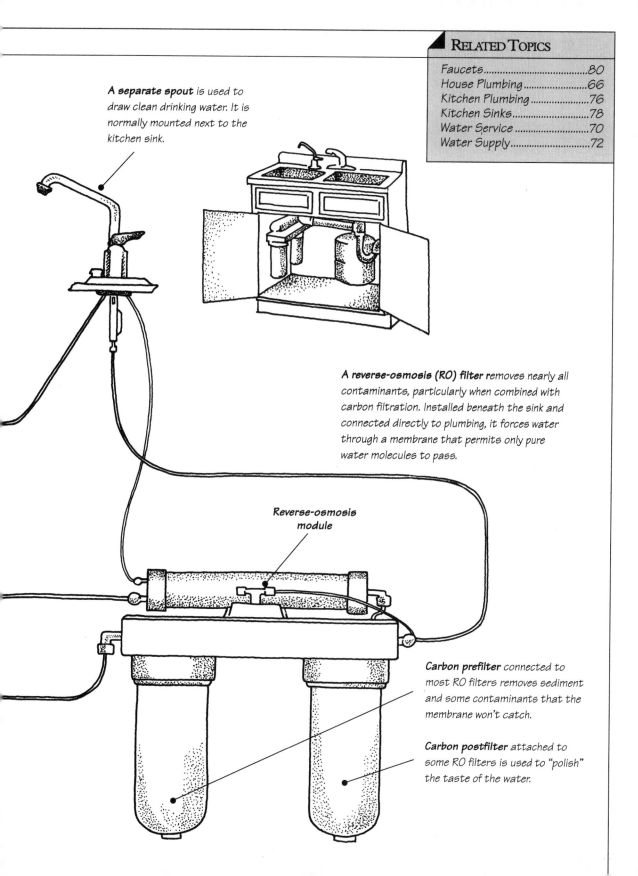

A separate spout is used to draw clean drinking water. It is normally mounted next to the kitchen sink.

A reverse-osmosis (RO) filter removes nearly all contaminants, particularly when combined with carbon filtration. Installed beneath the sink and connected directly to plumbing, it forces water through a membrane that permits only pure water molecules to pass.

Reverse-osmosis module

Carbon prefilter connected to most RO filters removes sediment and some contaminants that the membrane won't catch.

Carbon postfilter attached to some RO filters is used to "polish" the taste of the water.

Pipe Schemes

When it comes to energy efficiency, natural gas is the fuel of choice. It's the most affordable fuel to use; it requires less energy to extract, process, transport, convert, and deliver to homes than other fuels, and it is relatively clean burning, making it a responsible choice.

Natural gas is available in seven out of ten American houses, where it is used for space heating, water heating, cooking, clothes drying, and other tasks.

Natural gas is delivered to and throughout a house by pipes, in much the same way as water. Like water, it's under pressure. Because gas is both toxic and combustible, the piping and all fittings must be tight. Threaded iron pipe and fittings and flexible brass pipe with flare fittings (see page 69) or gray, epoxy-coated flexible tubing are the industry standards, although flexible corrugated stainless steel tubing that can be snaked through walls is a popular option.

Before gas is distributed to the various appliances throughout a house, it passes through a gas meter that has been installed by the utility company. This meter has dials that measure the amount of gas used.

On the pipe leading to the meter, normally right in front of the meter, there is a main shutoff valve that cuts off the gas flowing to the house. It's important to know where this valve is so you can turn off the gas in an emergency. In addition, there normally is an individual gas valve located just before every gas-fueled appliance so the gas may be shut off to that appliance without turning off the supply to the entire house.

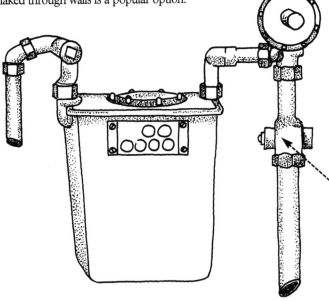

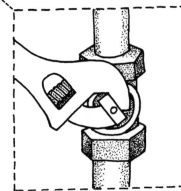

The main shutoff valve controls the gas supply to the house. When turned with a wrench so that the elongated head is perpendicular to the pipe, the flow is stopped. When the gas is turned back on, all pilot lights in appliances must be relit. (Follow appliance manufacturers' instructions.)

The gas meter measures the amount of natural gas used in a house. Each month, or interval, the gas company's meter reader notes the reading. This figure is compared with last month's to calculate usage. The dials, which measure cubic feet, are read from left to right. If an arrow is between two numbers, the lower number is the one recorded on each dial.

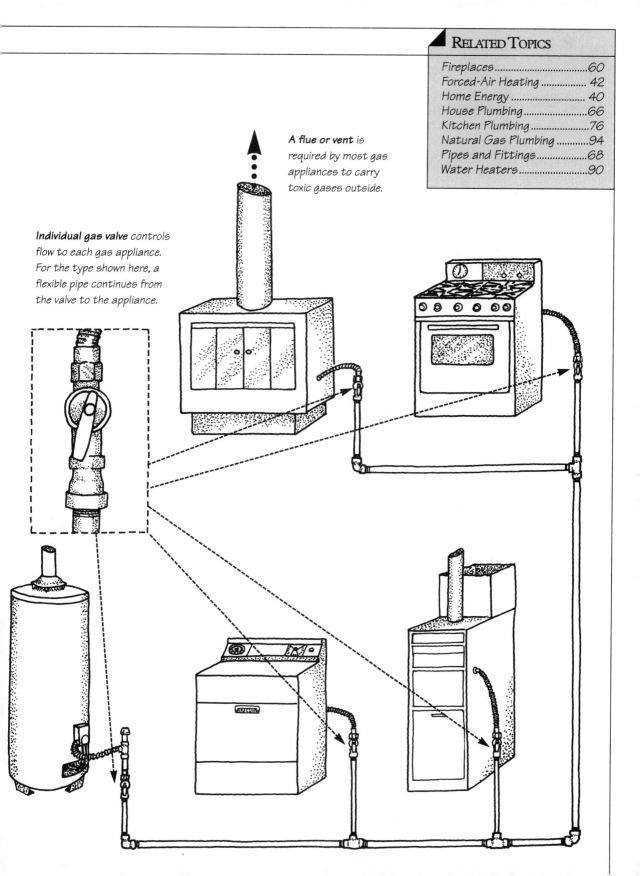

A flue or vent is required by most gas appliances to carry toxic gases outside.

Individual gas valve controls flow to each gas appliance. For the type shown here, a flexible pipe continues from the valve to the appliance.

Pipe Schemes

Although most houses have a hose bibb, many also have underground sprinklers that, when combined with a timer, can automatically irrigate the yard.

A sprinkler system consists of four main components: piping, valves, sprinkler heads, and a timer. Water supply piping—usually polyvinyl chloride (PVC)—routes water underground from the main supply pipe to valves and then to sprinkler heads. Valves control the flow to the heads; these may be operated manually or by an electric timer. An antisiphon device on the valves prevents any backflow of tainted water to the water supply system. Sprinkler heads deliver the water to the yard.

Two main types of sprinkler heads are available: spray and rotary. Spray heads are preferred for tightly controlled watering of shrubs and irregular areas; rotary heads require higher water pressure and work better for expansive lawns and densely planted areas because they throw water further, up to about 90 feet.

Pop-up heads automatically rise up when the water surges through them, then lower when the water shuts off. These are used where there is considerable foot traffic or on open lawns.

Sprinkler heads come in a wide assortment, each designed to emit a different amount or pattern of spray. Spray patterns include quarter circle, half circle, three-quarter circle, full circle, and rectangular strip patterns. A sprinkler's output is measured by its flow rate, the gallons of water it delivers in a minute (gpm).

In a typical sprinkler circuit, all the heads are served by a single valve. Sprinklers usually are grouped by type and output on separate circuits and they rely on several components to work smoothly and efficiently.

A riser is a vertical pipe, often threaded, that runs from the sprinkler supply pipe to the sprinkler head, raising the head up from the pipe to ground level or higher.

Sprinkler pipe, typically PVC, connects sprinkler heads to the water supply.

A _timer/control_ turns the automatic valves off and on. Timers may be either mechanical or programmable, digital models.

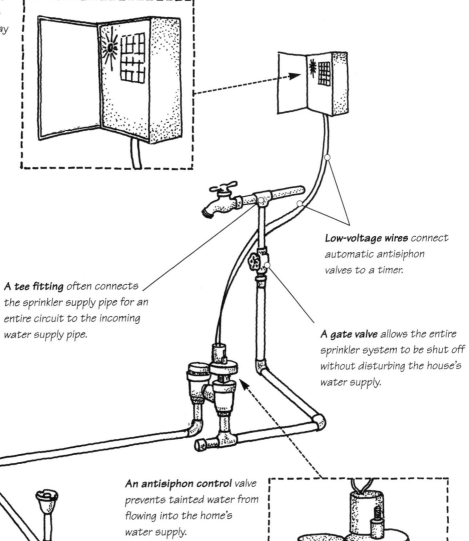

Low-voltage wires connect automatic antisiphon valves to a timer.

A _tee fitting_ often connects the sprinkler supply pipe for an entire circuit to the incoming water supply pipe.

A _gate valve_ allows the entire sprinkler system to be shut off without disturbing the house's water supply.

An _antisiphon control_ valve prevents tainted water from flowing into the home's water supply.

When it comes to watering outdoor plants and shrubs, no plumbing system delivers water more efficiently than drip irrigation. A drip system employs a network of flexible tubing and emitters to serve up water a drop at a time near the roots, according to the needs of the trees or plants. Water usage is cut substantially because the evaporation and overspray inherent in sprinklers and hand-watering are reduced.

Fundamentally, a drip system is similar to a sprinkler system (page 96). Like sprinklers, drip circuits are controlled by antisiphon valves that may be turned off and on by a timer and are designed to prevent any backflow of tainted water into the house's water supply.

But there are several differences. For one, drip systems operate under very low pressure—normally 20 to 30 pounds per square inch (psi) as opposed to a typical household water pressure of 50 to 100 psi. To reduce conventional water pressure to the low pressure required by a drip system, a pressure regulator normally is incorporated into the line.

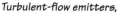

Turbulent-flow emitters,
*because of their makeup, are
resistant to clogging.*

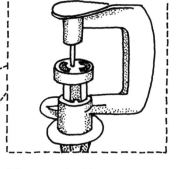

Misters and minisprays
*connect to tubing and operate
like small sprinklers to spray
water over a broad area.*

Because drip systems use tiny tubing and emitters, they also need filters to screen out sediment that might create clogs.

Drip systems may use plastic (PVC) pipe for part of the system, but the water ultimately is delivered through flexible tubing and tiny emitters.

Like sprinklers, drip systems can be controlled by a timer, but unlike sprinklers, they're used for relatively long periods of time, typically several hours.

Automatic controllers for drip systems can be set to water for several hours on a daily basis. Some will even repeat the cycle several times a day.

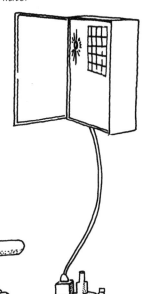

Diaphragm emitters adapt to changes in water pressure to deliver water in consistent amounts.

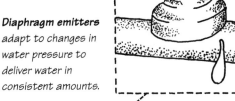

Various emitters are pushed into lengths of poly tubing where water is wanted. They're color coded by manufacturers according to their flow rate.

An antisiphon valve, which may be connected to a timer, controls a circuit of emitters.

In areas where terrain is flat and places for rain to runoff are limited, the ground can become saturated and eventually flood basements. To prevent this, many homes have sump pump systems. This special unit is designed to collect groundwater from around the foundation and under the basement floor and pump it safely away from the house.

A system of drain rock and drain tile, buried along the foundation and, in some homes, under the floor, collects groundwater. More drain tile or drainpipe routes the collected water to a sump tank that's buried at the low point of the basement floor. That tank, sometimes called a crock or basin, may be made of fiberglass, polyethylene, steel, concrete, clay, or tile. It generally has a sturdy cover that's easy to find.

There are two main types of electric sump pumps: submersible and pedestal. Submersible pumps are totally concealed, submerged in the bottom of the tank. A pedestal model stands on a column that extends above the floor level. Most sump pumps are activated by an automatic switch when the water level in the tank rises to a certain point.

Electric pumps plug into an electrical outlet. (Do not use extension cords with sump pumps, and be sure to disconnect the system before handling a pump.) Some pumps have a rechargeable 12-volt battery as an electrical backup in case the power goes out during a heavy rainstorm.

A sump pump draws in water through a filter and pumps it out through a discharge pipe or hose. A discharge pipe that's connected to a sewer has a check valve and may have an antisiphon device to prevent backflow of tainted water into the system.

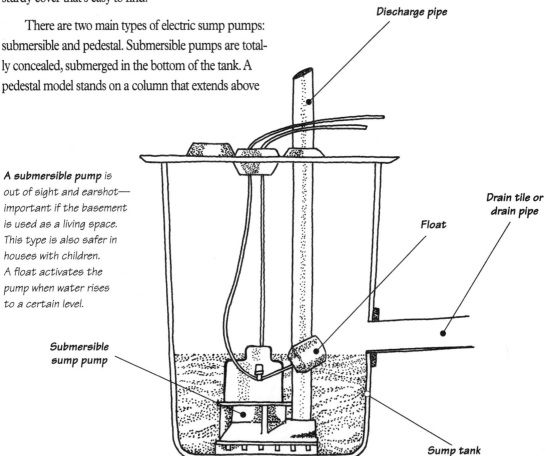

Discharge pipe

A submersible pump is out of sight and earshot—important if the basement is used as a living space. This type is also safer in houses with children. A float activates the pump when water rises to a certain level.

Drain tile or drain pipe

Float

Submersible sump pump

Sump tank

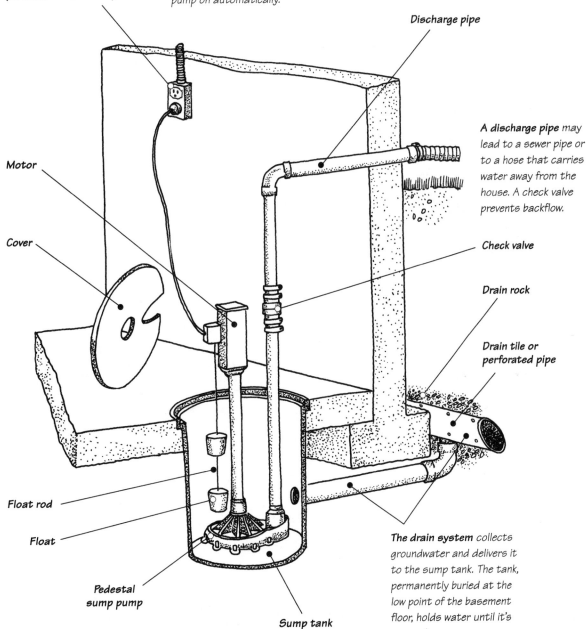

A pedestal pump is less expensive than most submersibles and lasts longer because it doesn't sit in the water. A float mechanism rises as the tank fills with water, switching the pump on automatically.

Electrical outlet (at least 4' from floor)

Discharge pipe

A discharge pipe may lead to a sewer pipe or to a hose that carries water away from the house. A check valve prevents backflow.

Motor

Cover

Check valve

Drain rock

Drain tile or perforated pipe

Float rod

Float

The drain system collects groundwater and delivers it to the sump tank. The tank, permanently buried at the low point of the basement floor, holds water until it's pumped away.

Pedestal sump pump

Sump tank

Pipe Schemes

Although central vacuum systems are still considered by many to be something of an extravagance, more and more builders and remodelers are finding their benefits worth consideration. Central vacuum systems take the drudgery out of vacuuming. They eliminate the noise, dust, and hassle of this less-than-favorite task.

A central vacuum system consists of a power unit that's coupled to a dust-collection canister, plastic piping, inlet receptacles, a long vacuum hose, and various vacuum heads and attachments.

The power unit can be mounted in the garage, basement, or utility room. Because it's installed in a remote location, it has several advantages over a portable vacuum. First, it can be larger, which means it's more powerful and has a greater capacity. Second, it doesn't recirculate fine dust back into the room, a problem with portable models. And third, the motor's noise is usually well out of earshot.

Vacuum brushes and attachments mount on the end of a particularly long hose. This hose plugs into special inlet receptacles that are positioned in the wall or floor at central locations on each level of the house. Some hoses include a power cord that can be plugged into an adjacent electrical outlet. With this type of unit, a rug attachment with a powered beater bar can be used.

Inlet receptacles are connected to the power unit by a network of plastic piping. Each story of most houses has one or more inlet receptacles. From each, the hose, typically 30-feet long, must be able to stretch to every corner of every room. Most receptacles are built with a low-voltage switch that activates when you plug in the hose, turning on the vacuum. When you pull out the hose, the power unit turns off.

*A **central vacuum system** consists of a power unit and collection canister, a network of plastic piping, and centrally located inlet receptacles. Houses with limited access below floors—two-story houses, for example—must have tubing routed elsewhere, perhaps vertically through laundry chutes or closets or through the attic. In a single-story house with a basement or crawl space, plastic piping can run under the floor and protrude through walls or directly serve floor inlets.*

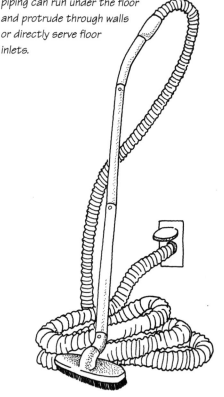

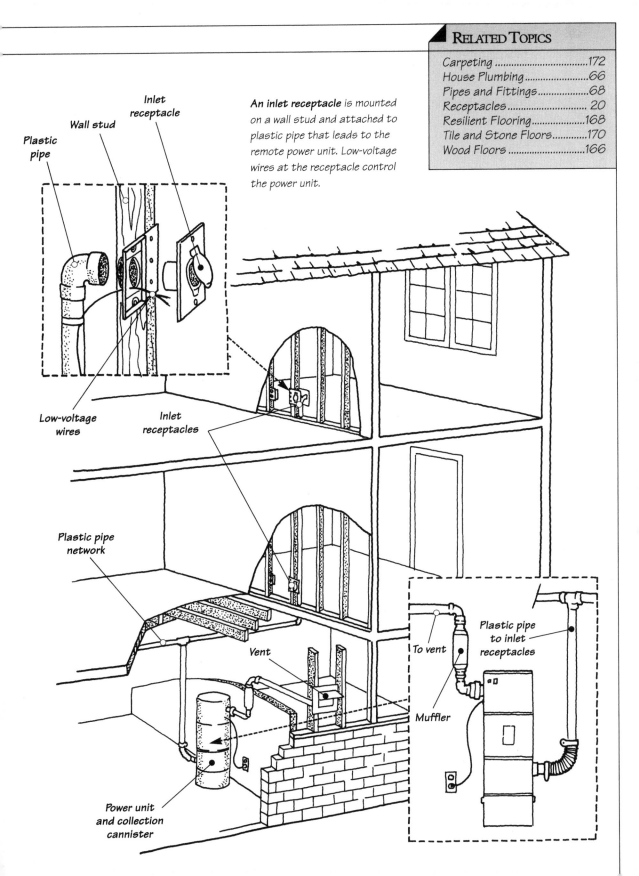

Plastic pipe

Wall stud

Inlet receptacle

An inlet receptacle is mounted on a wall stud and attached to plastic pipe that leads to the remote power unit. Low-voltage wires at the receptacle control the power unit.

Low-voltage wires

Inlet receptacles

Plastic pipe network

Vent

To vent

Plastic pipe to inlet receptacles

Muffler

Power unit and collection cannister

House Bones

Like the human body, a house has a skeleton that gives it support, and provides a framework for outer coverings. A house's skeleton is called the frame. Although some homes use steel framing, most are wood framed. A house's basic framework starts with a sound foundation, then beams, floor joists, wall studs, and roof rafters. To ensure the structure's strength, these parts are sized and connected in accordance with building codes, which are based on basic load engineering principles.

It's important to know which parts are critical to a house's structure so you don't compromise its strength when remodeling or doing work that involves cutting into the framing members. For example, if you remove part or all of a load-bearing wall without reinforcing the structure, the floors and roof may sag, forcing the windows and doors to stick. Or worse, part of the house might collapse.

Nonbearing walls may be perpendicular or parallel to joists or rafters. They often may be identified from under the house, because they're not supported by a foundation wall or beam. Because they don't support loads, they usually can be removed without compromising a structure's strength.

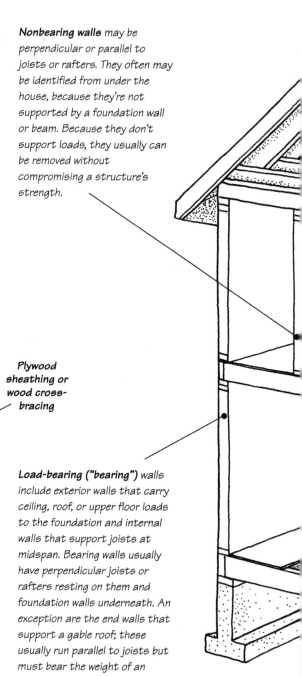

Steel strapping

Plywood sheathing or wood cross-bracing

Foundation bolts

Lateral stresses on a house, caused by wind and seismic loads, are managed by tightly interlocking framing members. Plywood sheathing, wood, or metal cross-bracing interconnect framing members, creating a sturdy triangular form and, together with foundation bolts, lock the walls to the foundation. The roof is secured and protected from wind uplift by steel strapping.

Load-bearing ("bearing") walls include exterior walls that carry ceiling, roof, or upper floor loads to the foundation and internal walls that support joists at midspan. Bearing walls usually have perpendicular joists or rafters resting on them and foundation walls underneath. An exception are the end walls that support a gable roof; these usually run parallel to joists but must bear the weight of an extended wall frame.

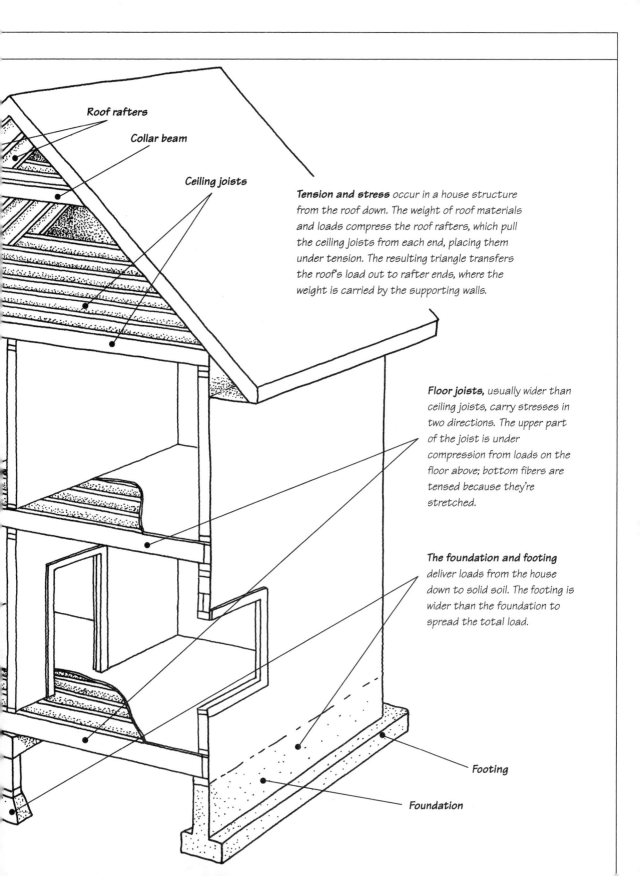

Roof rafters

Collar beam

Ceiling joists

Tension and stress occur in a house structure from the roof down. The weight of roof materials and loads compress the roof rafters, which pull the ceiling joists from each end, placing them under tension. The resulting triangle transfers the roof's load out to rafter ends, where the weight is carried by the supporting walls.

Floor joists, usually wider than ceiling joists, carry stresses in two directions. The upper part of the joist is under compression from loads on the floor above; bottom fibers are tensed because they're stretched.

The foundation and footing deliver loads from the house down to solid soil. The footing is wider than the foundation to spread the total load.

Footing

Foundation

House Bones

A house needs a foundation to shoulder its considerable weight; to provide a flat and level base for construction; and to separate wood-based materials from contact with the ground, which would otherwise cause rot and allow termite infestation.

Depending on when and where a house was built, the foundation may be made of stone, brick, preservative-treated lumber, concrete block, or poured concrete. By far the most common foundation material is concrete. There are three types of conventional concrete foundations: poured concrete, concrete block, and post-and-pier. Size and acceptable types are regulated by building codes. Everything in the foundation, from mesh to bolts, works together as a single unit to provide a singular, solid base that bears the load of the house.

Most houses have a raised perimeter foundation that supports floors and load-bearing walls. Some are built on a concrete slab that provides both a base for the structure and the bottom floor of the house. Still others, such as small vacation homes, rest on a series of concrete piers. Some houses utilize all of these methods for different portions of the house. Houses with perimeter foundations, for example, often have post-and-pier supports beneath a beam that runs under a load-bearing wall along the middle of the house.

The bottom of a foundation is called a *footing* or *footer*. It's generally wider than the foundation wall and is located about 12 inches below the frost line, the average depth at which soil freezes year after year. The footing distributes the house's weight to prevent future settling or movement.

A poured concrete foundation may be either a raised perimeter foundation, a slab, or a combination of the two. Houses in warm climates may have a *monolithic slab*—that is, the footings, foundation, and slab are a single, integral unit.

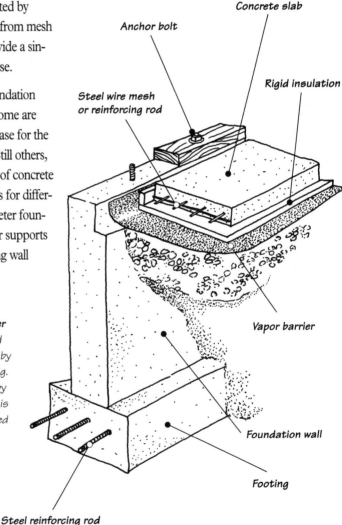

Concrete slab

Anchor bolt

Rigid insulation

Steel wire mesh or reinforcing rod

Vapor barrier

Foundation wall

Footing

Steel reinforcing rod

*A **conventional perimeter foundation** has a poured concrete wall supported by a poured concrete footing. Both are strengthened by steel reinforcing rods. This type of foundation is used in connection with both raised wood floors and concrete slabs.*

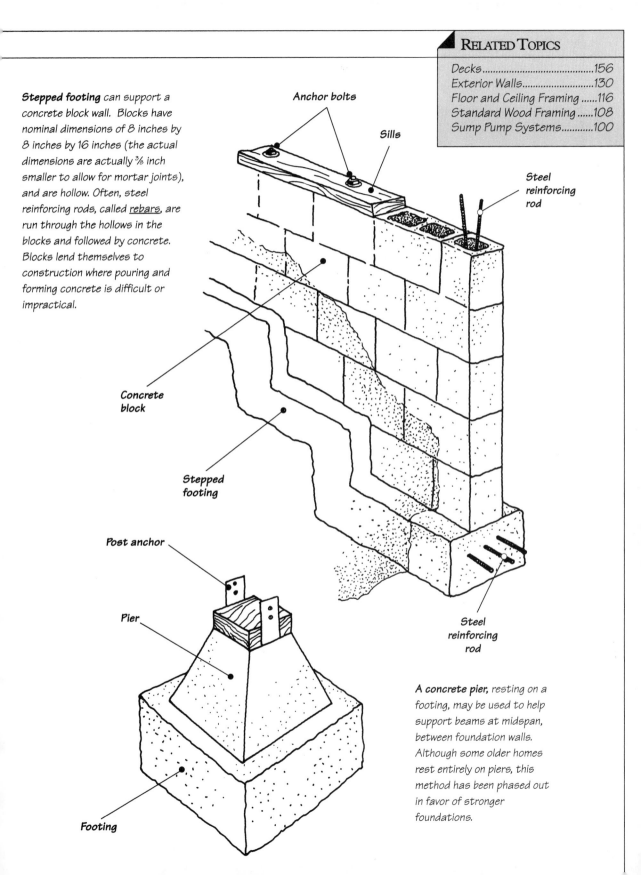

Stepped footing can support a concrete block wall. Blocks have nominal dimensions of 8 inches by 8 inches by 16 inches (the actual dimensions are actually ⅜ inch smaller to allow for mortar joints), and are hollow. Often, steel reinforcing rods, called <u>rebars</u>, are run through the hollows in the blocks and followed by concrete. Blocks lend themselves to construction where pouring and forming concrete is difficult or impractical.

Anchor bolts

Sills

Steel reinforcing rod

Concrete block

Stepped footing

Steel reinforcing rod

Post anchor

Pier

Footing

A concrete pier, resting on a footing, may be used to help support beams at midspan, between foundation walls. Although some older homes rest entirely on piers, this method has been phased out in favor of stronger foundations.

Most houses built since the 1920s have wood-frame construction: a system of wooden wall studs, floor joists, and other wooden members that provide a structure and a framework for attaching finished surfaces. The high cost of lumber is fueling an interest in steel and other alternatives, but wood is still the most popular framing material. In most cases, even houses that appear to have brick or stone walls actually have wood frame construction beneath their masonry facade.

There are two basic framing methods: *platform* and *balloon* construction. (Timber framing and log building are discussed on pages 110 and 112.) Platform construction is much more common than balloon framing, although balloon framing was employed in many two-story houses before 1930.

With both methods, wall studs, ceiling rafters, and floor joists occur every 16 or 24 inches, measured from center to center. These standardized layouts take advantage of floor, ceiling, and wall materials with the least cutting and waste. Most older houses have two-by-four wall studs spaced every 16 inches center to center; many newer houses have two-by-six wall studs spaced every 16 or 24 inches to make exterior walls stronger and allow a larger cavity for wall insulation.

With balloon framing, studs run full height from mudsill to the top plate, to a maximum of 20 feet. This method was popular before the 1930s and is still used on occasion for stucco and other masonry-walled two-story houses because such structures shrink and settle more uniformly than do platform structures. But balloon framing is more dangerous to erect, and the long, straight wall studs required have grown increasingly expensive and scarce.

The exterior wall sheathing adds rigidity to the structure and provides a flat base for siding, stucco, or other exterior wall finishes (see page 132). Older homes have diagonal sheathing—½-inch-thick boards nailed on the diagonal. Most newer homes have plywood or similar composite panel sheathing.

Exterior roof sheathing serves the same purposes for roofing. Most contemporary roof sheathing is plywood or oriented-strand board (OSB) panels; spaced wood sheathing is common for wood shingle roofs.

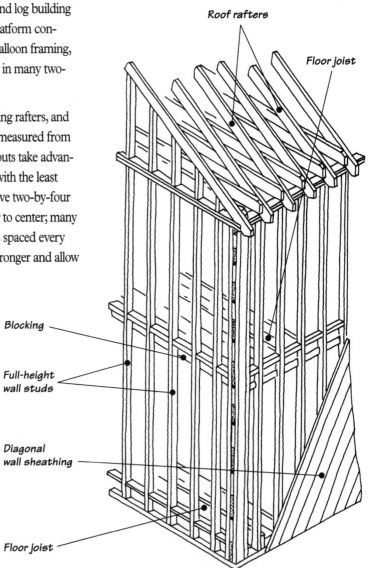

Roof rafters

Floor joist

Blocking

Full-height wall studs

Diagonal wall sheathing

Floor joist

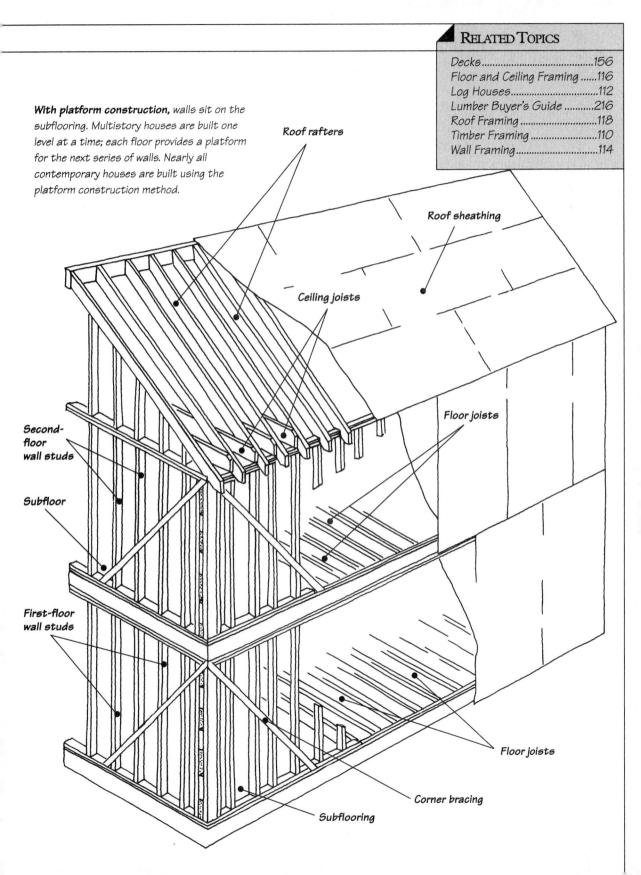

With platform construction, walls sit on the subflooring. Multistory houses are built one level at a time; each floor provides a platform for the next series of walls. Nearly all contemporary houses are built using the platform construction method.

Roof rafters

Roof sheathing

Ceiling joists

Floor joists

Second-floor wall studs

Subfloor

First-floor wall studs

Floor joists

Corner bracing

Subflooring

Houses, barns, town halls, and other buildings erected before the mid-nineteenth century were often structured with massive timbers connected with handcrafted wood joinery. Many of these classics stand today, proud survivors of the test of time.

With this type of construction, posts and beams carry heavy loads, reducing the number of framing members needed. The result is a building with large interior spaces, plenty of wall space for windows, and in most cases, a handsome display of heavy framing timbers.

Over the past fifteen years, timber framing has seen a revival. New timber-framed houses have exposed beams and other heavy framing members, yet they benefit from energy-efficient techniques of modern construction. Stress-skin panels—sandwiches of sheathing and rigid insulation—are applied to the outside surfaces of the framing to make the home energy efficient, and large, multipaned windows flood interior spaces with light and warmth.

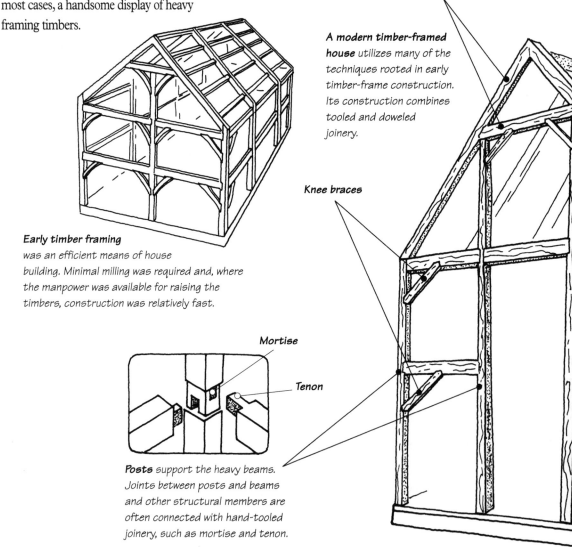

Bent or roof truss

A modern timber-framed house *utilizes many of the techniques rooted in early timber-frame construction. Its construction combines tooled and doweled joinery.*

Knee braces

Early timber framing
was an efficient means of house building. Minimal milling was required and, where the manpower was available for raising the timbers, construction was relatively fast.

Mortise

Tenon

Posts *support the heavy beams. Joints between posts and beams and other structural members are often connected with hand-tooled joinery, such as mortise and tenon.*

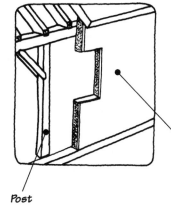

Stress-skin panels clad the roof rafters and framed walls for energy efficiency, leaving the posts and beams exposed inside.

Stress-skin panel

Post

Rafter beam

Ridge beam

Beams

House Bones

Log houses were once the natural solution to shelter in forested areas. The idea was to clear trees from a building site, cut away their branches and bark, notch the ends of the logs, and stack them to build cabin walls.

Now the term "log house" is applied to a wide range of construction techniques that may or may not use whole logs to yield a house that looks like it's built from logs. Although some are still made from peeled logs, most of today's log houses are made from logs that have been factory-milled in modified dowel shapes and sold as precut kits that can be owner-assembled. They run from small vacation-cabin sizes to large mansions.

Roofs may be framed with logs, using timber-framing techniques, or they can be built with conventional wood-frame construction.

Typical log species include white pine, ponderosa pine, cedar, cypress, and, rarely, hardwoods such as oak.

Log houses are often built from kits that include all framing, walls, roofs, windows, doors— everything but the foundation. There are more than 200 manufacturers; the method of construction depends on the maker.

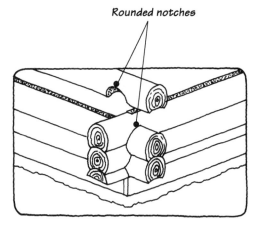

Rounded notches

Factory-milled logs are uniform in size and may have notched or dovetailed corners.

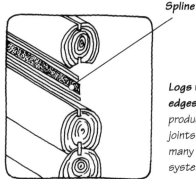

Spline

Logs with interlocking edges or splines that produce weathertight joints are common in many factory-milled systems.

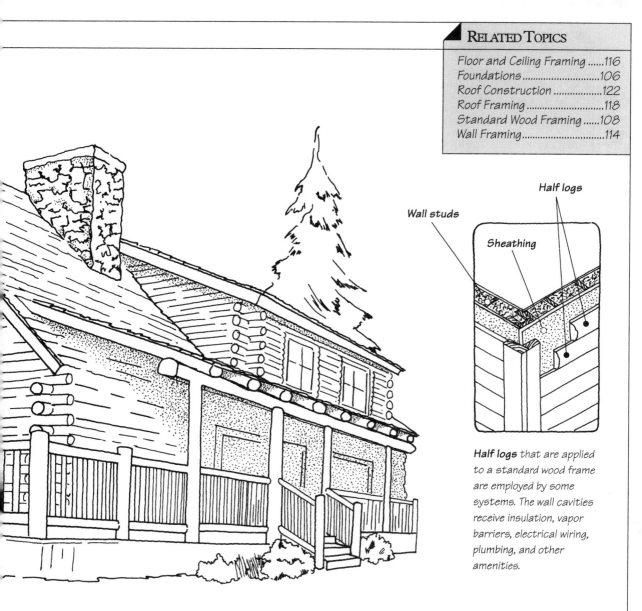

Half logs that are applied to a standard wood frame are employed by some systems. The wall cavities receive insulation, vapor barriers, electrical wiring, plumbing, and other amenities.

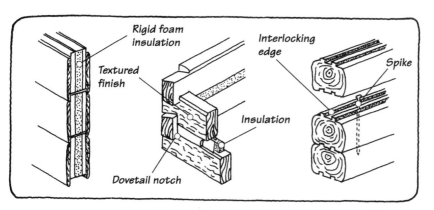

A wide range of milled profiles with sophisticated connections that seal out the weather is manufactured. For energy efficiency, many kits incorporate rigid foam insulation.

House Bones

Conventional house walls have an inner wooden framework. As discussed on page 108, this framework may or may not support part of the house, but it does support exterior and interior wall coverings, windows, and doors. It also provides cavities for electrical wiring, plumbing, ductwork, and insulation.

Although most walls are framed with two-by-four wall studs, two-by-sixes are used to provide more strength and larger cavities. Exterior walls, for example, may be framed with two-by-sixes to allow more room for insulation; some bathroom walls are framed with two-by-sixes to allow plenty of space for large pipes.

Not all houses are framed with wooden wall studs. Some newer homes are built with metal studs, a practice adopted from commercial construction methods.

Wherever windows, doors, or other openings occur along a wall, the regular studs are eliminated. Instead, a small beam, called a _header_, spans across the top of the opening, bridging the gap. Windows have a single or double _sill_ across the base, made of two-by-fours laid flat. _Trimmer studs_ support each end of the header, and _cripple studs_ fill in the areas above and below the openings. Cripple studs are placed every 16 or 24 inches, like wall studs.

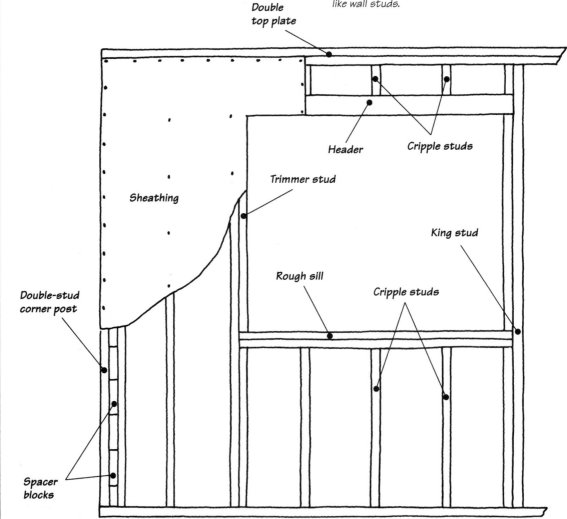

Double top plate

Header

Cripple studs

Trimmer stud

Sheathing

King stud

Rough sill

Cripple studs

Double-stud corner post

Spacer blocks

The wall frame generally consists of two-by-four or two-by-six _wall_ _studs_ placed every 16 or 24 inches, from center to center. Extra studs provide nailing area and sturdy support wherever walls intersect, such as at the corners. _Fireblocks_ (or _firestops_)—short horizontal blocks between studs—are required by some codes to slow down flame spread in the event of a fire. They also add rigidity to a center of a wall and may serve as a nail backing for wall coverings.

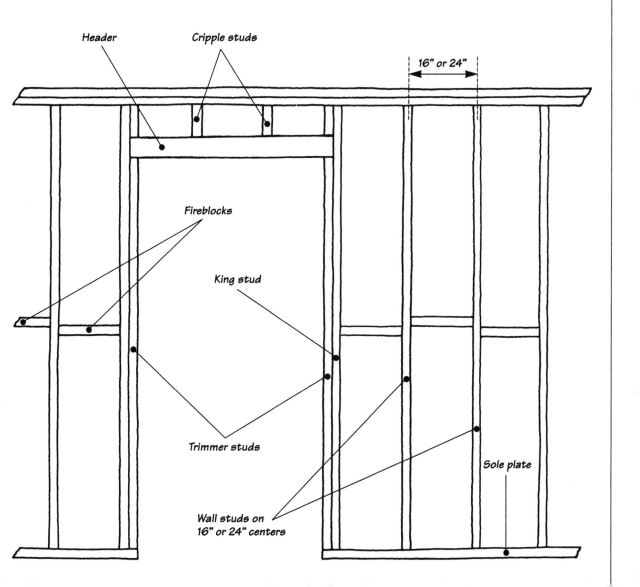

Header

Cripple studs

16" or 24"

Fireblocks

King stud

Trimmer studs

Sole plate

Wall studs on 16" or 24" centers

House Bones

Although some floors are built on a concrete slab, most are raised above the ground. Raised floors are more resilient under foot and provide room underneath for heating equipment, insulation, plumbing, and wiring.

A raised floor is constructed with a wooden framework that bridges from one exterior wall to another. This framework may be supported intermediately by girders, beams, or walls. On upper levels of a house, the underside of the floor framing serves to back the ceiling materials of the rooms below. Ceilings that have no floor above them are framed like floors, only they are constructed of lighter materials.

The framework is made of wooden *joists* that run parallel to one another at regular intervals. Floor joists are typically two-by-eights, two-by-tens, or two-by-twelves. Some newer homes have manufactured I-beam-shaped joists.

*The **subflooring** serves as a platform during construction then provides a base for the finish flooring. It may be made of boards laid at right angles or diagonally across the joists; or it may be made of plywood or other panel products that are laid perpendicular to the joists.*

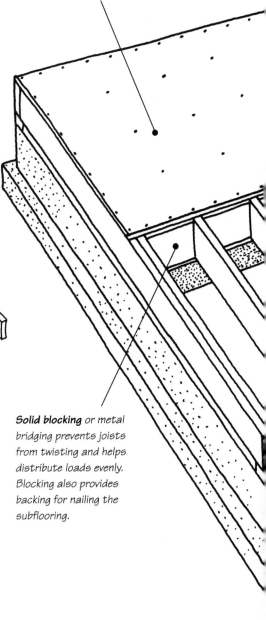

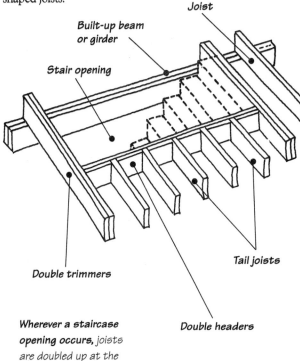

Joist

Built-up beam or girder

Stair opening

Double trimmers

Tail joists

Double headers

Solid blocking or metal bridging prevents joists from twisting and helps distribute loads evenly. Blocking also provides backing for nailing the subflooring.

Wherever a staircase opening occurs, joists are doubled up at the perimeter and capped with perpendicular doubled headers.

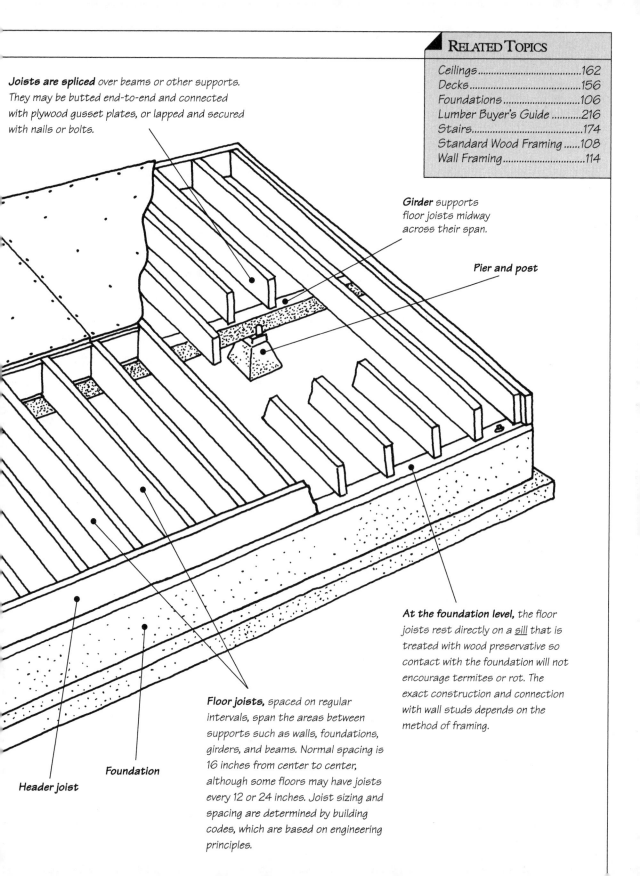

Joists are spliced over beams or other supports. They may be butted end-to-end and connected with plywood gusset plates, or lapped and secured with nails or bolts.

Girder supports floor joists midway across their span.

Pier and post

At the foundation level, the floor joists rest directly on a <u>sill</u> that is treated with wood preservative so contact with the foundation will not encourage termites or rot. The exact construction and connection with wall studs depends on the method of framing.

Floor joists, spaced on regular intervals, span the areas between supports such as walls, foundations, girders, and beams. Normal spacing is 16 inches from center to center, although some floors may have joists every 12 or 24 inches. Joist sizing and spacing are determined by building codes, which are based on engineering principles.

Foundation

Header joist

Drive through any neighborhood and you'll see that roofs have many different shapes. Houses have gable, hip, mansard, gambrel, flat, and shed roofs. Many homes combine roof types. It's quite common, for example, to see a hipped roof with gable dormers. A roof's shape is one of the key elements that sets the architectural style of a house.

Its shape also dictates how difficult and costly a roof is to build and how it will serve. Flat, shed, and some gable roofs tend to be less complicated to build and thus relatively affordable, but the more complicated and costly gambrel and mansard roofs offer more headroom in attics, making the space more functional.

Nearly all roofs are framed using one of two methods: standard stick framing or newer truss framing. Stick-framed roofs utilize individual rafters that span from the top of exterior walls to the ridge. Truss-framed roofs are built from triangular-shaped, premade truss units. Gable and hip roofs may be built primarily of

trusses; other roof shapes, particularly those with dormers or on houses with cathedral ceilings, attic rooms, or attic storage areas, are stick built. Truss construction is just as strong as stick framing but is lighter in weight and uses smaller sizes of lumber than does stick framing. Because trusses are carefully engineered units that shouldn't be cut, they are not a good choice for roofs that may be modified at a later date. And because they have several intermediate support members, they don't allow use of the attic space.

Like wall studs and floor joists, rafters and trusses are spaced every 16 or 24 inches from center to center. Most roofs utilize 16-inch spacings for strength and rigidity, and the rafters are usually positioned directly above the wall studs.

Hip rafter

Rafter tails

Roof style plays a major role in the overall look of a house. Shown here are six familiar styles. Many houses combine two or more of these shapes.

Shed **Flat** **Gable**

Gambrel **Hip** **Mansard**

7/12 Pitch

Rise **Run**

14/12 Pitch

12"

7"

14"

The angle of a roof is measured and referred to by either slope or pitch. The slope of a roof is the number of inches a roof rises in 12 inches of horizontal run. A roof with a "5-in-12 slope" rises 5 inches for every 12 inches of horizontal run. Pitch expresses the same two measurements as a fraction. The same roof has a "5/12 pitch."

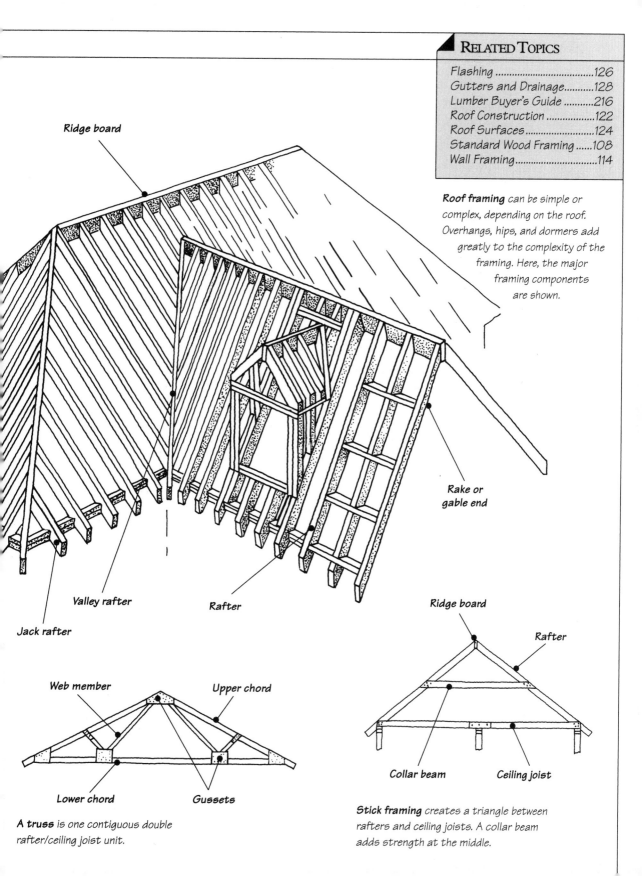

Ridge board

Roof framing can be simple or complex, depending on the roof. Overhangs, hips, and dormers add greatly to the complexity of the framing. Here, the major framing components are shown.

Rake or gable end

Valley rafter

Rafter

Jack rafter

Ridge board

Rafter

Web member

Upper chord

Lower chord

Gussets

A truss is one contiguous double rafter/ceiling joist unit.

Collar beam

Ceiling joist

Stick framing creates a triangle between rafters and ceiling joists. A collar beam adds strength at the middle.

The Outer Shell

In limestone caves nestled in the rolling hills near Johannesburg, archeologists discovered fossils of early humans that proved to be more than 2 million years old. From the time of those prehistoric cave dwellings to today's high-tech houses, people have been seeking shelter to protect themselves and their families from nature's extremes—wind-driven rain, bone-chilling cold, and scorching sun.

Shelter is the task of a house's exterior shell—the roofing, siding, windows, doors, and related components that provide a barrier between the indoors and outdoors. Additionally, today's houses are designed to be somewhat semitransparent shelters, providing the comfort and safety of an enclosure without the feeling of being "closed in." To this end, houses incorporate plenty of windows, doors, and skylights to bring in natural light, scenery, and a sense of connection with the outdoors.

Walls are faced with a durable siding. Beneath the siding, there is often building paper or a house wrap and, depending on the kind of siding, sheathing. Insulation provides an additional barrier against the heat and cold.

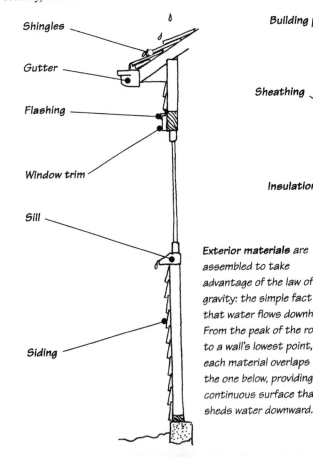

Shingles

Gutter

Flashing

Window trim

Sill

Siding

Building paper

Sheathing

Siding

Insulation

Exterior materials are assembled to take advantage of the law of gravity: the simple fact that water flows downhill. From the peak of the roof to a wall's lowest point, each material overlaps the one below, providing a continuous surface that sheds water downward.

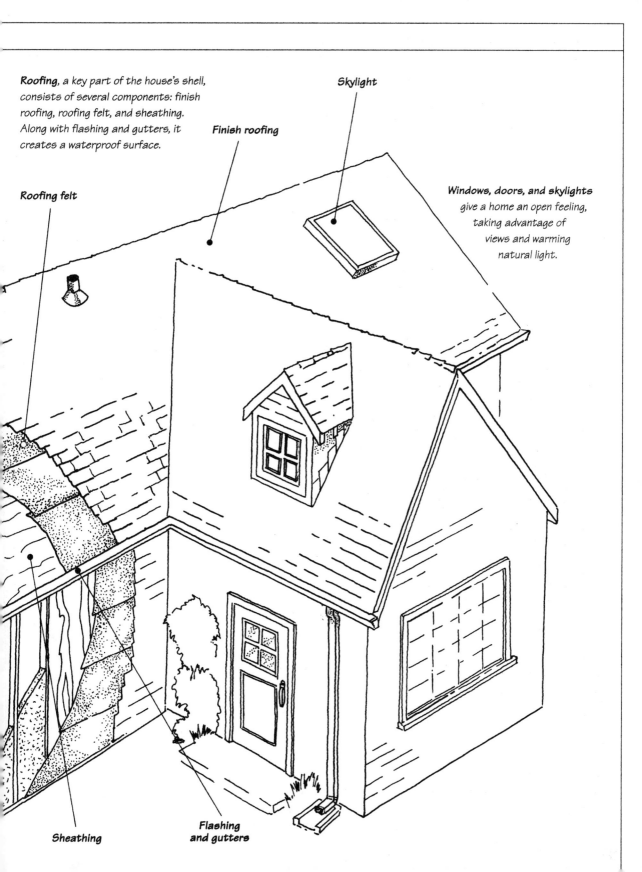

Roofing, *a key part of the house's shell, consists of several components: finish roofing, roofing felt, and sheathing. Along with flashing and gutters, it creates a waterproof surface.*

Skylight

Finish roofing

Roofing felt

Windows, doors, and skylights *give a home an open feeling, taking advantage of views and warming natural light.*

Sheathing

Flashing and gutters

Roofs take quite a beating. Fully faced toward the sky, they catch the brunt of weather's worst; they must be watertight, secure, durable, attractive, and elastic enough to withstand the elements and severe temperature shifts without cracking.

Over the centuries, techniques have been refined to yield roofs of considerable strength and durability. Materials have been developed that will last many years—in some cases, as long as the house.

A contemporary roof, regardless of its shape or surface material, consists of wood framing, sheathing, underlayment, flashing, gutters, and shingles or other roofing material. The illustration here shows how these materials work together to make a sound roof.

A roof's surface *must be able to withstand wind, rain, snow, hail, and sun. A wide variety of roof finishing materials is available; different types are discussed on page 124.*

Standard three-tab asphalt shingles *are a popular finishing material. They are made in 12-inch by 36-inch pieces that look like individual shingles. The exposed portion is called the <u>exposure</u>, and the lower edge is referred to as the butt.*

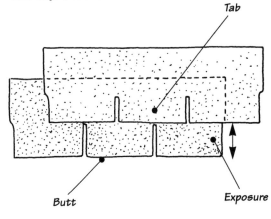

Tab

Butt

Exposure

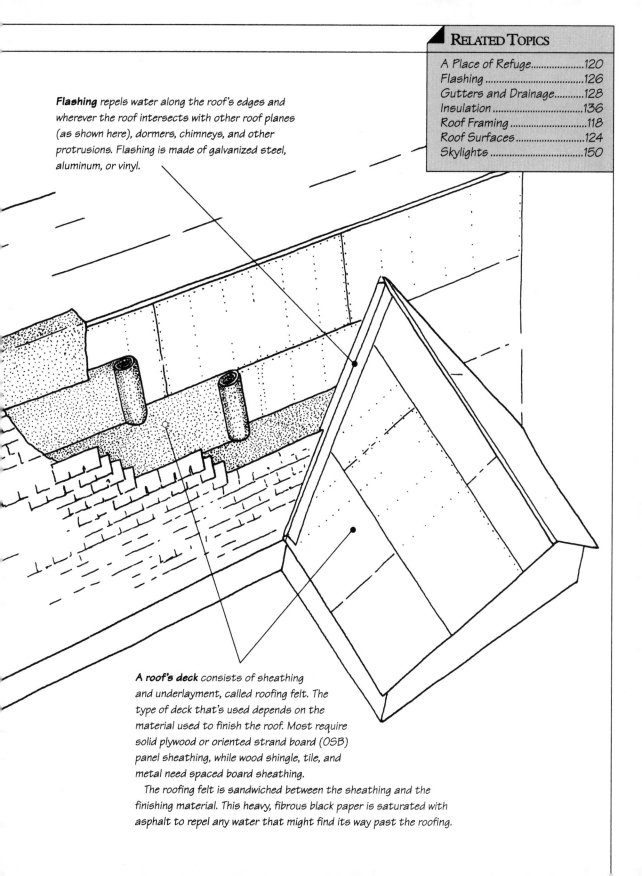

Flashing repels water along the roof's edges and wherever the roof intersects with other roof planes (as shown here), dormers, chimneys, and other protrusions. Flashing is made of galvanized steel, aluminum, or vinyl.

A roof's deck consists of sheathing and underlayment, called roofing felt. The type of deck that's used depends on the material used to finish the roof. Most require solid plywood or oriented strand board (OSB) panel sheathing, while wood shingle, tile, and metal need spaced board sheathing.

   The roofing felt is sandwiched between the sheathing and the finishing material. This heavy, fibrous black paper is saturated with asphalt to repel any water that might find its way past the roofing.

The Outer Shell

Throughout the ages, people surfaced their homes with just about anything that would keep out the weather, from animal skins to tree bark. Egyptians covered roofs with layers of rush, a method still used on the thatched roofs of European farmhouses. Ancient Greeks placed layers of reed-reinforced clay, a forerunner of tile roofing, on closely spaced timbers. They made these roofs watertight by applying bitumen, the main ingredient in today's asphalt roofing.

Modern roofing options are the result of eons of invention and experimentation. Some, such as slate and wood shakes, have remained virtually unchanged for centuries. Others, such as asphalt/fiberglass composites, lightweight concrete, and coated-metal tile, are products of the technological revolution. Each has slightly different durability, appearance, cost, and ease of application.

Although most contemporary roofs appear to be made almost entirely of shingles or tiles, they are actually waterproofing systems, made of components that work together. These systems include framing, sheathing, underlayment, flashing, and finish roofing.

Thatch **Hazel rod** **Lath**

Rafter

A **thatched roof** is built from layered bundles of straw or reeds. Hazel rods or steel rods run through the bundles horizontally; crooks or hooks fasten the bundles to hazel rods and rafters.

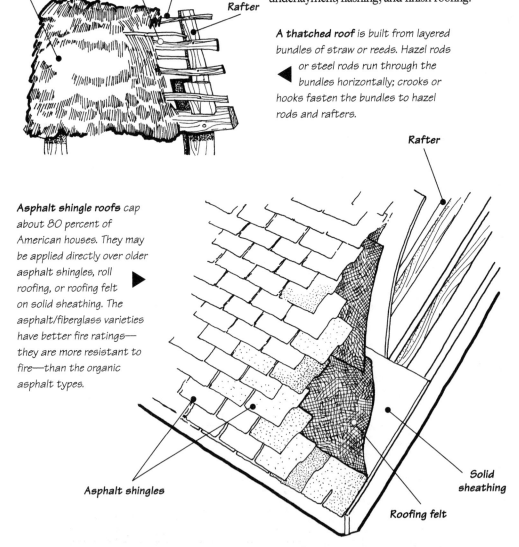

Asphalt shingle roofs cap about 80 percent of American houses. They may be applied directly over older asphalt shingles, roll roofing, or roofing felt on solid sheathing. The asphalt/fiberglass varieties have better fire ratings— they are more resistant to fire—than the organic asphalt types.

Rafter

Asphalt shingles

Solid sheathing

Roofing felt

Wood shingles and some wood shake roofs require open sheathing, one-by-six boards that are spaced apart. The spaces allow air to circulate around shingles to prevent moisture buildup underneath the wood.

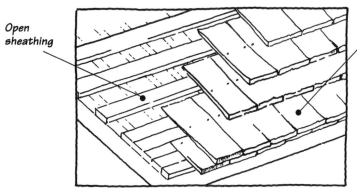

Open sheathing

Wood shingles

Wood shakes, with deeply grooved textures that allow air circulation, may be applied over solid sheathing with interlays of 30-pound roofing felt.

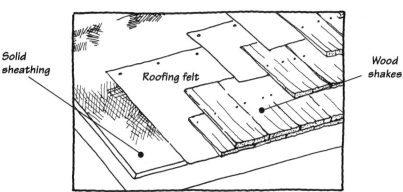

Solid sheathing

Roofing felt

Wood shakes

Tile and slate roofing is very heavy, sometimes requiring structural reinforcement. Most tile roofs go over solid sheathing and a 30-pound or heavier roofing felt. They're often hooked onto battens, strips of wood that run horizontally across the roof.

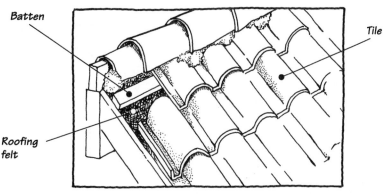

Batten

Tile

Roofing felt

A built-up roof is made from fiberglass-based asphalt sheeting, applied in layers with mopped-on hot bitumen between each. The surface is coated with bitumen and a layer of gravel or crushed rock to minimize damage from the sun and abrasion. Newer flat roofs may have coverings of single-ply bitumen or rubberlike materials.

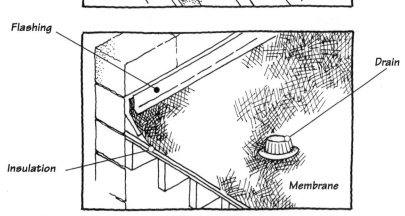

Flashing

Drain

Insulation

Membrane

Some parts of a roof and the exterior walls are particularly prone to leaks and water damage. These include roof valleys, the intersection between a dormer wall and roof surface, and chimney and skylight perimeters—nearly anywhere runoff water is heavy or where two surfaces meet. These and the other areas, shown here, require the extra protection that flashing provides.

Most flashing is made of galvanized sheet metal. Aluminum flashing is used with aluminum siding and roofing materials and, because it is easy to bend, for do-it-yourself installation. Copper flashing is custom fabricated for use with copper roofs and on some specialty applications.

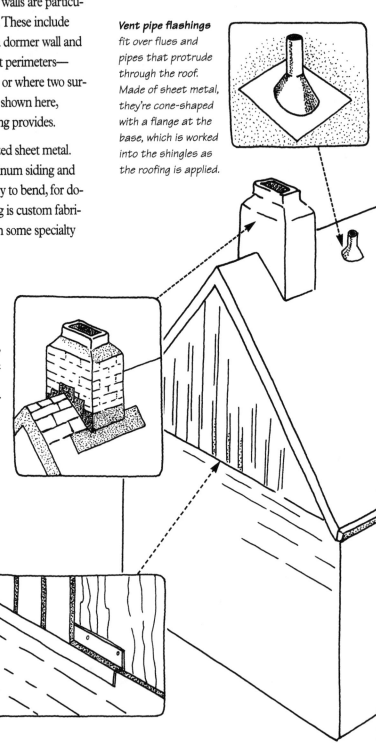

Vent pipe flashings fit over flues and pipes that protrude through the roof. Made of sheet metal, they're cone-shaped with a flange at the base, which is worked into the shingles as the roofing is applied.

Chimney flashing is applied around the base of a chimney in several parts: continuous flashing along the bottom, step flashing up the sides, and a saddle flashing at the top. Cap flashing, mortared or caulked into the chimney, laps over the top edges of the other flashings to prevent water from running behind them.

Z-flashing seals the horizontal seams between plywood or hardboard siding panels.

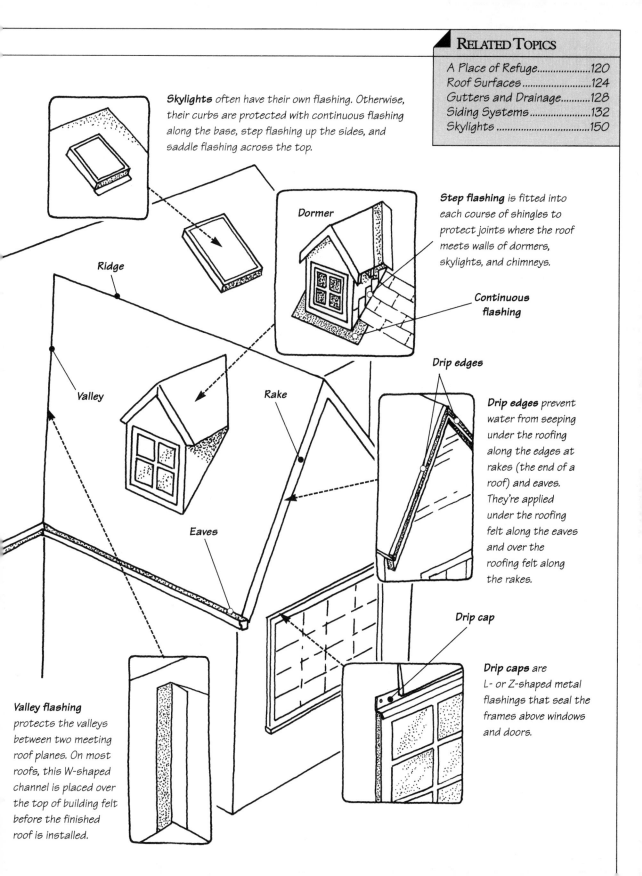

Skylights often have their own flashing. Otherwise, their curbs are protected with continuous flashing along the base, step flashing up the sides, and saddle flashing across the top.

Step flashing is fitted into each course of shingles to protect joints where the roof meets walls of dormers, skylights, and chimneys.

Dormer

Continuous flashing

Ridge

Drip edges

Drip edges prevent water from seeping under the roofing along the edges at rakes (the end of a roof) and eaves. They're applied under the roofing felt along the eaves and over the roofing felt along the rakes.

Valley

Rake

Eaves

Drip cap

Drip caps are L- or Z-shaped metal flashings that seal the frames above windows and doors.

Valley flashing protects the valleys between two meeting roof planes. On most roofs, this W-shaped channel is placed over the top of building felt before the finished roof is installed.

The Outer Shell

A heavy rain, flowing down house walls to the ground below, can cause a great deal of damage. At the very least, it taxes paint and wriggles into cracks, contributing to eventual, long-term decay. At its worst, it foils windows, invades walls, and undermines foundations. Gutters and drainage systems handle rainwater removal to keep these things from happening.

Gutters are long troughs that catch water at the house's eaves; they slope slightly toward downspouts that pipe the water to the ground. Depending on the drainage around the base of the house, water is then routed into underground drainpipes or other means to disperse it away from the foundation.

Gutters on older homes may be wood, galvanized sheet metal, or copper. Newer gutters are usually aluminum or vinyl. Do-it-yourself metal and vinyl types are fitted together from 10-foot-long gutter sections and a variety of corner connectors, end caps, and other components. Vinyl gutter systems are favored by do-it-yourselfers because they are lightweight and can be easily snapped or glued together. Professionally installed seamless gutters are extruded from precoated aluminum in very long single runs at the site.

Gutters and downspouts carry rain off the roof and deliver it a safe distance away from the house. They're fitted together from a variety of standardized parts.

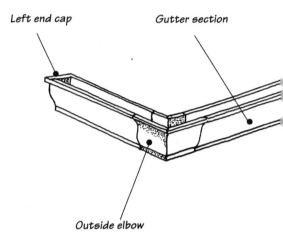

Left end cap   Gutter section

Outside elbow

A gutter's profile depends on the material from which it's made. Wooden gutters are milled; galvanized metal gutters are formed; aluminum and vinyl gutters are extruded.

A gutter's attachment depends on the type of system. Gutters are either hung from the sheathing along the eaves before the roof is shingled or nailed to the fascia with a clip hanger or spike-and-ferrule hanger.

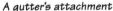

Spike-and-ferrule hanger

Wooden

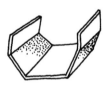

Vinyl

Clip hangers

Galvanized steel

Aluminum

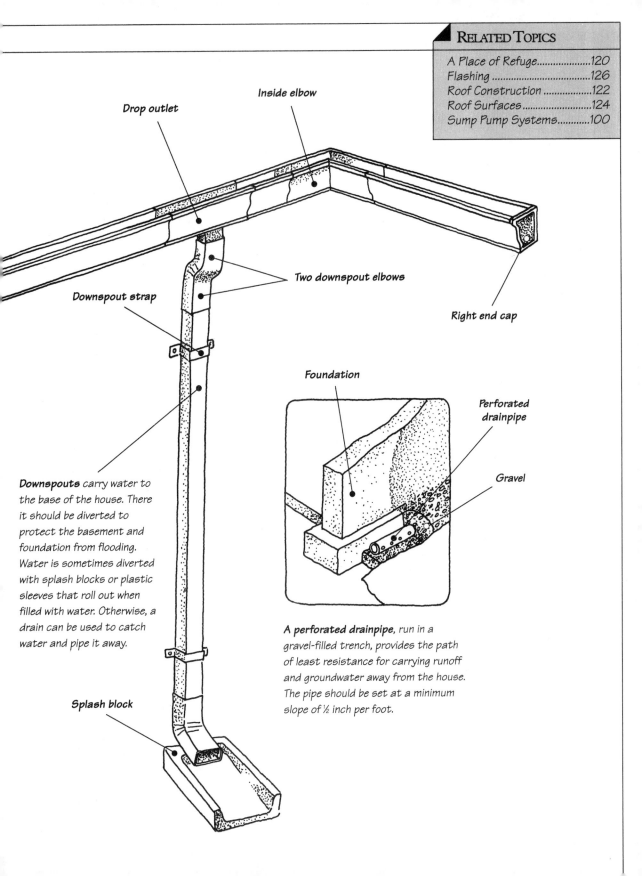

Inside elbow

Drop outlet

Two downspout elbows

Right end cap

Downspout strap

Foundation

Perforated drainpipe

Gravel

Downspouts carry water to the base of the house. There it should be diverted to protect the basement and foundation from flooding. Water is sometimes diverted with splash blocks or plastic sleeves that roll out when filled with water. Otherwise, a drain can be used to catch water and pipe it away.

Splash block

A perforated drainpipe, run in a gravel-filled trench, provides the path of least resistance for carrying runoff and groundwater away from the house. The pipe should be set at a minimum slope of ½ inch per foot.

Keeping nature's extremes at bay is no small task. Exterior walls must reject rain, wind, and cold in the winter and block excess heat in the summer. To do this, they must be well insulated and leak-free. Various siding systems have been developed to accomplish these tasks, as discussed on page 132.

In addition, exterior house walls are designed to support the structure. With few exceptions, house walls are framed with wooden wall studs, then clad with some type of siding system. This method provides the necessary strength and allows numerous design options.

Although many older homes don't have insulated walls, the exterior walls of most homes built since 1970 are insulated. Insulation may be located in the cavities between wall studs or applied as rigid board panels over the top of, or in place of, sheathing.

But exterior walls must be more than just heat efficient; they must contain windows for views and natural light and doors for access. Through these elements, they provide a connection with the world outside. (Windows and doors are also discussed in this section.)

Wall studs *provide the structural framework of a wood-frame wall.*

Insulation

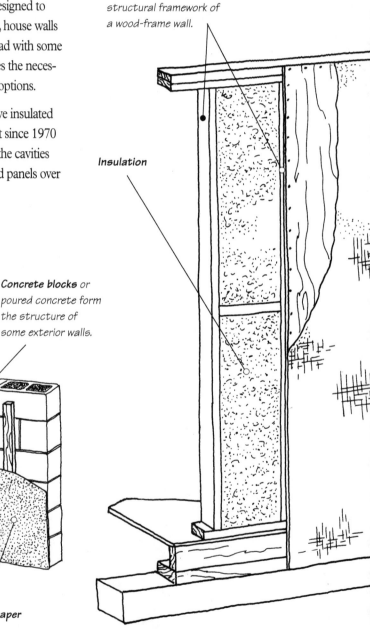

Furring strips, a gridwork of one-by-twos or one-by-threes, provides a flat nailing base for some types of siding. Furring is required for nearly all vertical siding patterns.

Concrete blocks or poured concrete form the structure of some exterior walls.

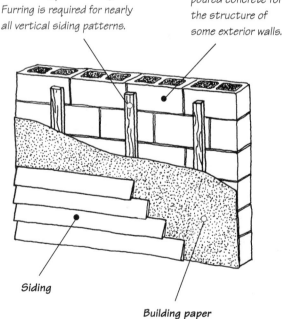

Siding

Building paper

Housewrap, a relatively new material, significantly reduces heat loss caused by air infiltration. The material, sold in 12-foot-wide rolls, is stretched over sheathing or wall studs and stapled or nailed in place. Because it is made from spun-bonded or woven polymer, it rejects water and wind but doesn't trap indoor humidity in the walls.

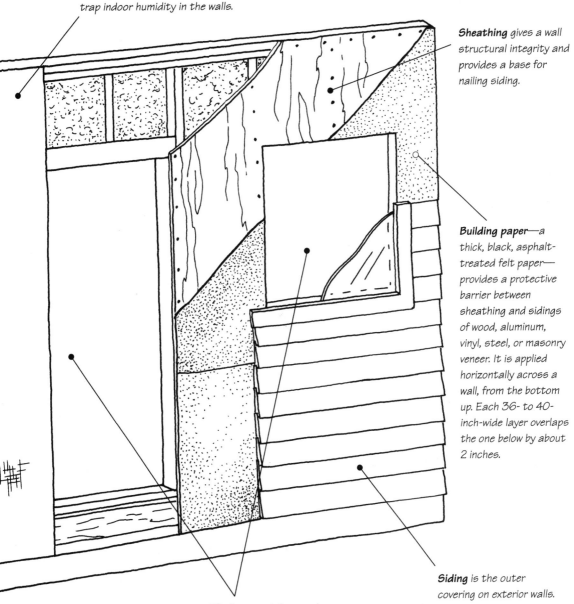

Sheathing gives a wall structural integrity and provides a base for nailing siding.

Building paper—a thick, black, asphalt-treated felt paper—provides a protective barrier between sheathing and sidings of wood, aluminum, vinyl, steel, or masonry veneer. It is applied horizontally across a wall, from the bottom up. Each 36- to 40-inch-wide layer overlaps the one below by about 2 inches.

Siding is the outer covering on exterior walls.

Windows and doors, also part of exterior walls, provide the openings for light, views, and access.

The predominant material on the outside of a typical house is siding. Spanning from corner to corner and from ground to eaves, siding sets the tone for how a house looks. In addition, it's responsible for shedding rain, rejecting wind, and surviving sun.

Many different kinds of sidings are used on houses: clapboard and similar wood sidings; sheet sidings made of plywood, hardboard, and oriented-strand board (OSB); synthetics such as vinyl, aluminum, and steel; wood shingles; masonry veneers; and stucco.

Some sidings are applied over a base of solid panel sheathing, while others go directly over the wall studs. Some are even applied over existing siding. Between sheathing and siding, a thin layer of building felt or housewrap often provides an additional barrier between air and water infiltration. Here is a more detailed look at how these siding systems work.

Wood sidings are milled in various patterns for both horizontal and vertical application. Wood siding is usually, but not always, applied over solid sheathing and a layer of building paper. Horizontal patterns are nailed through sheathing into studs; vertical patterns generally are nailed to horizontal nailing or furring strips. Horizontal sidings are always applied so that each board overlaps the one below it; in some cases, the edges are milled to interlock, as they are with all vertical patterns.

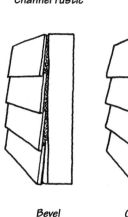

Channel rustic

Shiplap

Tongue and groove

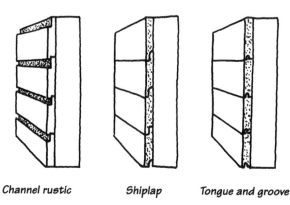

Bevel

Clapboard

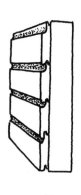

Dolly Varden

Drop

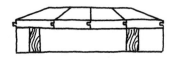

Tongue and groove

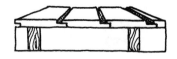

Channel

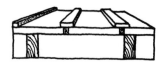

Board and batten

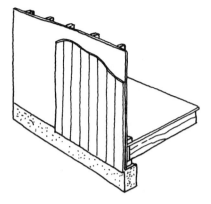

Hardboard and plywood sidings are manufactured in sheet form. They are available in a standard width of 4 feet and lengths of 8, 9, and 10 feet. Made in a variety of thicknesses and patterns, sheet sidings are often applied directly to wall studs, without sheathing.

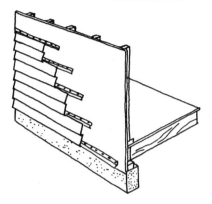

Vinyl, aluminum, and steel siding systems look similar to horizontal wood siding but don't require as much maintenance. These systems can be applied right over old siding but are easier to apply over solid sheathing.

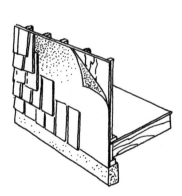

Wood shingles are used as a siding material for a wide range of house styles, from contemporary to Victorian. They're usually installed over solid sheathing or horizontal furring strips and a protective layer of building paper.

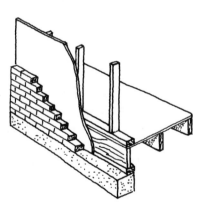

Brick and stone walls are usually built of wood-frame construction with a thin veneer of brick or stone. These walls almost always have solid sheathing and special ties that connect into the areas of grout between bricks and stones.

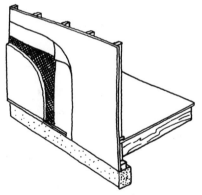

Conventional stucco, a mixture of sand, cement, lime, and water, is troweled onto a metal lath that is attached to wall studs. Newer types of stuccolike coverings are sprayed or troweled onto a base of fiberglass mesh, fiber-cement board sheathing, or foam board insulation. They're less likely to crack.

The Outer Shell

Filigree, gingerbread, columns, and moldings bring an ornate sense of charm to some traditional houses, particularly those influenced by highly crafted, decorative architectural styles such as Victorian and Arts and Crafts. (See page 180 for more about various architectural styles.)

There are many different types of moldings and architectural details used on houses. The traditional material for this purpose is wood, typically pine, fir, redwood, or cedar. Ornate patterns of molding and millwork are created by combining a variety of simpler wood molding profiles.

Newer architectural detailing is often formed from high-density polyurethane. Although it isn't as authentic as wood, polyurethane foam is equally workable and not subject to many of wood's vulnerabilities. Polyurethane moldings don't expand and contract, warp, decay, or require heavy maintenance. And because intricate polyurethane moldings are made as single-piece units, they're also much cheaper to install.

Some vinyl siding manufacturers also offer a range of decorative classic millwork that coordinates with their systems. These include door and window surrounds, shutters, corner posts, dentil moldings, and more.

Columns may be structural or merely decorative. Structural columns are made from wood, extruded aluminum, or fiberglass composites. Nonstructural, decorative columns, made from polymers, are hollow in the center to allow for a wood or metal post.

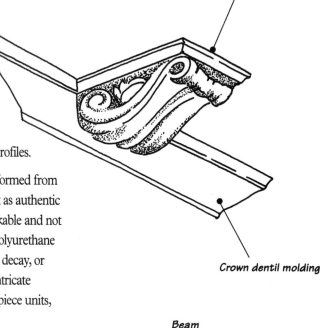

Dentil block

Crown dentil molding

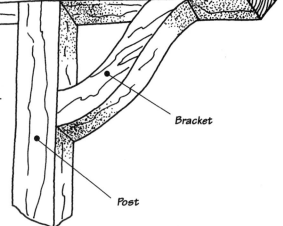

Beam

Bracket

Post

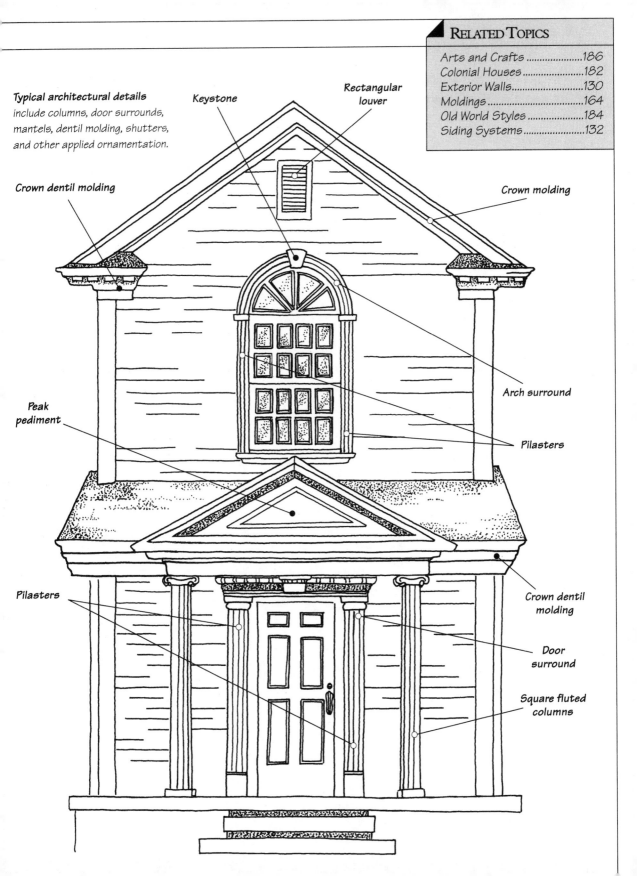

Typical architectural details
include columns, door surrounds,
mantels, dentil molding, shutters,
and other applied ornamentation.

Keystone

Rectangular
louver

Crown dentil molding

Crown molding

Peak
pediment

Arch surround

Pilasters

Pilasters

Crown dentil
molding

Door
surround

Square fluted
columns

The Outer Shell

As discussed on page 38, heat travels by convection, conduction, and radiation. Because homeowners spend a great deal of money and make use of much energy generating warm and cool air, it's important to prevent the air from escaping through the walls, ceilings, roof, and floors. The idea is to trap heat, or slow its flow. Materials that resist heat flow better than others—insulation materials—are installed in a house's shell to keep winter warmth in and summer heat out.

Materials used as insulation have tiny air cells that slow heat's movement. In addition, some have foil facings that reflect radiant heat and retard the movement of water vapor that travels in heated air. A vapor retarder, faced toward the warm-in-winter side of a house, keeps moisture from condensing inside walls, ceilings, and floors and damaging both the insulation and the structure itself.

Several types of insulation are available. Batts and blankets of fiberglass or rock-wool insulation are affordable and easy to install in open framing.

Loose-fill insulation, which is poured or blown into attics or closed-up walls by machine, is manufactured from a variety of materials, including fiberglass, rock wool, cellulose, perlite, and vermiculite.

Some walls are filled with plastic foam. Polyurethane, which is sprayed on during construction, has an excellent R-value and blocks drafts caused by air infiltration. Urea-formaldehyde, an older type of spray foam, is no longer installed because of its potentially dangerous vapor emissions.

Rigid foam board insulation is also used during new construction; it's usually installed as roof or wall sheathing before the roofing or siding is applied.

Reflective insulations, made from aluminum foil, are used mostly in hot climates for blocking radiant heat gain through roof and walls.

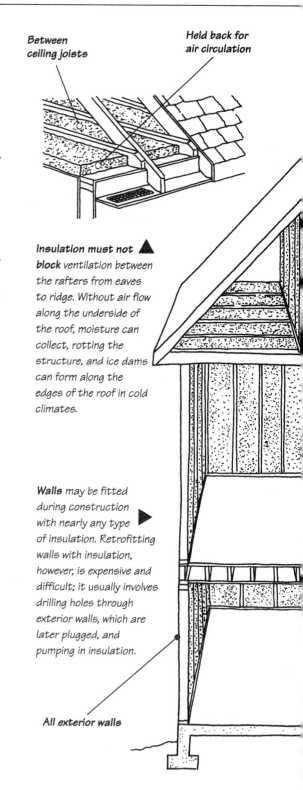

Between ceiling joists

Held back for air circulation

Insulation must not ▲ **block** ventilation between the rafters from eaves to ridge. Without air flow along the underside of the roof, moisture can collect, rotting the structure, and ice dams can form along the edges of the roof in cold climates.

Walls may be fitted during construction with nearly any type ► of insulation. Retrofitting walls with insulation, however, is expensive and difficult; it usually involves drilling holes through exterior walls, which are later plugged, and pumping in insulation.

All exterior walls

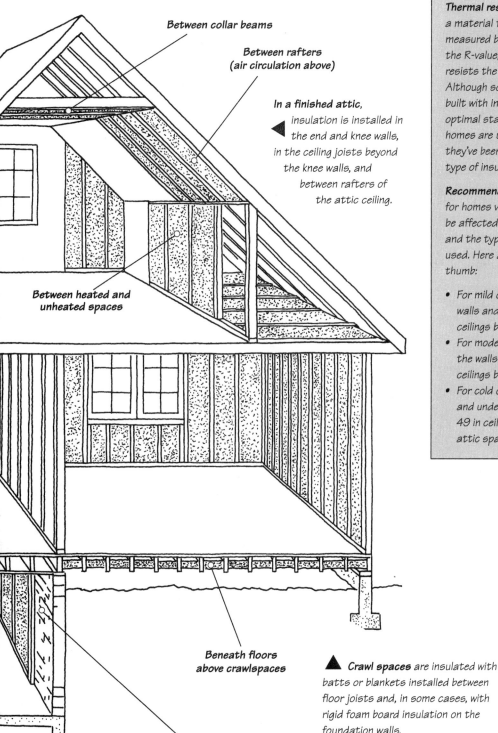

Between collar beams

Between rafters
(air circulation above)

In a finished attic,
insulation is installed in
the end and knee walls,
in the ceiling joists beyond
the knee walls, and
between rafters of
the attic ceiling.

Between heated and
unheated spaces

Beneath floors
above crawlspaces

Walls in heated
basement

Crawl spaces are insulated with
batts or blankets installed between
floor joists and, in some cases, with
rigid foam board insulation on the
foundation walls.

The Outer Shell

Most houses have several different kinds of doors, each designed to address a particular need. All doors are classified as exterior or interior, differentiated by construction, weathertightness, weight, and related factors that determine whether or not they can survive exposure to the elements.

Typical weathertight exterior doors include front entry doors, back doors, French doors, glass sliders, and patio doors. Interior doors are lighter in weight and are less durable.

A door's function determines its construction, appearance, and operation. If it's meant for security, it features solid, durable construction and highly effective hardware. If, in addition to providing access, it's intended to permit natural light or views, it incorporates glass—a French door or glass slider, for example. If ventilation is important, the door may have a louvered construction or a portion that swings open, like the half-acting "Dutch" door. For dividing rooms, a lightweight, economical hollow-core door is often preferred.

Doors are also distinguished by their action. Although most swing on hinges, some slide along tracks or fold and unfold, as shown here.

Exterior sliders
have one fixed panel and another that glides along top and bottom tracks. These doors operate easily, seal out the weather, and admit plenty of light.

A terrace or patio door *is hinged and has glass lights. Hinged glass-light doors mounted in pairs that swing independently are called French doors.*

Exterior doors *allow access, provide security, and maintain a comfortable indoor climate. They're made to be particularly strong, weather-resistant, and energy efficient. In addition, a front door is designed to project a handsome first impression.*

Folding doors are often used to conceal a wide space where a conventional door's swing would be cumbersome or restricted. Mounted in pairs that are hinged together, they combine the actions of both sliders and hinged doors, using end pivots and overhead tracks.

Bypass doors, often used on closets or storage areas, are lightweight indoor sliders that hang from rollers that run along an overhead track. They're typically mounted in pairs or threes; they bypass one another to allow access.

A pocket door is another type of slider that is ideal for places where there isn't room for a door to swing. It slides into a space or "pocket" installed in the wall.

Conventional hinged doors may be either right- or left-handed.

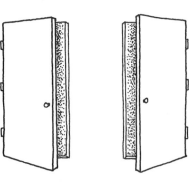

Right handed   **Left handed**

Most doors are designed to look like wood. Materials such as steel and fiberglass can simulate the look of wood, plus they are more affordable, have a greater insulation value, and require far less maintenance.

All-wood doors are made from softwoods or hardwoods, which are more durable and elegant. Fiberglass-composite doors, made from a core of rigid insulation clad with a fiber-reinforced polymer, are often embossed with artificial wood grain so they look like wood. Steel doors, made of heavy-gauge, galvanized steel over a core of rigid foam, are strong but look less like wood. Their surfaces usually are coated with polymer or vinyl and are wood-grain embossed. You can also buy doors that consist of veneer applied over solid wood, or veneer applied over a hollow core.

Standard doors are 6-foot, 8-inches tall and vary in width from 12 inches for cupboards to more than 8 feet for sliders.

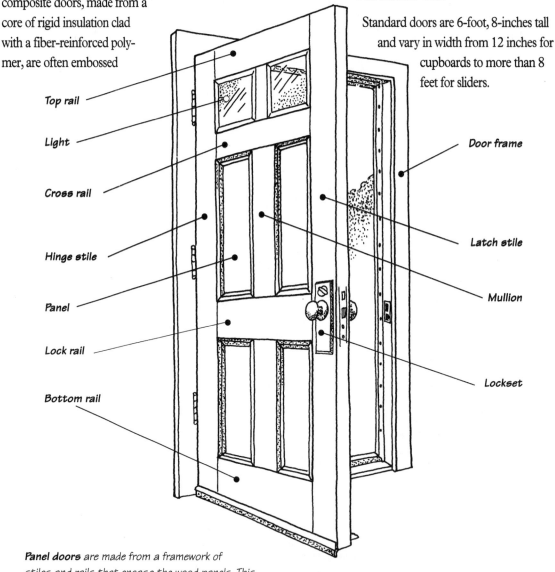

Top rail

Light

Cross rail

Hinge stile

Panel

Lock rail

Bottom rail

Door frame

Latch stile

Mullion

Lockset

Panel doors are made from a framework of <u>stiles</u> *and* <u>rails</u> *that encase the wood panels. This construction method is common because it minimizes the effects of wood's tendency to shrink, warp, and swell with variations in humidity.*

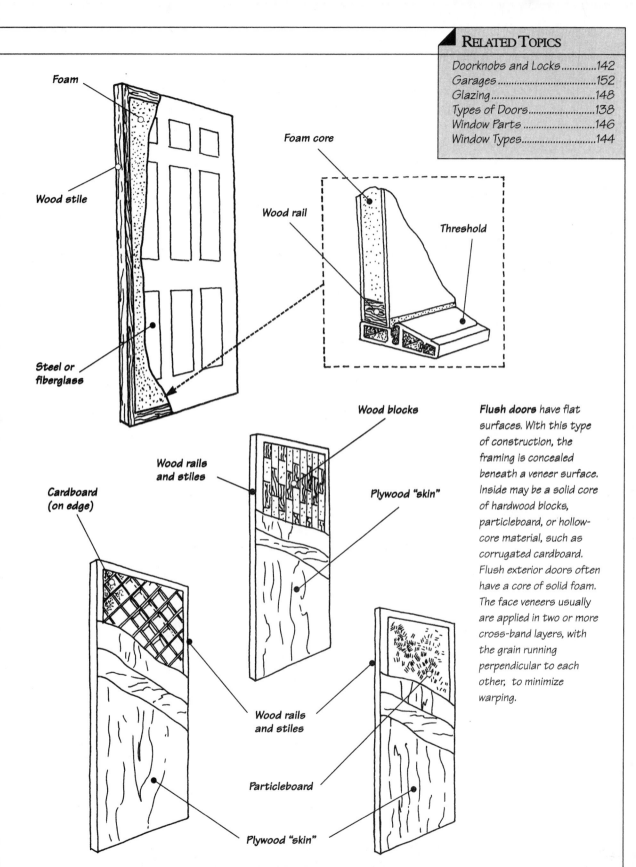

Foam

Wood stile

Steel or fiberglass

Foam core

Wood rail

Threshold

Wood blocks

Wood rails and stiles

Plywood "skin"

Cardboard (on edge)

Wood rails and stiles

Particleboard

Plywood "skin"

Flush doors have flat surfaces. With this type of construction, the framing is concealed beneath a veneer surface. Inside may be a solid core of hardwood blocks, particleboard, or hollow-core material, such as corrugated cardboard. Flush exterior doors often have a core of solid foam. The face veneers usually are applied in two or more cross-band layers, with the grain running perpendicular to each other, to minimize warping.

The Outer Shell

Some of a house's most important hardware are doorknobs and locks. Highly visible and used on a daily basis, they are critical to a home's appearance and convenience and provide the first line of defense against intruders.

In the construction trade, doorknobs are sometimes called locksets. The type on interior doors may be called passage locksets, spring-latch locks, interior knobs, or tubular locks. A knob with a push-button lock is called a privacy lock. This is often found on bathroom and bedroom doors.

Locksets for exterior doors may be called entry locksets, keyed locks, or exterior locks. A key-operated lock that has no doorknob or lever is called a deadbolt lock. Entry locksets can be locked or unlocked from both sides of the door, using a key, a button, or a throw latch, depending on the lock's construction.

Lockset bodies are classified as either cylindrical or mortise. Cylindrical locksets have a rounded body designed to fit into intersecting holes bored into the door. Mortise locksets have a large, rectangular body that slides into a mortise cut into the door's edge. With a mortise set, the knob generally is interconnected with a security deadbolt.

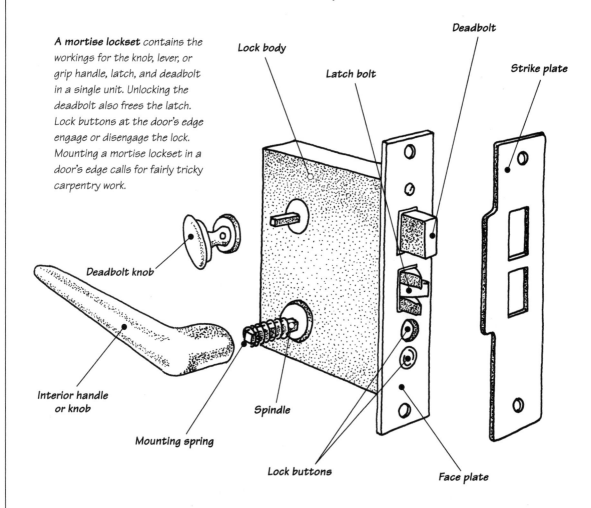

A mortise lockset contains the workings for the knob, lever, or grip handle, latch, and deadbolt in a single unit. Unlocking the deadbolt also frees the latch. Lock buttons at the door's edge engage or disengage the lock. Mounting a mortise lockset in a door's edge calls for fairly tricky carpentry work.

Lock body

Deadbolt

Latch bolt

Strike plate

Deadbolt knob

Interior handle or knob

Spindle

Mounting spring

Lock buttons

Face plate

The level of security a lockset offers depends on its construction. Any type with a key in the knob or handle is only marginally secure; it can be easily foiled by a burglar. For a significant level of security, a deadbolt should be installed with at least a 1-inch "throw"—that is, it should extend a minimum of 1 inch beyond the door's edge—and be made of case-hardened steel.

A double-cylinder deadbolt requires the use of a key from both sides of the door. This is the safest type to use for doors with windows. The key should be left in the interior lock when you are home to allow quick exit in case of fire or emergency.

*A **cylindrical lockset** is operated by a knob, lever, or grip handle. To provide better security, it can be paired with a deadbolt. A deadbolt should have at least a 1-inch throw, and the strike plate that receives it should be mounted into the frame with 3-inch-long screws.*

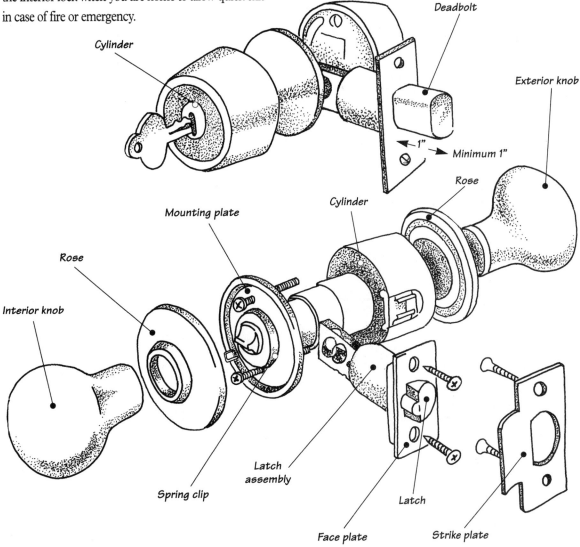

Cylinder

Deadbolt

Exterior knob

1" Minimum 1"

Mounting plate

Cylinder

Rose

Rose

Interior knob

Latch assembly

Spring clip

Latch

Face plate

Strike plate

A window does more than bring light and views to a room. It can also define a room's shape, provide an architectural focal point, allow ventilation, and provide for emergency escape. To serve these needs, windows come in a variety of types and sizes that operate and function differently.

Broadly speaking, windows are either fixed or operable. Fixed windows are used mostly for accents or where light and views, but not ventilation, are important.

Most round-top, triangular, and other unusually shaped windows are fixed, as are large picture windows.

Operable windows may slide up, down, or sideways, or they may hinge outward or inward.

Windows are available in a number of innovative styles; you can buy bent-glass corner windows, curved-glass windows, or casements with no center stile, for example. Some beautiful bow and bay windows are made by combining fixed and operable units.

A slider offers a contemporary appearance. It's made from two separate sashes—one is fixed, the other slides in a track. Half opens for ventilation. A slider is easy to operate and most types are particularly water- and air-tight.

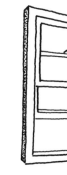

A double-hung window, classic in appearance, offers excellent control of ventilation. Both sashes are movable. With a single-hung window, only the lower sash can move.

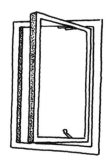

A casement window is hinged on one side and swings out; some are inward-swinging. Because it opens fully, it affords good ventilation and is easy to clean.

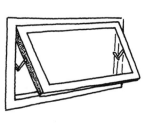

An awning window hinges at the top and tilts out at the bottom, providing partial ventilation. These are often used above doors or other windows.

Jalousie or louvered windows are excellent for ventilation but are poor insulators, as they leak a great deal of air.

A hopper window hinges at the bottom. It normally is used for ventilation above a door or window, where it's protected by eaves.

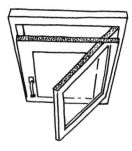

A tilt-turn is a fairly new type of window. It tilts out for ventilation but also can be opened fully for cleaning or as an emergency escape.

The round-top and other geometrically shaped windows are used as architectural accents. They are stationary.

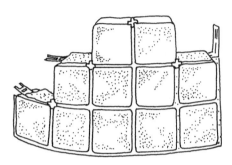

Glass block is a light-allowing alternative to conventional windows, used both in exterior and interior walls. Various patterns allow degrees of view or privacy. Typical sizes are 6, 8, and 12-inch squares and 4 by 8 and 6 by 8 rectangles for 4-inch-thick walls.

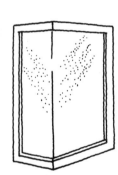

The seamless bent-glass corner window is a fairly new product that offers unobstructed views at the corner of a house.

A bow window is made from several windows positioned together to create an arcing form. Similar to a bay window, it adds drama to a room.

A bay window, made from a central sash and two angled side sashes, is a classic favorite for expanding a room with light, views, and drama. Angled side windows are often operable casements or double-hung windows.

The Outer Shell

On first glance, a window looks like a pretty simple piece of equipment. It has a frame, glass, and some basic hardware. But if you look a little closer, you'll find there's much more than first meets the eye. A window must be designed to allow light and views—and in some cases ventilation—yet seal out the weather. It must shed heavy rain and block powerful winds without leaking. And if it's operable, it must open and close easily. To handle all these tasks effectively, it requires many parts and a surprisingly complex construction.

The drawings here identify the various components of two typical windows: a double-hung wood window and a metal casement window. These are the major components of most standard windows.

The window frames and sashes are made of wood, aluminum, vinyl, or a combination of these materials. Of these, wood is the best insulator and tends to be the most attractive indoors. Vinyl and aluminum are more durable and maintenance free outdoors; some makers apply a cladding of these materials to wood windows.

Some windows have real divided lights; others have snap-in wood grilles that imitate the look of divided panes. Although snap-in grilles don't appear to be as substantial as real muntins, windows with grilles are less expensive and are easier to clean than real paned windows because they're actually a single sheet of glass.

The type of glass in a window has a great deal to do with how the window performs. For a full discussion of glazing, see page 148.

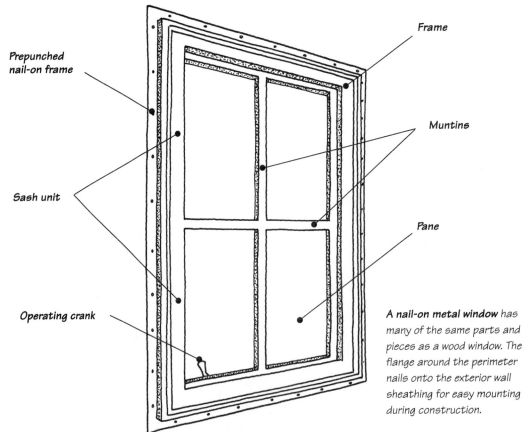

Prepunched nail-on frame

Sash unit

Operating crank

Frame

Muntins

Pane

A nail-on metal window has many of the same parts and pieces as a wood window. The flange around the perimeter nails onto the exterior wall sheathing for easy mounting during construction.

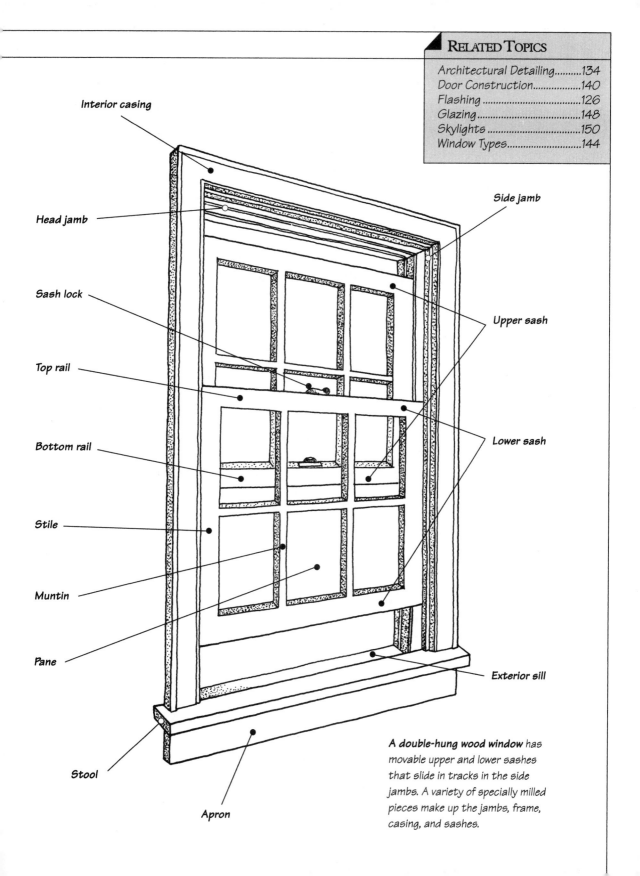

Interior casing

Head jamb

Sash lock

Top rail

Bottom rail

Stile

Muntin

Pane

Stool

Apron

Side jamb

Upper sash

Lower sash

Exterior sill

A double-hung wood window has movable upper and lower sashes that slide in tracks in the side jambs. A variety of specially milled pieces make up the jambs, frame, casing, and sashes.

The Outer Shell

Glass makes possible many of the best features of houses: natural light, views, and a visual connection with the outdoors. But as the amount of glass used in a house increases, its energy efficiency usually decreases, simply because glass windows and doors are not as effective as walls for insulating. Because of this, a great deal of effort has been made in recent years to improve the efficiency of glazings.

Now when you buy or replace a window or glazed door, you can choose from a variety of glazings. Generally speaking, the more energy efficient the glazing, the more expensive it is.

Heat loss through glass is measured by an *R-value* (see page 137). The way a window is glazed has a great deal to do with its R-value: the higher the R-value, the more efficient the glass.

The *U-value* measures the amount of heat that can escape per hour through a given window. Two U-values are usually given: one for the glass and one for the entire window, including the frame. The lower the U-value, the more energy efficient the window.

Although single glazing—a single sheet of glass—was once the standard, dual glazing or insulating glass is now more common for quality windows. This type of glass consists of two panes of glass separated by a thin air space and offers twice the R-value. You can also buy even more effective triple glazing with dual air spaces.

There is a variety of high-performance glazings on the market today. Low-E glazing is perhaps the most common. This employs an imperceptibly thin metallic film or coating between two glass panes that selectively rejects some energy wavelengths, greatly reducing heat transfer through the

Trapped gas

Suspended reflective film

High-performance glazing utilizes two low-E coatings or suspended reflective films to achieve ultra-high values of R-8.

Glass pane

Sash

Glass pane

glass and minimizing fading of furniture and carpets that can be caused by ultraviolet rays.

Argon gas-filled windows are even more energy efficient. When a window is injected with this natural, colorless, nontoxic gas, its insulating qualities are doubled. New *super windows* use two low-E coatings or films to achieve incredibly high R-8 insulation values.

Where ultraviolet fading is a real problem—in especially sunny climates—a solar bronze- or gray-tinted glass can reject unwanted heat and UV rays. Glass may also be purchased with a polymer coating that repels dirt, minimizing the need for washing windows.

Some windows are sold with integral shades. You can even buy dual-glazed windows that have louvered mini-blinds between the glass panes. As an option in most cases, nearly all operable windows are sold with screens.

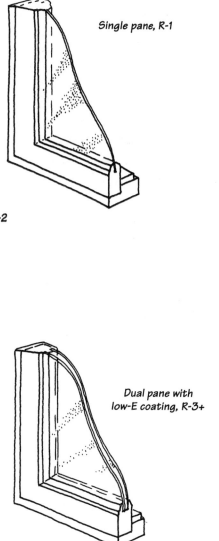

Single pane, R-1

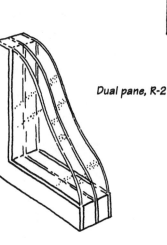

Dual pane, R-2

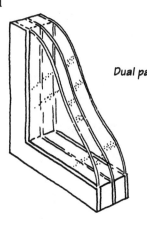

Triple glazing, R-3

Dual pane with
low-E coating, R-3+

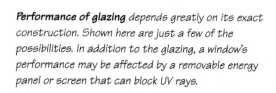

Performance of glazing depends greatly on its exact construction. Shown here are just a few of the possibilities. In addition to the glazing, a window's performance may be affected by a removable energy panel or screen that can block UV rays.

By letting natural light stream in, a skylight gives a room a feeling of spaciousness and light. By reducing the need for electric lighting, it can help trim energy bills.

A skylight is basically a window in a roof. Its frame is designed to withstand the rigors of weather, and its flashing works with the roofing material to seal out rain and snow. A roof window, which pivots at the center, is designed for use in an attic room.

Some older skylights leak because of poorly sealed flashings. Others drip because of unchecked condensation that collects when warm room air comes in contact with a skylight's cold inner surface. Leaks can usually be fixed by resealing the flashings. Condensation is tougher to correct; it calls for improving a house's ventilation. (See page 58 for more information on ventilation.)

Newer skylights are virtually leak-free, thanks to rugged construction and easy-to-install, integral flashings. They're also equipped with channels that carry away condensation.

Although some frames are solid wood or aluminum, most new skylights are made of a combination of metal, vinyl, and wood. The exterior frames tend to be aluminum cladding with a durable finish; the part visible from inside is often made of solid wood, plywood, or white vinyl.

Some skylights are glazed with acrylic or polycarbonate, others with glass. Plastic versions are lightweight and economical and are often used where a glass skylight could be easily broken. Because they are molded, however, they come only in standard sizes and shapes: flat rectangles, bubbles and domes, pyramids, and dormer models, for example.

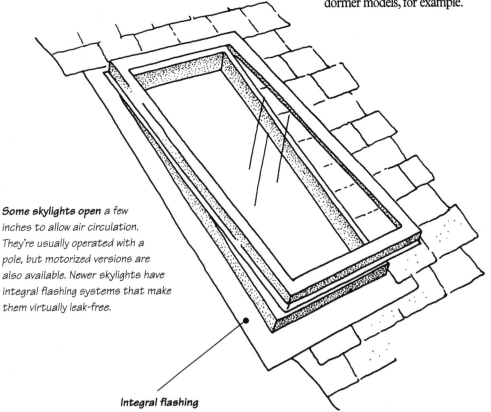

Some skylights open a few inches to allow air circulation. They're usually operated with a pole, but motorized versions are also available. Newer skylights have integral flashing systems that make them virtually leak-free.

Integral flashing

Glass is usually preferred because it doesn't scratch as readily as plastic and because it's available in nearly limitless sizes and types. Versions include single, double, or triple glazing with energy-saving low-E glass or argon gas filled panes. Bronze-tinted or other UV-blocking glass is available to protect carpets and furniture from direct sunlight. Other options for eliminating or reducing the sun's effects are built-in blinds and horizontal curtains or shades.

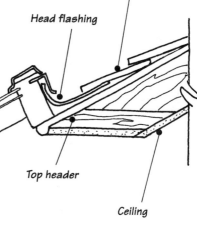

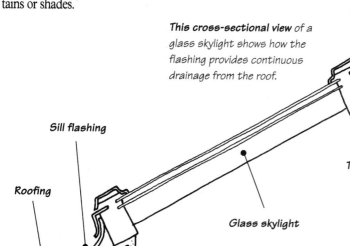

This cross-sectional view of a glass skylight shows how the flashing provides continuous drainage from the roof.

Roofing

Head flashing

Top header

Ceiling

Glass skylight

Sill flashing

Roofing

Rafter

Bottom header

Ceiling

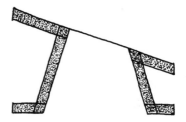

Flared

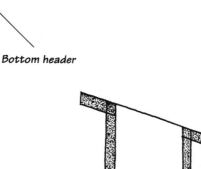

Perpendicular to ceiling

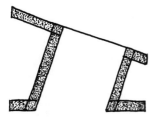

Perpendicular to roof

A skylight's shaft controls the way light is delivered to the room below. If all four sides are flared, light is spread over a wide area. If the sides are perpendicular to the roof, the light is focused below it. If the shaft is flared on only one or two sides, light is somewhat diffused and directed toward the flared side.

No longer the icon of middle-class success, the two-car garage has become essential. More often than not, it is an overflow storage building—a shelter for bicycles, recycling bins, kayaks, and much more. Unfortunately, most garages are so crammed with stuff that the family's beloved car is left out in the cold.

A garage is considered an "unfinished space." As such, it is built a little more simply than the rest of the house. For example, most garages have a concrete floor, sloped slightly toward the door for drainage. They generally have few windows and exposed rafters or roof trusses.

A garage is fitted with a home's largest moving part—the garage door. There are two main types: sectional, *roll-up* doors and single-piece, *tilt-up* doors.

Garage doors are built of wood, steel, aluminum, or fiberglass. Wood sets the standard for appearance, as most people prefer its natural look. Wood is also relatively inexpensive and easily tooled; the frames of some tilt-up doors are built right in the driveway. The problem with wood is that it's vulnerable to the weather; to keep it in good condition, it must be repainted periodically.

Wood doors may have flush, raised-panel, or recessed-panel construction. With flush construction, a frame is covered with plywood. With panel construction, a series of panels are fitted into a softwood framework. The most durable panels are made of composites and are guaranteed to last for twenty years or more.

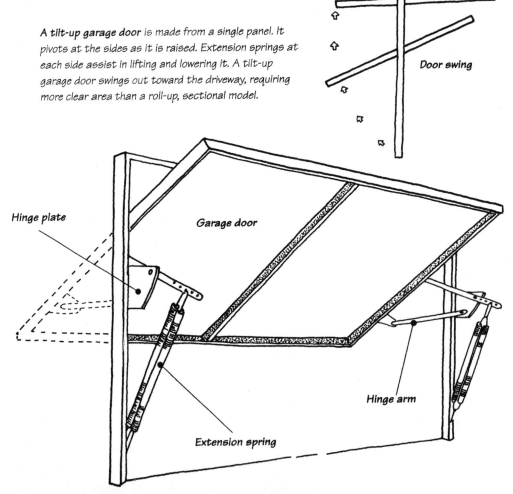

*A **tilt-up garage door** is made from a single panel. It pivots at the sides as it is raised. Extension springs at each side assist in lifting and lowering it. A tilt-up garage door swings out toward the driveway, requiring more clear area than a roll-up, sectional model.*

Door swing

Hinge plate

Garage door

Hinge arm

Extension spring

Steel is strong, durable, and easy to maintain. Because of wood-grain embossing, vinyl-cladding, and baked-on finishes, steel successfully imitates the look of wood yet offers finishes that are guaranteed not to rust. Steel doors may feature single-skin and frame construction or double-skin "sandwich" construction. The first type looks less finished from inside the garage. The double-skin construction, which contains rigid insulation between interior and exterior steel panels, looks finished from both sides, and provides a better weather barrier.

Roller

Door section

Track

Rollers fixed at both ends of each section guide the garage door along tracks at the sides of the doorway.

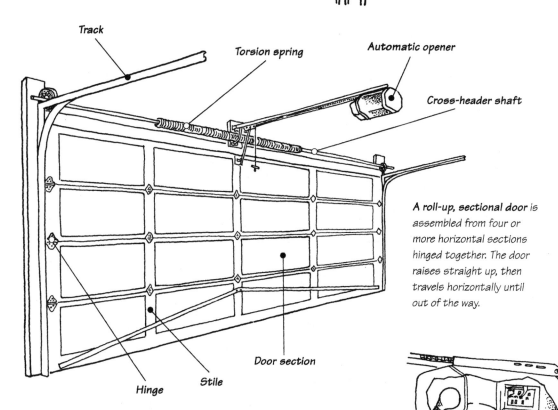

Track

Torsion spring

Automatic opener

Cross-header shaft

A roll-up, sectional door is assembled from four or more horizontal sections hinged together. The door raises straight up, then travels horizontally until out of the way.

Door section

Stile

Hinge

An electric garage door operator can be attached to either tilt-up or sectional garage doors. The operator is simply an electric motor mounted above the door and controlled by either a key, a switch, or a remote control. The motor drives a device that's hooked to the door—a worm-drive shaft, for example—raising and lowering the door.

The Outer Shell

When life was slower and simpler, many houses had substantial front porches. These were places to rest a spell, catch up on the latest neighborhood gossip, or cool down in a summer breeze. But with the industrialization and inventions of the twentieth century—cars, television, air conditioning—the desire for front porches waned. By the 1930s, real porches were being replaced by small entries or simple canopies for the front door.

In recent years, porches have had something of a rebirth. Whether because of nostalgic memories or a new practicality, porches now make sense for several reasons. First, they help save energy. A porch provides shelter for the front door; in fact, an enclosed porch is essentially an air lock. A porch is also a relatively inexpensive space that expands a home's usability; it's a place for kids to play or to stow gear out of the rain. And, depending on its design, a porch can add a wonderful dimension and character to the facade of a house.

A porch may be open, with a simple roof, or partly enclosed, with low walls. A screened porch keeps the bugs out. An enclosed porch also keeps out drafts.

One variation on the porch is the sunspace, also called a sunroom, conservatory, greenhouse, or solarium. Although these all-glass enclosures are seldom used as front porches, they serve some of the same purposes as an enclosed porch. They provide an air lock between indoors and out and extend a home's usable space. When used as a breezeway, a sunspace can also link an addition or garage to the house.

Sunspaces have frames of aluminum or decay-resistant red cedar that hold the glass panels. Glazing may be single-pane, but in newer, more energy-efficient sunspaces, double glazing is nearly always used. Sunspaces generally rest on a concrete foundation and slab floor.

Front porches *may be open, screened, or enclosed. When properly designed, they effectively enhance a home's architecture.*

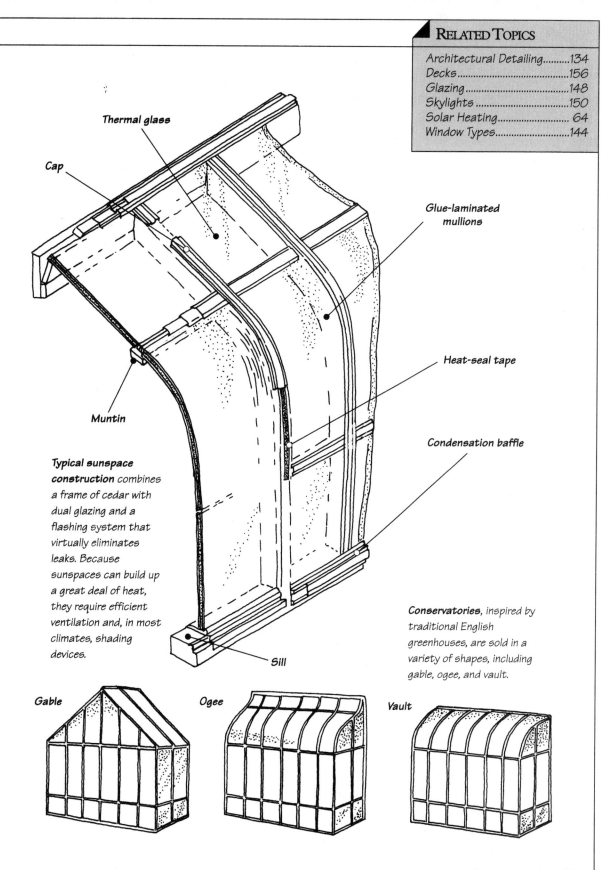

Thermal glass

Cap

Muntin

Glue-laminated mullions

Heat-seal tape

Condensation baffle

Typical sunspace construction combines a frame of cedar with dual glazing and a flashing system that virtually eliminates leaks. Because sunspaces can build up a great deal of heat, they require efficient ventilation and, in most climates, shading devices.

Sill

Conservatories, inspired by traditional English greenhouses, are sold in a variety of shapes, including gable, ogee, and vault.

Gable

Ogee

Vault

A deck expands a house outward, making outdoor spaces more comfortable. It can integrate the house with a patio, a pool, and a garden or provide a private retreat.

Although many decks are attached to at least one wall of a house, freestanding garden decks are also common. An attached deck may perch high off the ground, serving rooms that overlook a hillside or, like a freestanding deck, sit virtually at ground level.

A deck is essentially an outdoor floor. Accordingly, most decks are built using construction practices almost identical to those employed for floors (see page 116), with a few notable exceptions that provide for the harsher outdoor conditions.

The framing, often built from conventional lumber, consists of an arrangement of joists, beams, and posts. Their sizes depend on specific building codes. The surface material on most decks is two-by-six lumber that is laid flat and spaced about ⅛ inch between boards to allow drainage. The preferred species are redwood and cedar, which have a natural resistance to decay, or pine that has been pressure-treated with a preservative. Although there are several variations for special effect, the surface lumber is normally laid perpendicular to supporting joists and nailed or screwed to each joist.

Railings are used on all decks more than 3 feet off the ground and on stairs. Many patterns are possible, but all railings must measure 36 to 42 inches from the deck's surface. Local building codes may have different requirements.

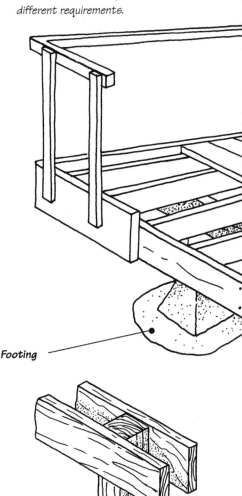

Footing

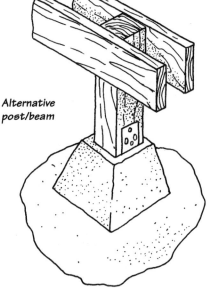

Alternative post/beam

Surface decking often consists of two-by-sixes laid parallel to joists, but a number of other materials and designs are possible.

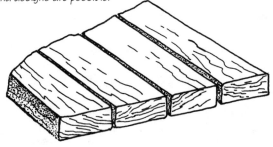

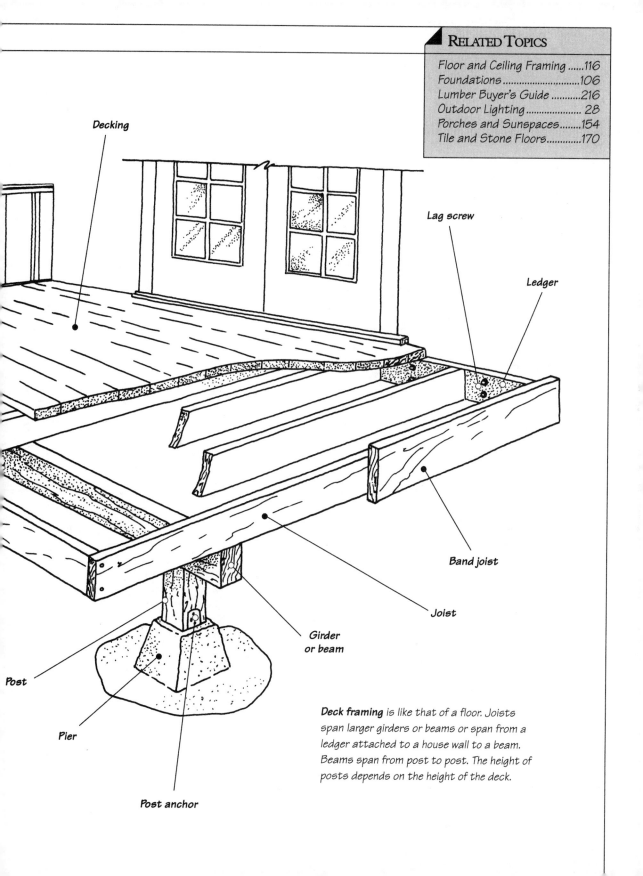

Decking

Lag screw

Ledger

Band joist

Joist

Girder
or beam

Post

Pier

Post anchor

Deck framing is like that of a floor. Joists span larger girders or beams or span from a ledger attached to a house wall to a beam. Beams span from post to post. The height of posts depends on the height of the deck.

Inner Surfaces

Walls, ceilings, floors, cabinets, and countertops are the most familiar surfaces in our homes, the ones that make up the interior. Both highly functional and decorative, they buffer the daily wear-and-tear of busy families and give a house its true personality. These are the elements that determine a home's durability, elegance, comfort, maintenance requirements, and, of course, expense.

Understanding how these elements are constructed can be helpful in maintaining your home and making decisions about improvements, simple or complex. And basic knowledge can be critical when the inevitable time comes to make choices about wall coverings, floorings, and so forth—not only in choosing the right materials but in discussing your needs and wishes with contractors or installers.

This chapter looks at the surfaces of a home's interiors: walls, ceilings, moldings, floorings, stairs, cabinets, and countertops.

Moldings stylize a room and hide the gaps and transitions between various wall, ceiling, and floor coverings. (See page 164.)

Stairs may be dramatic interior statements or a purely utilitarian means of passage from one floor to the next. Many different styles are found in houses. (See page 174.)

Floorings come in many different styles, each with its own advantages. Some are foot friendly, others are incredibly durable, and still others are character-filled. All are guaranteed to set the tone of a room, from a playroom to a formal living room. (See pages 166 through 173.)

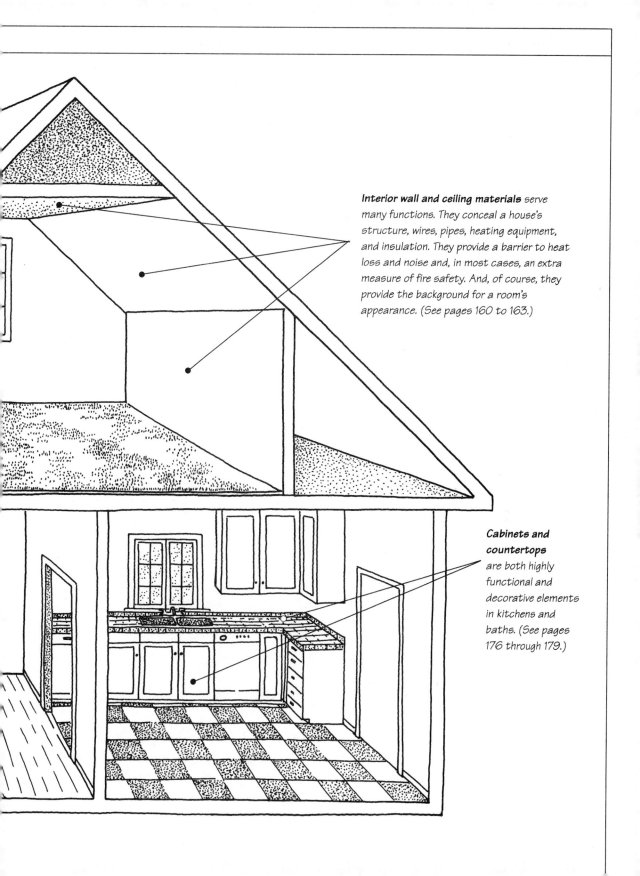

Interior wall and ceiling materials serve many functions. They conceal a house's structure, wires, pipes, heating equipment, and insulation. They provide a barrier to heat loss and noise and, in most cases, an extra measure of fire safety. And, of course, they provide the background for a room's appearance. (See pages 160 to 163.)

Cabinets and countertops are both highly functional and decorative elements in kitchens and baths. (See pages 176 through 179.)

Inner Surfaces

Whether you're remodeling a kitchen or simply hanging a mirror, a clear understanding of how interior walls are built is essential. As discussed on page 108, most houses have wood-frame construction— a wooden framework is clad on the outside by siding and finished inside with an interior wall surface material. The two most common interior wall surfaces are gypsum wallboard, usually referred to as *drywall* or *gyp board*, and plaster. Wood is also employed, both as paneling and as *wainscoting* along the lower portion of walls.

Drywall panels cover most walls built over the last forty years. These panels have a layer of gypsum sandwiched between heavy paper facings. A waterproof type—sometimes called *green board*—is used in bathrooms and other areas subject to heavy moisture. The sheets, which are relatively inexpensive, are 4 feet wide, ¼ to ⅝ inch thick, and 6 to 16 feet long. The standard size is ½ inch thick and 8 feet long.

Drywall sheets are applied to studs, joists, or rafters with drywall nails or screws, or with adhesive. Joints between the panels are covered with a paper or fiberglass tape and coated with several layers of smooth, plasterlike joint compound.

In older homes, plaster walls are common. Plaster is a mixture of portland cement, sand, and water that is applied in layers to a base of wood or metal lath or perforated plasterboard. First, a *scratch coat* is troweled onto the lath; the plaster oozes through the lath and grips the backing when it hardens. Then a *finish* or *white coat* is troweled onto the scratch coat for the final surface.

Wood also is used as a wall covering, although primarily as an accent for a study or family room, where its warmth and character are wanted. Wood paneling is made both in sheets and in individual, interlocking strips.

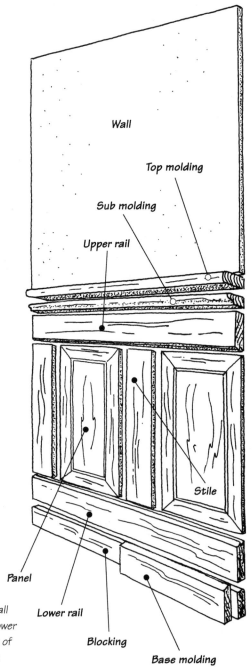

Wall

Top molding

Sub molding

Upper rail

Stile

Panel

Lower rail

Blocking

Base molding

Classic wainscoting, which not only gives a wall elegance and warmth but also protects the lower portion, is made up of several different pieces of milled hardwoods that are fastened together.

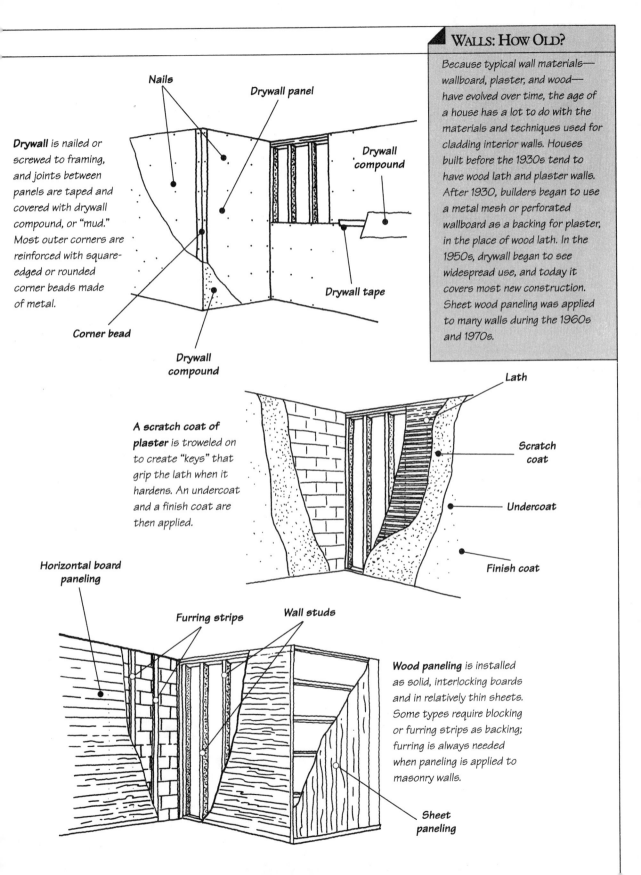

Nails

Drywall panel

Drywall is nailed or screwed to framing, and joints between panels are taped and covered with drywall compound, or "mud." Most outer corners are reinforced with square-edged or rounded corner beads made of metal.

Drywall compound

Drywall tape

Corner bead

Drywall compound

Because typical wall materials—wallboard, plaster, and wood—have evolved over time, the age of a house has a lot to do with the materials and techniques used for cladding interior walls. Houses built before the 1930s tend to have wood lath and plaster walls. After 1930, builders began to use a metal mesh or perforated wallboard as a backing for plaster, in the place of wood lath. In the 1950s, drywall began to see widespread use, and today it covers most new construction. Sheet wood paneling was applied to many walls during the 1960s and 1970s.

A scratch coat of plaster is troweled on to create "keys" that grip the lath when it hardens. An undercoat and a finish coat are then applied.

Lath

Scratch coat

Undercoat

Finish coat

Horizontal board paneling

Furring strips

Wall studs

Wood paneling is installed as solid, interlocking boards and in relatively thin sheets. Some types require blocking or furring strips as backing; furring is always needed when paneling is applied to masonry walls.

Sheet paneling

Most ceilings are built with the same materials and methods as walls, their vertical counterparts; they consist of wood framing members—joists rather than wall studs—and normally are clad with drywall or plaster. The conventional ceiling is 8 feet high and flat, corresponding to standard construction practices and material sizes.

Some ceilings depart from these norms for either structural, spatial, or decorative reasons. Perhaps the most familiar departure is the cathedral ceiling that angles upward from walls to a peak, following the roof's pitch. Such a ceiling adds drama and a sense of spaciousness to a room. On the downside, a room with cathedral or higher-than-normal ceilings can be more expensive to heat because warm air rises.

More decorative ceilings may be covered with wood paneling or, in the case of some old, classic ceilings, pressed metal.

Another familiar variation is the suspended ceiling. This type, often used to lower a too-high ceiling or to hide cracks and mechanical equipment, consists of a metal grid that supports removable panels. The entire apparatus is suspended from the ceiling joists or the existing ceiling.

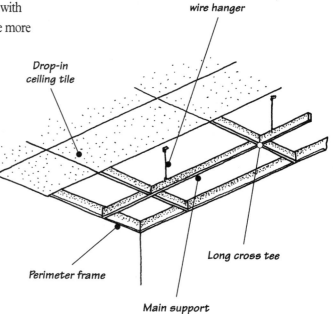

Bracket and wire hanger

Drop-in ceiling tile

Suspended ceilings are lower than the original ceiling and often cover up old cracks or mechanical equipment. A metal grid, suspended from joists or the old ceiling and attached at the walls, supports lightweight ceiling panels. These panels may be made of mineral fiber or fiberglass acoustical board in plain and decorative patterns, or they may be any of several types of translucent plastic panels for above-the-ceiling lighting.

Perimeter frame

Long cross tee

Main support

Ceilings are built in a variety of shapes. A conventional dropped ceiling is flat and 8 feet high. Cathedral and shed ceilings follow the roofline. A coved ceiling is rounded at the corners; a tray ceiling has a vertical or angled soffit around the perimeter. A dome ceiling rolls up into a half-barrel shape. A suspended ceiling is a second, flat ceiling that hangs beneath the original ceiling.

Cathedral

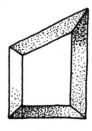

Shed

Solid wood paneling

Ceiling joist

Several different materials may be fastened to the existing ceiling or directly to ceiling joists, if they're strong enough. These materials include wood planks and paneling and classic pressed metal panels.

Blocking

Nails

Drywall

Drywall

A conventional drywall ceiling consists of drywall panels screwed or nailed to ceiling joists. Joints between the panels are taped and finished with drywall compound using the same methods as for walls. These ceilings are normally hung before the drywall is applied to the walls. Older ceilings often have lath-and-plaster construction.

Blocking

Ceiling joist

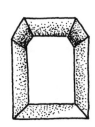

Coved

Tray

Dome

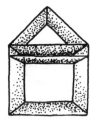

Suspended

Inner Surfaces

Moldings are both functional and decorative. Although they give a room distinctive style and detailing, they also serve a purpose: to hide the joints between walls and floors, ceilings, doors, and windows.

Many different patterns and styles are made from a variety of both softwoods and hardwoods. These profiles can be used individually or in combination—called "built up" moldings—to create intricate patterns.

Moldings in older homes may be made of plaster, particularly cornice and crown moldings, or any of the several hardwoods or softwoods.

New moldings are sold at lumberyards and mill-work shops, the best places to see the wide selection available. Hardwood moldings that are meant to be stained or finished naturally are relatively expensive; much less expensive are paint-grade pine or fir moldings made from short pieces that are "finger joined" together. You can also buy a range of ready-to-paint, highly decorative moldings made from high-density polymers.

Most moldings are nailed in place with finishing nails; nailheads are set beneath the wood's surface and filled with spackling compound or, for moldings meant to be stained rather than painted, pigmented wood filler.

Typical moldings include crown moldings, chair rail, baseboard, and window and door casing. Some of these are mitered together at the corners and some are coped. (See page 160 for information on wainscoting.)

Basic profiles of moldings run the gamut from simple rectangles to intricate patterns. Many of these styles are combined with one another to form base moldings, ceiling moldings, casings, chair ▼ *rails, and other styles.*

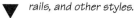

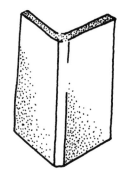

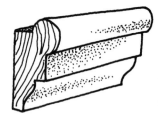

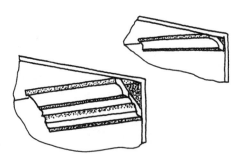

Ceiling moldings add a decorative element and provide a gentle transition from wall to ceiling. ◀ *Depending on a room's style, these may be a simple cove pattern or a highly intricate crown molding.*

Chair rail

A chair rail is attached to a wall at 33 inches to 35 inches from the floor. It protects the wall from marring by chair backs and may provide a transition from a wainscoting at the base to the wall above.

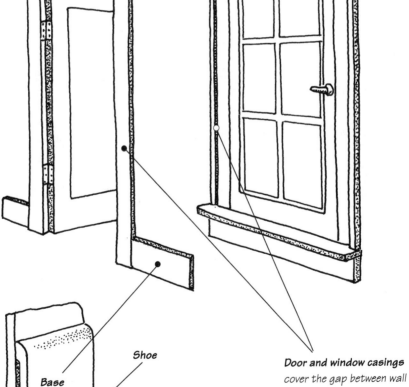

Base and base-with-shoe styles hide the joint between wall and floor and protect the bottom of the wall from shoes, vacuum cleaners, and the like.

Base

Shoe

Door and window casings cover the gap between wall and door or window jambs. Styles range from simple to intricate.

Carpet colors and vinyl patterns may come and go, but one flooring material that never falls from grace is wood. Tough, durable, natural, and warm, wood is perhaps the most practical of all flooring materials.

There are three main types of wood flooring: strip, plank, and parquet. Strip flooring, the standard for homes built during most of the twentieth century, is made from 1½-inch or 2¼-inch-wide by ¾-inch thick strips of hardwood that are laid parallel. They have interlocking tongue-and-groove edges. Planks are wider—from 3 to 8 inches wide—and may be laid in random lengths or with real or simulated pegs at the ends. Parquet flooring is made from small pieces that are laid in intricate patterns, such as herringbone.

Although softwoods, such as pine and Douglas fir, are used for some floors, most wood flooring is made from durable hardwoods, such as oak, maple, ash, and a few exotic woods, such as walnut, teak, and cherry.

Solid hardwood flooring is a favorite, but in recent years laminated wood flooring has soared in popularity. Laminated flooring has a ⅛-inch layer of hardwood bonded to two layers of less costly wood backing, reducing the amount of expensive hardwood needed. It's also easier to install because, unlike conventional solid wood flooring which must be blind-nailed to subflooring and sanded before finishing, laminated flooring is prefinished and may be glued down or applied over a thin foam pad laid on the subfloor. Some types are adhesive backed.

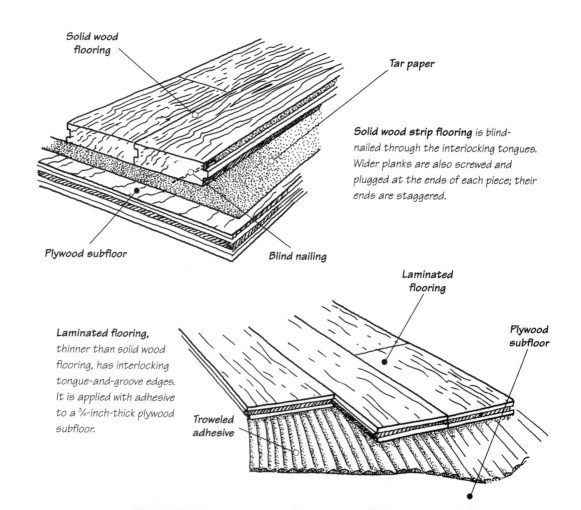

Solid wood flooring

Tar paper

Plywood subfloor

Blind nailing

Solid wood strip flooring is blind-nailed through the interlocking tongues. Wider planks are also screwed and plugged at the ends of each piece; their ends are staggered.

Laminated flooring

Plywood subfloor

Laminated flooring, thinner than solid wood flooring, has interlocking tongue-and-groove edges. It is applied with adhesive to a ¾-inch-thick plywood subfloor.

Troweled adhesive

Another advantage of laminated flooring materials is that, because they're made up of multiple layers, they're less likely to suffer from expansion and contraction problems that commonly occur in moisture-prone areas, such as bathrooms and kitchens. Most laminated floors are installed over plywood subflooring but they can also be applied to a smooth concrete slab or a sound existing vinyl floor.

Its thickness gives a solid-wood flooring an advantage over a laminated one. Solid-wood flooring may be sanded and refinished numerous times. Laminated floors have a surface layer that's no more than ⅛ inch thick. Once this goes, the floor goes.

Most of today's hardwood floors are coated with water-borne urethanes and impregnated acrylics that are durable, highly resistant to water, and require very little care.

Parquet flooring *is made up of short pieces arranged in patterns. Although older floors may be designed of pieces that are individually laid, modern parquet floors are laid in 6- to 12-inch tiles. Because parquet is completely nonstructural, it is most solid when laid on an extra sturdy base of both underlayment plywood and a ¾-inch subfloor.*

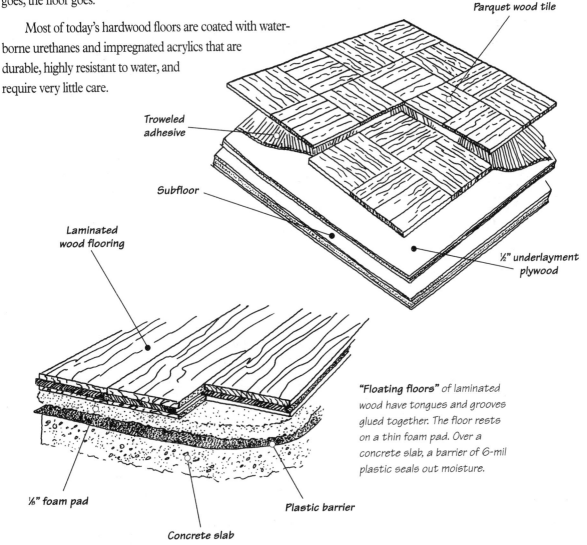

Parquet wood tile

Troweled adhesive

Subfloor

½" underlayment plywood

Laminated wood flooring

"Floating floors" *of laminated wood have tongues and grooves glued together. The floor rests on a thin foam pad. Over a concrete slab, a barrier of 6-mil plastic seals out moisture.*

⅛" foam pad

Plastic barrier

Concrete slab

Resilient flooring is one of the most practical flooring materials. With resilient flooring, a dropped milk glass has a chance of survival, and the resulting spill is easy to clean up with a damp cloth. Underfoot, resilient flooring is comfortable, skid-resistant, quiet, and warm. In addition, it's relatively inexpensive and readily available in an unbelievable array of patterns and colors. Resilient flooring is made from vinyl, rubber, cork, linoleum, and composites, but vinyl is by far the most common. (In fact, the industry uses the term "resilient" to refer to vinyl.)

In older homes, linoleum is commonplace. This natural material is made from linseed oil, pine resins, wood flour, granulated cork, and a burlap backing.

Vinyl flooring is laid as either sheets or tiles. They may be a composition, a mixture of vinyl, mineral fibers, and clay or, for more durability, they may be solid vinyl.

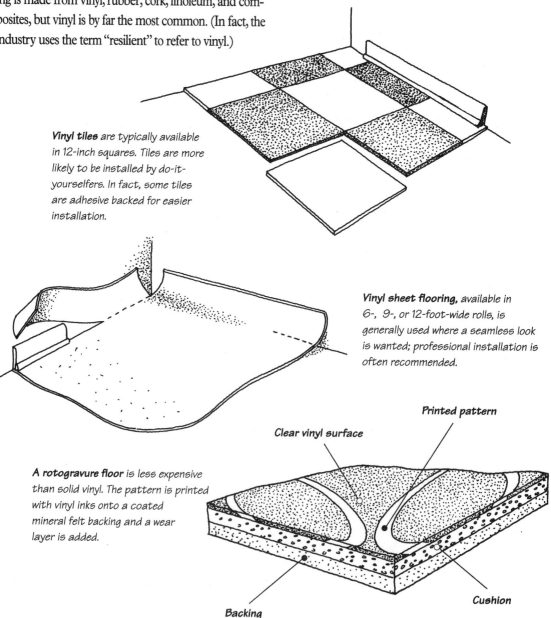

Vinyl tiles are typically available in 12-inch squares. Tiles are more likely to be installed by do-it-yourselfers. In fact, some tiles are adhesive backed for easier installation.

Vinyl sheet flooring, available in 6-, 9-, or 12-foot-wide rolls, is generally used where a seamless look is wanted; professional installation is often recommended.

A *rotogravure floor* is less expensive than solid vinyl. The pattern is printed with vinyl inks onto a coated mineral felt backing and a wear layer is added.

Clear vinyl surface

Printed pattern

Cushion

Backing

Quality vinyl flooring has a clear, protective wear layer for durability and to help in repelling dirt and spills. A urethane finish comes closest to meeting the "no wax" promise but even it may eventually lose its shine. A vinyl finish is a bit more stain resistant.

Vinyl is applied over a flat, smooth, clean surface such as plywood, wood, concrete, or an older resilient floor. (Because older resilient floors or their adhesives may contain asbestos that is dangerous when airborne, leaving an old floor in place and covering over it is common practice.)

With inlaid flooring, the pattern goes all the way through to the backing. In manufacturing, vinyl granules are generally applied to a backing through a series of templates, giving the design substantial visual depth. Multiple layers are fused together. Then the surface is given a wear layer for protection.

◣ VINYL CARE

With a little bit of care, you can keep vinyl floorings looking great for a long time. Here are a few general tips:

Cleaning. Dullness comes from small scratches caused by everyday dirt that gets ground in, so sweep or vacuum often and occasionally mop with clean, warm water. Avoid soap—it leaves a dull film.

For more rigorous cleaning, add clear ammonia to water. Remove scuffs with a bristle brush or abrasive pad; dip it into the water/ammonia solution, then scrub the floor in a circular motion.

To reinstate a high-lustre shine, you can buff some floors with a rented power buffer fitted with a lamb's wool pad. High-traffic areas may require this once or twice a year; low-traffic areas once every two years. On a high-gloss floor covering, never use mechanical buffers, abrasive cleaners, or steel wool, as they will ruin the finish. Some manufacturers make or recommend cleaners and finishes you can use to reinstate the shine.

Protection from damage. Ultraviolet rays, over extended periods of time, can fade or discolor vinyl, so protect it from excessive exposure to direct sunlight. Inside, you can manage protection using shades and drapes. Outside, trees, trellises, and overhangs can help shade.

Protect vinyl from permanent dents or grooves caused by furniture and appliances. Tables and other stationary furniture should rest on wide-bearing, hard plastic floor protectors. Rolling chairs, serving carts and other mobile furniture should be equipped with casters that have at least ¾-inch of flat surface width.

Before moving a refrigerator or other heavy appliances across a vinyl floor, lay hardboard or plywood runways on the floor for protection.

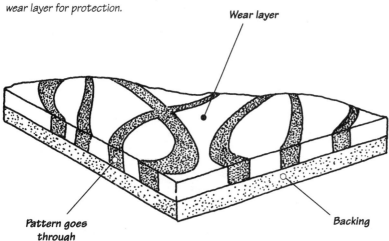

Wear layer

Pattern goes through

Backing

The most durable of all floorings are tile and stone—materials that, when properly installed, last the lifetime of a house. This toughness combined with the natural beauty of stone and the incredible array of tile types, colors, patterns, and textures makes tile and stone the materials of choice where quality and character are most important consideration.

Tile and stone are fundamentally different. Stone is just what its name implies: quarried slate, limestone, flagstone, granite, or marble. Tile is made from slabs of clay that are fired for hardness. A third material, stone tile, is made from real stone aggregate suspended in a polymer binder. This is a relatively affordable alternative to stone.

Tile may be either glazed or unglazed. Glazed tiles have very hard, smooth surfaces that reject water and stains. The glaze, applied between the first firing and a second one, gives the tile color and texture. Glazed tile comes in every color of the rainbow and may have a surface that is high gloss, satin, matte, or dull and may be smooth or textured.

Unglazed tile is unfinished, so is usually the color of the fired clay or an added pigment. It doesn't scratch as easily as glazed tile, but because it doesn't have the hard surface finish it is more likely to stain. It is generally treated with a sealer or wax for protection.

Tile is made in many different sizes, from 12-inch by 12-inch pavers to tiny mosaic tiles that are sold pre-arranged on a webbed backing.

The joints between tiles are filled with grout. The type of grout most commonly used is a very fine, thin mortar that is sometimes colored, but epoxy-base grouts are also used on occasion.

Conventional mortar bed installation is the method used by most professional tile installers. Tar paper and reinforcing wire mesh are installed over a ¾-inch plywood subfloor. A ¾-inch mortar bed is laid, sometimes in two coats, then the tile is adhered to this base with thin-set adhesive. Finally, grout is added between the tiles.

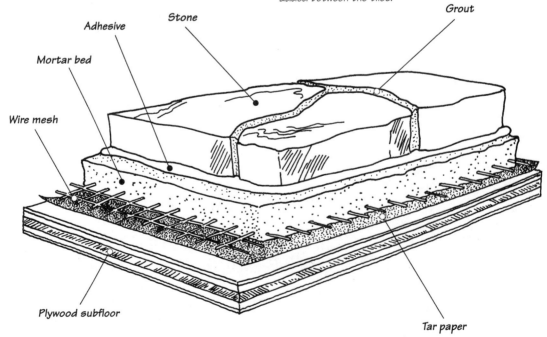

Adhesive · Stone · Grout

Mortar bed

Wire mesh

Plywood subfloor

Tar paper

Flooring tile should have a nonskid, stainproof surface (if it's only stain-*resistant*, it should be sealed and routinely resealed for protection). The slipperiness of a particular tile is rated by a friction coefficient and, more than anything, this is a factor that limits where or whether a tile should be used as a floor material.

Because tile and stone floors are heavy, rigid, and unforgiving of movement, they are applied over a strong, unyielding base; otherwise, they will crack. Wood subfloors are either reinforced with a secondary underlayment of plywood, cement backer board, or for a more durable application, a bed of mortar. Tile may be laid on a concrete slab using a thin-set adhesive.

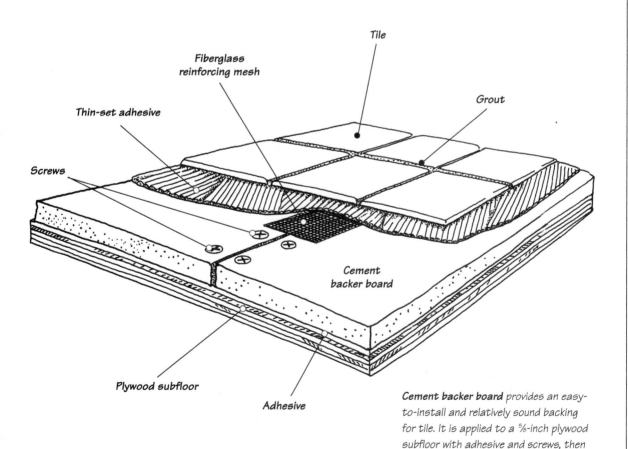

Cement backer board provides an easy-to-install and relatively sound backing for tile. It is applied to a ⅝-inch plywood subfloor with adhesive and screws, then the tile is bonded to the backer board with thin-set adhesive.

Where comfort underfoot is key, carpet is the floor covering of choice. It's relatively affordable, quick to install, soft and warm to walk on, and sound absorbing.

Carpeting is like a heavy fabric made from face yarns and backing. Most carpets today are tufted on huge machines that stitch face yarn to a synthetic backing with hundreds of high-speed needles working simultaneously. Once completely stitched, the carpet backing is usually coated with latex adhesive and reinforced with a second backing of jute, polypropylene, urethane foam, or rubber.

Depending on how the face yarns are finished, the carpet may have a pile that is looped, cut, cut looped, or tip-sheared.

Face yarns are made from both synthetic fibers and natural wool. Wool generally is considered to be the ultimate fiber, although it costs two to three times the price of synthetics; it's particularly durable and natural in appearance.

Synthetic fibers are made from several materials. Although these are given trade names, generically they are called nylon, olefin, polyester, or acrylic. Nylon is the most popular because of its durability. Olefin is an easy-care material that's often used outdoors and in basements. Polyesters are softer but a bit less durable than nylon. Acrylics resemble wool more than other fibers and resist static electricity and fading, but they are more expensive than nylon.

Carpeting is applied over padding most of the time. Dense, but not necessarily thick, padding prolongs a carpet's life, reduces noise, and adds a cushion.

Before a carpet is laid, *tackless stripping*, also called "tack strips" for short, are nailed around the perimeter of the floor. These thin strips of wood have short tack points that grab onto the carpet's backing. The carpeting is then stretched between the stripping. Any seams are joined from behind with fiberglass adhesive seam tape or a thermal plastic seam tape applied with a special iron.

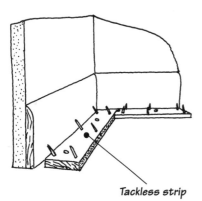

Tackless strip

Tackless stripping, *nailed to the floor around every nook and cranny of a room's perimeter, holds wall-to-wall carpeting in place. One edge of the carpet is hooked onto the protruding points of the stripping, then the carpeting is stretched tight, hooked onto the tackless strips at the opposite wall, and trimmed.*

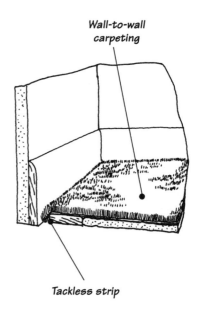

Wall-to-wall carpeting

Tackless strip

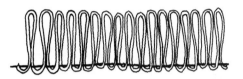
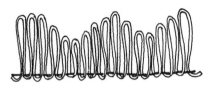

Loop carpet, the result of tufting, has complete yarn loops that stand upright. Loops tend to wear better than cut-pile carpets. High-level loops, such as Berbers, create a nubby texture, while low loops offer a smoother surface. Sculptured carpets have both high and low loops.

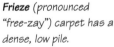

Cut-pile carpet has loops trimmed off so that yarn ends poke up. Saxony plush, one of the most popular varieties, has short tufts that are densely packed. Textured plushes have slightly taller pile and are less dense.

Frieze (pronounced "free-zay") carpet has a dense, low pile.

Cut-loop pile carpets combine loops with cut pile. The cut-loop pile has cut ends that are taller than the loops, creating an informal look.

Tip-sheared carpets have both cut and uncut loops at the same level.

A staircase is an integral part of the home's design and style. There are, of course, many different kinds of stairs, differing by their materials, construction, general shape, design, and a number of other features. Stairs may be steep or gradual, narrow or wide, purely functional or grand and showy. Some are built in place by woodworkers, finish carpenters, or stairmakers; others are factory manufactured and shipped to a building site.

A stair's design is heavily dictated by its function. An entry stairway that handles all up-and-down foot traffic and is placed in a highly-visible location is bound to be much more grand than a basement stairway that is hardly ever used, or where economy is imperative.

The available space is key in determining a stair's shape. Straight stairs are the easiest and most affordable type to build. But because stairs with a landing—L-shaped or return stairs—are safer and easier to climb, they're often preferred where space allows. Spiral stairs take the least space but are also the hardest to climb; in fact, rooms served by a spiral stair often also have a primary stair for easier access for furniture.

Stairs are built according to basic rules and principles intended to make them safe to use. These rules, governed by building codes, stipulate the permissible heights of risers, depth and width of treads, construction, placement of handrails, and similar concerns.

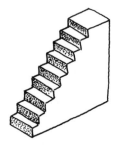

*A **straight stair** stretches from the lower to upper levels in one straight run. Although this is the easiest type of stair to build, it can be difficult to squeeze into a floorplan.*

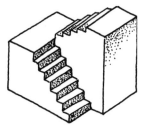

*A **return stair** divides the run, reversing direction a full 180° at a landing.*

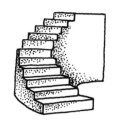

*A **circular stair** generally sweeps in a broad curve from one level to another.*

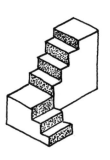

*An **"L" stair** makes a 90° turn at a landing. A <u>winder</u> stair serves like an "L" stair, but requires less space (and is less safe to use) because the landing is divided into pie-shaped steps.*

*The **common spiral stair** has a straight center pole with steps radiating out from it; a <u>helix-style</u> <u>spiral</u> has a center support that curves and follows the sweeping twist of the stair. Spiral stairs are relatively economical and take up minimal space.*

The fundamental parts of stairs
*are the same, regardless of type. It is how these
parts are built and combined that gives a
stairway its style and individuality. Of course, not
all stairways have all these parts—for example,
some stairways have open risers (no risers).*

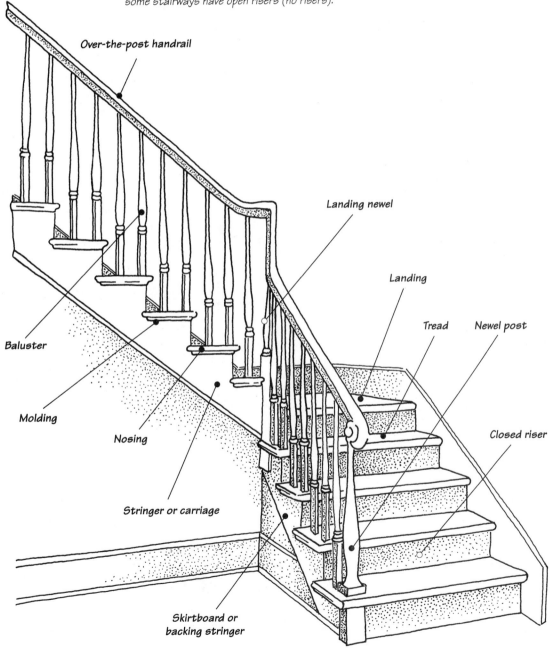

Over-the-post handrail

Landing newel

Landing

Tread

Newel post

Baluster

Molding

Closed riser

Nosing

Stringer or carriage

Skirtboard or
backing stringer

Cabinets are the heart of a kitchen's organization and the key contributor to its appearance. In addition, they supply important storage in bathrooms, offices, and other rooms. Hundreds, if not thousands, of styles are made from a broad range of materials: fine hardwoods, laminates, veneers, painted particleboard, and more.

From the highest quality models to the bottom-of-the-line units, all cabinets have one thing in common: fundamentally, they're simply boxes. Some of the boxes stand on the floor and are capped with countertops; others hang from the walls. Some are fitted with doors and shelves; others hold drawers or other kinds of specialty accessories.

There are two types of cabinet construction: *face frame* and *frameless* (also called European-style). Face frame cabinets, as their name implies, have a frame around the front of the cabinet. Frameless cabinets don't. You can usually tell the difference between the two types of

cabinet construction by the way the doors and drawers fit against the front. Bathroom cabinets are made using these same techniques.

Because a face frame adds rigidity to a cabinet's construction, it usually won't have a top panel or a full back, or the back may be made of quite thin material. Also, frameless base cabinets are usually mounted on top of a separate *plinth* or *toekick*; face frame cabinets have integral bases.

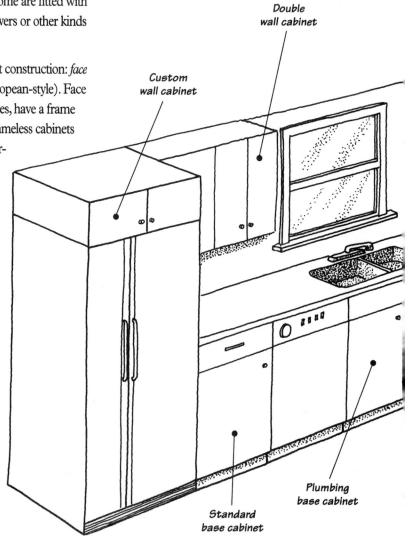

Double wall cabinet

Custom wall cabinet

A kitchen cabinet system is made up from several separate units, joined together. Base cabinets may have all drawers, doors and shelves, pullouts, or a combination of these. Plumbing bases have no shelves or drawers, reserving the space for a sink and plumbing. Upper wall cabinets offer storage above counters and appliances. Full-height cabinets, such as a pantry, provide tall storage.

Plumbing base cabinet

Standard base cabinet

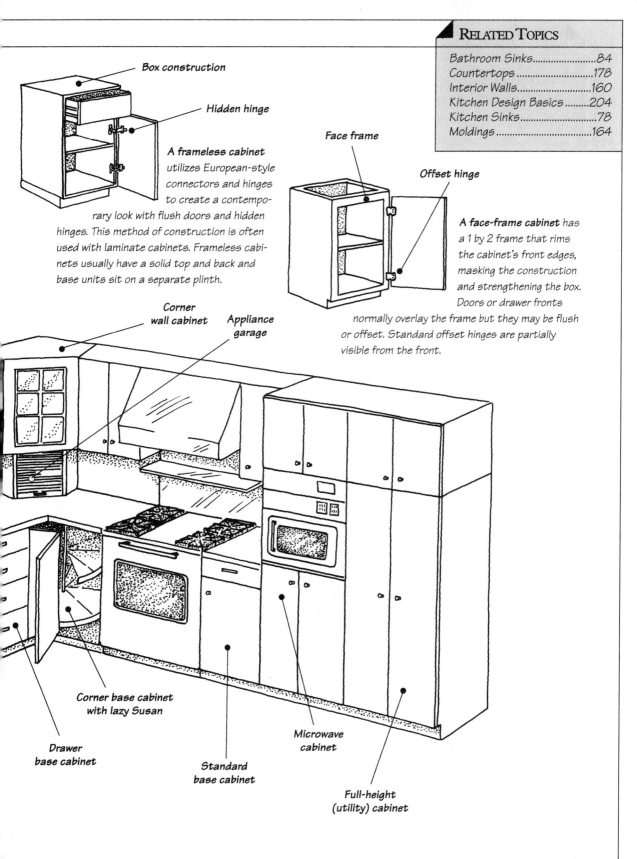

Box construction

Hidden hinge

A frameless cabinet utilizes European-style connectors and hinges to create a contemporary look with flush doors and hidden hinges. This method of construction is often used with laminate cabinets. Frameless cabinets usually have a solid top and back and base units sit on a separate plinth.

Face frame

Offset hinge

A face-frame cabinet has a 1 by 2 frame that rims the cabinet's front edges, masking the construction and strengthening the box. Doors or drawer fronts normally overlay the frame but they may be flush or offset. Standard offset hinges are partially visible from the front.

Corner wall cabinet

Appliance garage

Corner base cabinet with lazy Susan

Drawer base cabinet

Standard base cabinet

Microwave cabinet

Full-height (utility) cabinet

Inner Surfaces

Like a workbench in a woodshop, a countertop is perhaps the most necessary piece of equipment in a kitchen. Countertops are essential for just about every aspect of kitchen work. Here we'll look at the various types of counters used in kitchens. (These same materials and construction techniques are used in bathrooms.)

Countertops are made from materials that are durable and, in most cases, easy to maintain. Most combine a base of plywood or particleboard that spans across the top of a cabinet and the finish surface material. Of course, they also include any mastic, glue, mortar, or grout needed to adhere the surface to the base and keep it impervious to water and stains.

Standard kitchen counters are 24 inches deep and 36 inches from the floor. Bath counters are often shorter (30 inches high) and less deep (about 18 inches). Some have backsplashes, short vertical sections along the back that protect the wall.

The most common materials are high-pressure laminate, ceramic tile, wood, solid surfacing, and natural stone. If you're looking to buy new countertops, the material you choose will depend on your budget and the appearance and serviceable qualities you want.

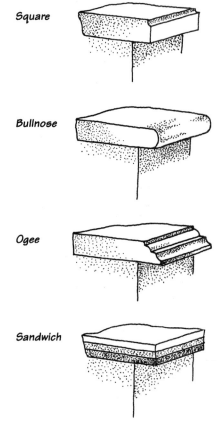

Square

Bullnose

Ogee

Sandwich

Woods such as maple, oak, and other hardwoods applied in butcherblock fashion, make handsome and durable countertops in some situations. Wood requires a finish to maintain its original patina. It can warp, scorch, and allow bacteria to grow.

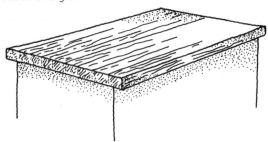

Edge treatments for countertops may vary. Depending upon the materials they're made from, countertops may have any of several edges. The square edge is the most common, particularly with laminates, wood, and tile. Bullnose is a safe, practical edge that makes a countertop look substantial. Ogee is more decorative, but possible only with certain materials. For a more decorative appearance, a detail of wood, metal, or a different color is sometimes sandwiched between layers of laminate, solid surfacing, or stone.

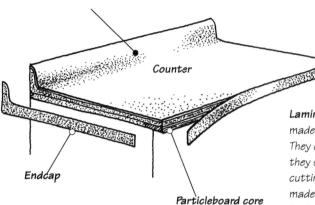

Backsplash

Counter

Endcap

Particleboard core

Laminates, inexpensive and durable, are made in hundreds of colors and patterns. They can be scorched by hot utensils and they show scratches; they're not suitable as cutting surfaces. Laminate countertops are made from a thin surface of high-pressure laminate that is applied to a base of particleboard or plywood.

Ceramic tile is available in practically any color and is extremely durable, easy to clean, and scorch-proof. Tiles are applied with mastic or, even better, with mortar to a plywood or tile backer board base.

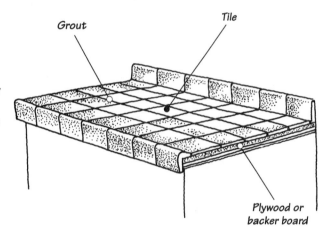

Grout

Tile

Plywood or backer board

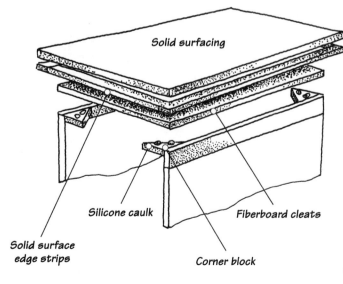

Solid surfacing

Silicone caulk

Fiberboard cleats

Solid surface edge strips

Corner block

Solid surfacing, a relatively newer countertop material, is quite durable and offers seamless, easy-care surfaces that often imitate the look of natural stone, such as marble, granite, or slate. Although these materials can be machined with standard woodworking tools, installation requires a professional.

Natural stone, such as granite, is considered to be the height of elegance and will last longer than most kitchens. Stone, however, is very expensive and requires some care: grease will stain granite and acidic foods, such as orange juice, will etch the finished surface of marble.

Architectural Style

If you've ever wondered whether your house is an example of Colonial, Queen Anne, or Greek Revival architecture, this chapter is for you. It examines the roots of American design so you can better understand your own home. Using this information, you should be able to identify its style or combination of styles. And with it, you should be able to understand more clearly why your house is built the way it is, how it works, and, if you intend to remodel or add on to it, how you can be true to its character.

Architecture is born from what works. The construction of walls, the pitch of a roof, the design of windows and doors: these all have developed from the materials and practices that have succeeded over time. Normally, building materials are intrinsic to the area in which a house is built. And construction practices align with the talents of local builders.

Although all houses share one universal purpose—to provide shelter—they differ greatly in how they approach this task. A house, after all, is a very specific answer to a particular problem. It is designed and built to address a certain climate, to meet a family's taste and budget, and to utilize available building materials and technologies.

The United States has a rich architectural history. Since colonial times, American homes have been founded both on regional resources and on the heritage of immigrants. This chapter looks at the vernacular of American homes, both past and present.

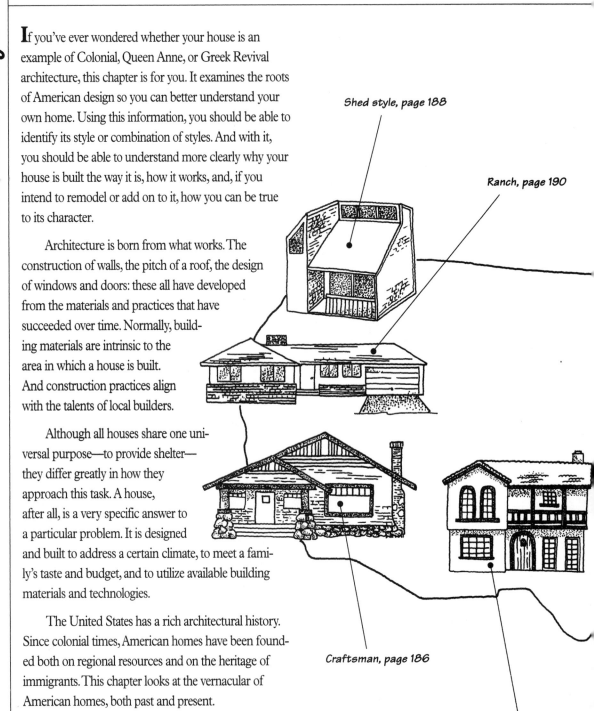

Shed style, page 188

Ranch, page 190

Craftsman, page 186

Spanish, page 184

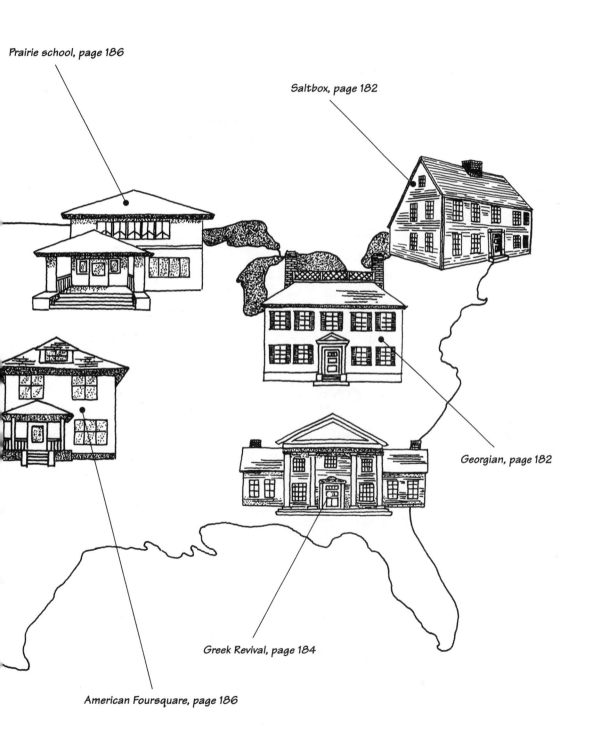

Prairie school, page 186

Saltbox, page 182

Georgian, page 182

Greek Revival, page 184

American Foursquare, page 186

Architectural Style

In building their homes, the first settlers in America were more interested in security and warmth than in architecture. They raised simple, practical dwellings using local materials. Although these homes were influenced by European traditions, early colonial houses were clearly big on function, small on pretension. The first houses often consisted of a single room with a central fireplace, and few amenities were considered.

House shapes and materials varied from one region to another, depending on climate, local materials, and European roots. Split-shingle or clapboard-covered wood frame construction became the norm in New England; southeastern Pennsylvania and the Hudson River valley utilized local quarry stone or fieldstone; Philadelphia and Virginia took advantage of brick.

As these houses developed, rooms were added and shed roofs were extended, creating the familiar "saltbox" style common in the Northeast.

Residences grew more sophisticated in the eighteenth century, and more attention was paid to architectural details. Proportions became more balanced and formal, ornamentation was added, and many houses grew in size. The Georgian and Southern Colonial houses shown here are characteristic of that period.

All these styles—and several other related forms of Colonial architecture—are mimicked today.

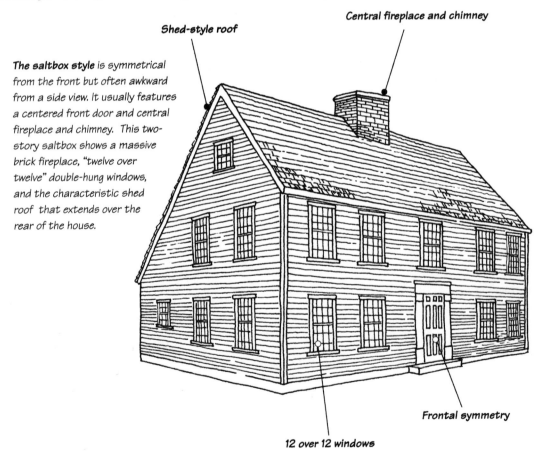

Shed-style roof

Central fireplace and chimney

The saltbox style is symmetrical from the front but often awkward from a side view. It usually features a centered front door and central fireplace and chimney. This two-story saltbox shows a massive brick fireplace, "twelve over twelve" double-hung windows, and the characteristic shed roof that extends over the rear of the house.

Frontal symmetry

12 over 12 windows

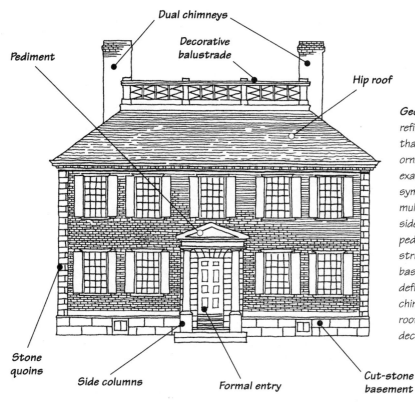

Dual chimneys

Decorative balustrade

Pediment

Hip roof

Stone quoins

Side columns

Formal entry

Cut-stone basement

Georgian architecture is an early refinement of the Colonial style that introduced elements of ornamentation and design. This example, built of brick, shows the symmetry, formal entry with multipaneled door and side lights, side columns, and overhanging pediment typical of this style. The structure has a cut-stone basement and stone quoins that define the house's corners. Two chimneys extend through the hip roof, bookends for a roof deck with decorative balustrade.

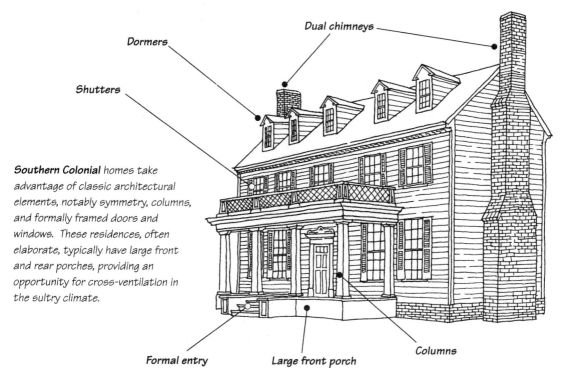

Dormers

Shutters

Dual chimneys

Southern Colonial homes take advantage of classic architectural elements, notably symmetry, columns, and formally framed doors and windows. These residences, often elaborate, typically have large front and rear porches, providing an opportunity for cross-ventilation in the sultry climate.

Formal entry

Large front porch

Columns

Architectural Style

As the population expanded and prosperity grew, Americans experimented with a growing range of styles from Europe. Many of these Old World styles drew on classical architecture, which Europeans had been rediscovering since the time of the Renaissance.

Some Old World architecture appealed to Americans because it symbolized Western civilization's great achievements, such as the development in ancient Greece of democratic government. In the young United States, proud of representative government, Greek Revival architecture received an enthusiastic reception that lasted from the 1820s through the 1850s. So popular was Greek Revival that it came to be considered for a time as the national style.

During the early nineteenth century, there were few professional architects in the United States, but pattern books for builders and carpenters circulated widely, supplying the instruction necessary for mastering the Greek Revival style.

A Greek Revival house commonly had a low or moderately pitched roof with a gable in front, above the entrance. If the gable was trimmed into a triangle, known as a pediment, it resembled in shape, if not in detail, the peak of a Greek temple. In many American towns, the grandest Greek Revival house had a pediment supported by columns, effecting a tone of sober dignity.

As the nineteenth century progressed, home building converted from heavy post-and-beam construction to much lighter balloon framing. Expansion of the railroads helped bring precut architectural components within reach of most of the nation. In addition, machines like the jigsaw made it easy for local carpenters to turn out intricate wooden ornaments. The result was that in the last part of the century, a host of styles, some of them quite decorative, each had a brief heyday. Gothic Revival, Italianate, Stick style, and Queen Anne were among them.

In the early 1920s, when inexpensive techniques were developed for adding a thin veneer of brick or stone to the exteriors of wood-frame houses, it became possible to mimic Old World styles more precisely than ever. Houses assumed styles such as English Tudor, in which surfaces of brick, stone, or stucco might be subdivided by false "half timbering" on the facade. A number of period styles found a following. In regions that Spain had once controlled—California, parts of the Southwest, and Florida—builders avidly adopted Spanish styles of architecture.

European-influenced styles have continued to be built to the present day, although they are often substantially modified to fit contemporary construction practices and current concepts of comfort.

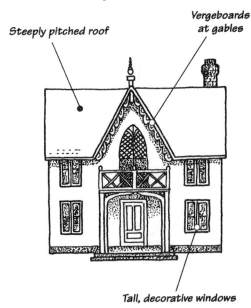

Steeply pitched roof

Vergeboards at gables

Tall, decorative windows

Gothic Revival has a steeply pitched roof, often with decorated <u>vergeboards</u> that give the gables a frilly look. Windows are long and narrow, and some have pointed tops, especially those beneath a front gable.

The Spanish style favors stuccoed exteriors and orange or red tile roofs. Some houses have windows or doorways with round arches. Different names have been given to the varieties of Spanish architecture in the United States, including Mission, Spanish Colonial, Spanish Eclectic, and Monterey. Mission style commonly features quatrefoil windows, curving dormers, and roof parapets. Spanish Eclectic houses often have arched doors and primary windows; doors may be elaborately carved.

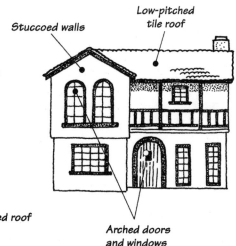

Stuccoed walls

Low-pitched tile roof

Arched doors and windows

Chimney pot

Steeply pitched roof

Half timbering

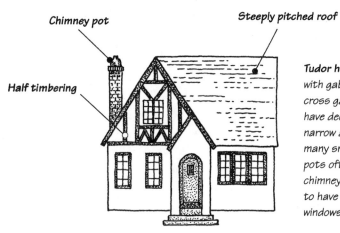

Tudor houses typically have steeply pitched roofs with gables to the sides and with one or more steep cross gables on the facade. Gables and walls may have decorative half timbering. Windows are tall and narrow and are grouped together; they often have many small panes. Interestingly shaped chimney pots often provide picturesque peaks for massive chimneys. Tudor houses built since World War II tend to have lower-pitched roofs, more conventional windows, and less elaborate chimneys.

Greek Revival architecture usually features a gable or hip roof with a low to moderate pitch. Beneath the roofline is a wide band of trim, typically divided into two parts: the frieze above and the architrave below. There may be an elaborate door surround. Window sashes typically are divided into six panes each. Columns, most commonly plain and Doric, support entry porches on many Greek Revival houses. On elaborate houses, a formal pediment tops the entrance. A lower wing may extend from the house's side.

Gable roof, moderate pitch

Formal pediment

Columns

Frieze

Architrave

Mulitipaned sash

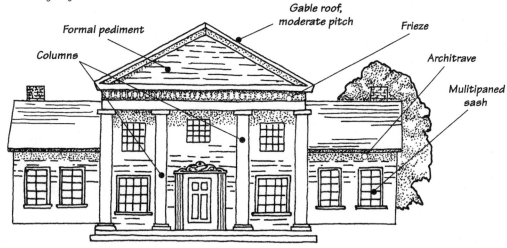

Architectural Style

At the beginning of the twentieth century, a burst of home building was inspired by the Arts and Crafts movement, which extolled objects that were honest and well made. Arts and Crafts downplayed the use of historic antecedents for design and decoration. In the Chicago area, Frank Lloyd Wright set out to create a new and distinctively American architecture that would harmonize with its landscape. Flat, open land characterized the Midwest. Wright and other architects thus pioneered the Prairie school, a form of domestic architecture that emphasizes horizontal lines, spreading out across the land rather than reaching up to the sky.

A low-pitched roof with widely overhanging eaves does much to establish the horizontal character of Prairie-style houses. Patterns in the walls also emphasize horizontal lines. Although the houses may be two stories high, many of them have one-story porches or wings that help to reduce their verticality. An elaborate Prairie house may have planters or low walls that extend outward, anchoring the house further to the ground. Prairie-style houses achieved their greatest popularity in the Midwest. They flourished, especially in newly developing suburbs, until about 1920.

A second distinctive style arose almost simultaneously on the West Coast. About 1903, two brothers—Charles Sumner Greene and Henry Mather Greene—began designing houses in Pasadena, California. These houses had extraordinary wooden detailing. Greene and Greene houses featured low-pitched roofs with deep overhangs and exposed roof supports. The style became known as Craftsman and spread nationwide in the 1910s and 1920s. Most Craftsman houses were one or one and one-half stories high and were called bungalows.

Related is the American Foursquare. This is a house that usually is two and one-half stories high with a roughly square floorplan and a pyramidal roof. The Foursquare, popular from 1900 to about 1930, often had a hip-roofed porch across its front and a hip-roofed dormer in the attic. The Foursquare does not blend into its surroundings like a Prairie house; on the contrary, it impresses viewers with its bulk. But it often shares the Prairie style's deeply overhanging eaves and some of the window and door details used on Prairie houses.

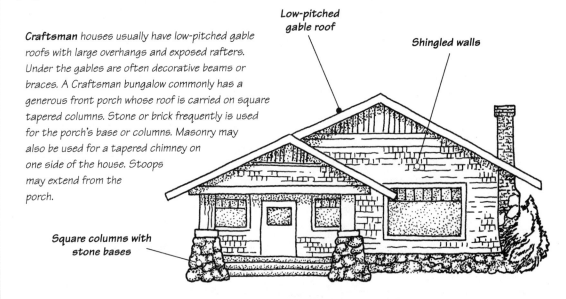

Craftsman houses usually have low-pitched gable roofs with large overhangs and exposed rafters. Under the gables are often decorative beams or braces. A Craftsman bungalow commonly has a generous front porch whose roof is carried on square tapered columns. Stone or brick frequently is used for the porch's base or columns. Masonry may also be used for a tapered chimney on one side of the house. Stoops may extend from the porch.

Low-pitched gable roof

Shingled walls

Square columns with stone bases

Prairie school houses feature a low-pitched roof with deep overhangs. Two-story houses often have single-story wings or porches that contribute to a sense of horizontal lines. The grouping of several casement windows in a row and lines in the exterior further emphasize the horizontal character. Windows may contain small panes in geometric patterns. A prominent central fireplace that culminates in a large, low chimney is often the focal point of the interior.

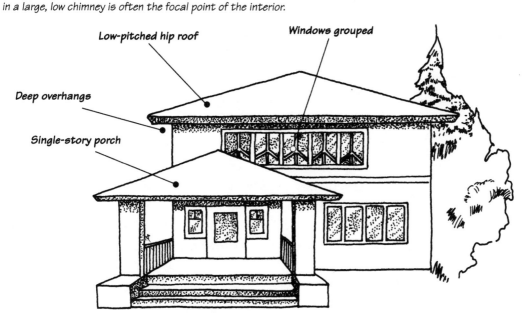

Low-pitched hip roof

Windows grouped

Deep overhangs

Single-story porch

Pyramid-shaped hip roof

Deep overhangs

Boxy shape

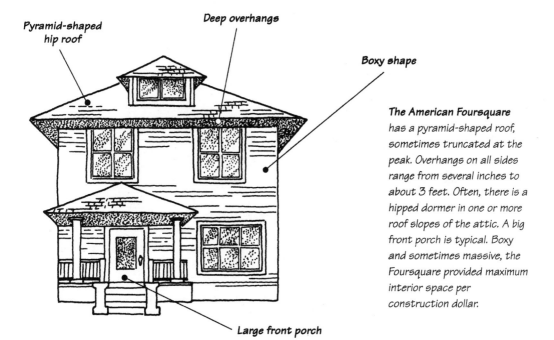

The American Foursquare has a pyramid-shaped roof, sometimes truncated at the peak. Overhangs on all sides range from several inches to about 3 feet. Often, there is a hipped dormer in one or more roof slopes of the attic. A big front porch is typical. Boxy and sometimes massive, the Foursquare provided maximum interior space per construction dollar.

Large front porch

Architectural Style

Modern houses—those built since the mid-1920s—aim for a functional design that avoids the trappings of historic architecture. One of the most influential trends in architecture, the International style, was employed by a relatively small number of pacesetting designers from the 1920s to the 1940s. International style houses favor flat roofs and smooth exterior walls with little or no applied ornamentation. Facades are usually asymmetrical, determined more by the demands of the interior layout than by the desire for a particular exterior appearance.

A less austere variant, Art Moderne, was built in the 1930s, distinguished by rounded corners, horizontal grooves or lines in the exterior, and often a small ledge along the edge of its flat roof. Art Moderne is a Machine Age esthetic, with flowing contours that give a streamlined effect, the same visual that was developed in the thirties for moving objects, such as trains and airplanes.

In the 1950s, designers, while continuing to experiment with new materials and novel structural systems, began to relent on the question of whether Modern buildings must have flat roofs. Many houses by prominent architects started to incorporate visible roofs into their profiles—but not gable roofs or any that closely resembled those in traditional architecture; Modernists preferred bolder, less conventional shapes. Natural materials, such as stone or flat cedar, also began to appear on exterior walls. The modified version of Modern architecture was often called Contemporary.

In the 1960s, architects introduced the Shed style, so named for its brusque, angular roofs. The Shed style showed up in individual houses, apartment complexes, and town house developments. A style still employed, it often gives the impression of geometric shapes that have been jumbled together.

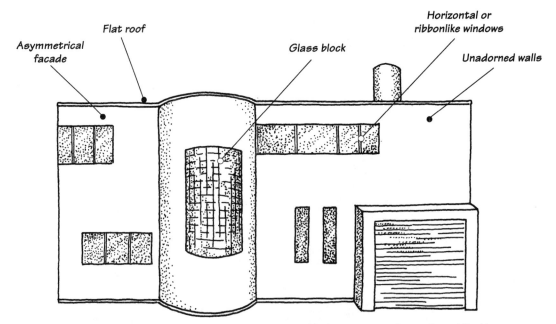

Asymmetrical facade · Flat roof · Glass block · Horizontal or ribbonlike windows · Unadorned walls

International style houses have smooth, machinelike unadorned walls with flat roofs and flexible, open interior layouts. The facade is often asymmetrical. Windows are often arranged as horizontal ribbons, flush with the wall surface. The entrance may be downplayed.

Art Moderne, sometimes called Modernistic, favors flat roofs, smooth stucco walls, and horizontal ribbon windows. Glass block is popular in this style. Either glass block or curving transparent window glass may be set in a wall. Balconies may have sleek railings of metal tubing.

Shed roofs

Angular forms

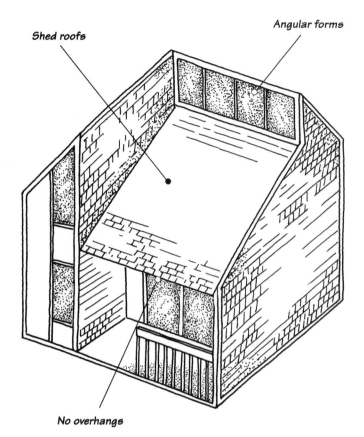

No overhangs

Shed style houses, inspired by starkly expedient rural buildings, have simple roofs that terminate abruptly where they meet the walls; overhangs are minimal or nonexistent. Often, the exteriors are clad with wood shingles, panels, or boards. Boards may run at the same angle as the roofline to accentuate the angular look. Some Shed style dwellings were designed so that solar energy panels or large expanses of glass would receive maximum exposure to the sun, cutting heating costs.

Contemporary houses have abstract shapes devoid of historical ornament. The roof may be flat or have a dramatic shape. There may be floor-to-ceiling glass or glass in ribbons, strips, or other nontraditional shapes. Interiors feature open plans. The expanses of glass bring large views of the outdoors inside.

Flat roof

Large windows

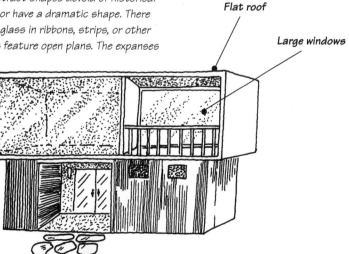

Architectural Style

Following World War II, rising incomes stimulated a sustained boom in home building. Builders and homeowners now exerted more influence over popular house styles than did architects. In the 1950s and 1960s, in particular, one of the most popular contractor styles was the ranch house, an asymmetrical one-story dwelling with a low-pitched roof and an attached garage. The development of the ranch house was made possible by the rapid growth of the suburbs, which in turn was the result of Americans' exodus from urban areas and their love affair with cars.

Instead of a front porch, the ranch house typically featured a patio to the rear. Outdoor life was shifting from front porches, sidewalks, and streets to the more private backyard, often outfitted with a swimming pool, a barbecue, and other leisure-time accoutrements.

The ranch house, with its hip roof and deep overhangs, looks like a greatly simplified adaptation of the Prairie school house; indeed, it expresses the same emphasis on the horizontal line. The ranch house has also been described as echoing the low, rambling Spanish house of the American Southwest.

Immediately after the war, new houses were compact, often 1,000 square feet or less. But through most of the postwar decades, people demanded increasingly larger houses, without necessarily larger lots. So builders found ways to squeeze more house onto each suburban lot, generally by adding a full or partial second story. Thus was born the split-level. Introduced in the 1950s, it remained extremely popular into the 1970s.

The split-level combines one and two-story segments set side by side. The design was promoted as giving families three distinct areas: one for noisy activities,

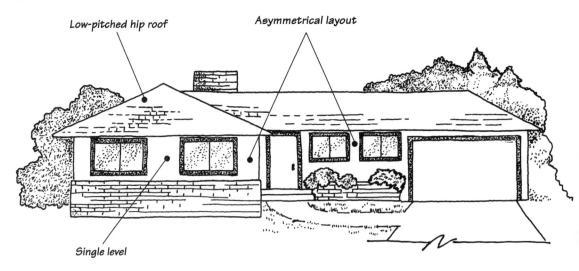

Low-pitched hip roof

Asymmetrical layout

Single level

*A **ranch** house is all on one level, under a gently sloping hip or gable roof, usually with moderate to deep eaves. A garage typically is attached to one end of the house. There may be one or more large windows at the front of the living area. Large ranch houses often have one or two wings at right angles to the main facade. This helps to separate the bedrooms from the living areas. Exterior materials and decoration vary widely.*

such as children's play and television viewing; one for more formal activities, as found in the living room, dining area, and kitchen; and one for sleeping.

Another offshoot of the ranch house was the raised ranch, a two-story dwelling with its lower level a daylight basement. The entrance to a raised ranch usually was midway between the upper and lower floors.

Many people who could not afford a site-built house bought a mobile home, which was assembled in a factory and which came equipped with appliances and often other furnishings. A mobile home is long and boxy because the complete unit has to be narrow enough to be hauled over roads. Increasingly, however, mobile homes have been upgraded for those able to afford more than basic shelter. Two units can be attached to form a one-story dwelling with more conventional dimensions. On some mobile homes, low-pitched gable roofs have succeeded the old standard, a flat roof. Decorative touches have been added to make mobile homes resemble traditional houses.

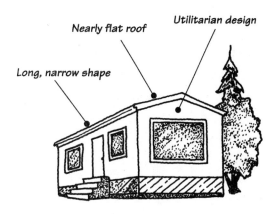

Nearly flat roof | Utilitarian design

Long, narrow shape

*A **mobile home** is typically long and one room deep; its narrowness is dictated by its need to be hauled from the factory to its lot. Its name notwithstanding, a mobile home moves few times during its years of use. When two units are connected side to side as a "double wide," the mobile home assumes more conventional house proportions.*

*The **split-level** house has a two-story segment joined to the side of a one-story portion. The one-story segment most often contains the living room, dining area, and kitchen. The top of the two-story portion contains bedrooms, while the bottom of that segment often contains a garage, family room, and utility room. The split-level commonly has a low-pitched hip or gable roof with overhanging eaves.*

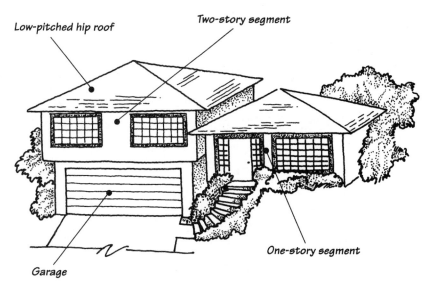

Low-pitched hip roof | Two-story segment

Garage

One-story segment

Home Design Basics

As discussed in the previous chapter, studying a house's inner workings requires looking at the overall architectural design. That chapter dealt with the roots of design. Here, we look at design fundamentals and the building plans that employ them.

If you think of a house as a complex mechanism, an assemblage of many parts, then design is the general plan that allows everything to work together. When done well, home design produces a residence that's pleasing to the eye, comfortable, easy to maintain, durable, relatively affordable, and ecologically responsible.

If you've dug up old blueprints for your house but you're not sure how to read them, this chapter will unravel the mystery. And if you're getting ready to build a new house, or modify or improve an existing

one, this information can help with your planning. It discusses building codes and zoning and even looks at a few specific design considerations for the kitchen—the area that requires the most thought during building or remodeling—and home safety.

In designing a house, architects factor in space requirements, cost, construction techniques, and local codes. They communicate with builders and homeowners primarily through drawings. During the conceptual phase, they create schematics and preliminary drawings that detail how a house will look and work. Through discussions with the builder and homeowners, the architects then refine their plans and prepare a set of working drawings, or blueprints, and specifications.

Site plan

Floor plan

Elevation and section view

Views used in drawings include plans, elevations, and sections. A plan view is from directly above, looking down. An elevation view is a straight-on look at a vertical surface, such as an exterior wall. A section view slices open part of a building to see its construction; there are both elevation and plan sections. Drawings may also incorporate three-dimensional views that show complex details.

Blueprints and specifications detail the house plans. A full set of drawings usually consists of a site plan; a foundation plan; structural plans; floor plans; elevations and sections; HVAC plans, plumbing and electrical plans or notations; reflected ceiling plans; and all necessary construction details, such as kitchen, bath, and built-in elevations. Full sets are usually given to the builder, the owners, the bank or other financial institution, and the local building codes department.

Knowing how to read these drawings will help you visualize the finished house, eliminate surprises, and minimize disputes with the builder. Once you understand views, symbols, and abbreviations, you should be able to comprehend most drawings.

On the following pages are some of the key parts of a set of working drawings: a site plan, a floor plan, elevations, sections, and an electrical plan.

Scale is used to reduce dimensions in drawings to a manageable proportion. Most blueprints are drawn so that ⅛ inch, ¼ inch, or ½ inch equals 1 foot.

Symbols are used to reduce the amount of description needed. Typical symbols are shown here.

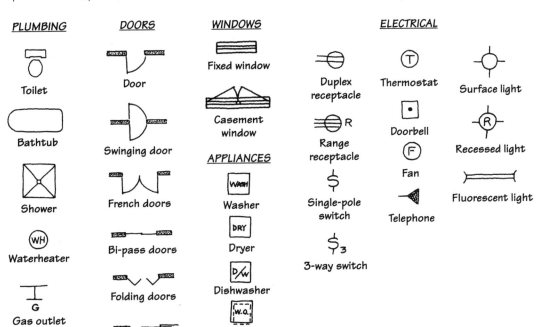

PLUMBING

Toilet

Bathtub

Shower

Waterheater

Gas outlet

DOORS

Door

Swinging door

French doors

Bi-pass doors

Folding doors

Pocket door

WINDOWS

Fixed window

Casement window

APPLIANCES

Washer

Dryer

Dishwasher

Oven

ELECTRICAL

Duplex receptacle

Range receptacle

Single-pole switch

3-way switch

Thermostat

Doorbell

Fan

Telephone

Surface light

Recessed light

Fluorescent light

Home Design Basics

A site plan, required by the building department in most areas for new construction, shows the shape, dimensions, and contours of a particular site, and where the house and other structures on the property are (or will be) located. It includes property lines, setbacks (see page 202), utilities, drainage, sewer, or septic lines, and a bird's-eye view of the "footprint" of the buildings. A site plan also shows trees and may even include circular drip lines around them that indicate the root spread so roots may be avoided during excavation.

Perhaps the most confusing parts of a site plan are contour lines, the wavy lines that show variations in grade. What's important to know is this: between each two lines, the ground rises or drops 1 foot. This means that where the contour lines are close together, the site is hilly or steep; where they are far apart, it's flatter.

A site plan utilizes the same types of symbols as a floor plan to reference other drawings and details.

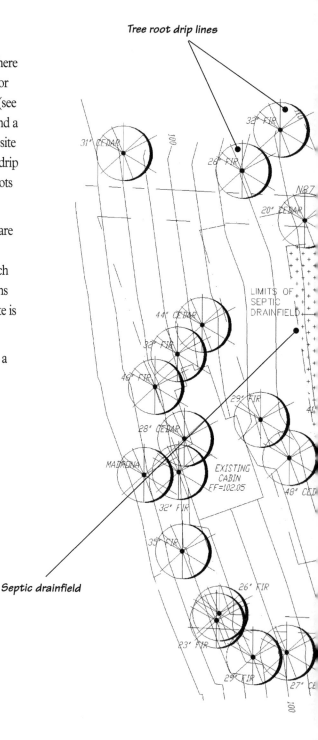

Tree root drip lines

Septic drainfield

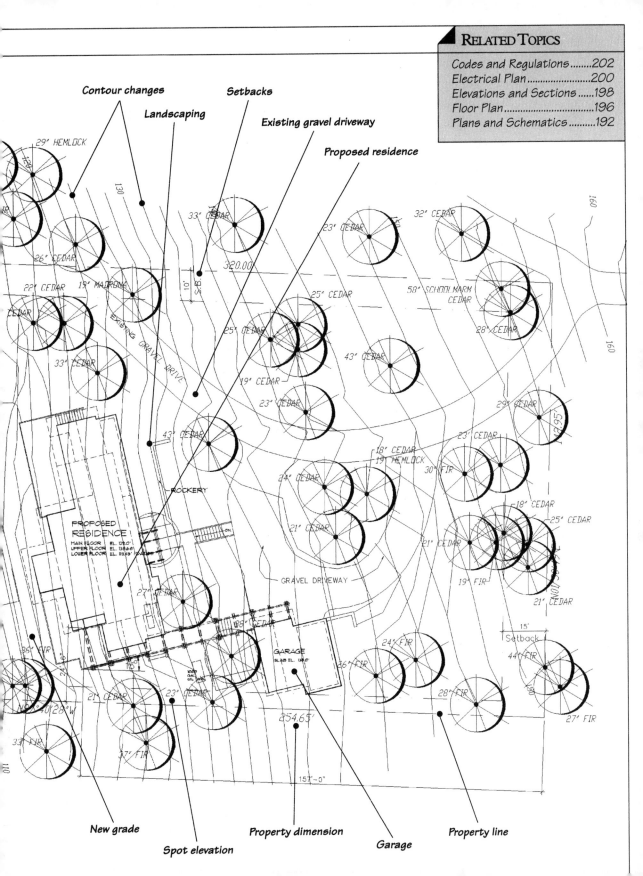

Contour changes

Landscaping

Setbacks

Existing gravel driveway

Proposed residence

29' HEMLOCK

26' CEDAR

22' CEDAR   15' MADRONE

33' CEDAR

33' CEDAR

43' CEDAR

PROPOSED
RESIDENCE
MAIN FLOOR EL. 120.0'
UPPER FLOOR EL. 130.0'
LOWER FLOOR EL. 110.0'

ROCKERY

27' CEDAR

36' FIR

21' CEDAR   23' CEDAR

33' FIR

17' FIR

33' CEDAR

25' CEDAR

25' CEDAR

19' CEDAR

23' CEDAR

43' CEDAR

18' CEDAR
19' HEMLOCK

24' CEDAR

21' CEDAR

21' CEDAR

GARAGE
SLAB EL. 110.0'

18' CEDAR

36' FIR

24' FIR

28' FIR

23' CEDAR

32' CEDAR

58' SCHOOLMARM
CEDAR

28' CEDAR

29' CEDAR

23' CEDAR

30' FIR

18' CEDAR

25' CEDAR

19' FIR

21' CEDAR

44' FIR

27' FIR

15'
Setback

15'
Setback

320.00'

GRAVEL DRIVEWAY

854.65'

157'-0"

EXISTING GRAVEL DRIVE

160

160

110

130

130

New grade

Spot elevation

Property dimension

Garage

Property line

Home Design Basics

Despite its name, the floor plan is much more than a plan of the floor. It's a bird's-eye view of the floors, walls, doors, windows, stairs, counters, built-ins, and other key elements. It shows the sizes of all rooms and spaces, the direction of door swings, the location of plumbing fixtures, and more. In addition, it usually includes the locations of lighting elements, switches, and other electrical devices, although more detailed drawings of the electrical system are often done separately (see page 200). A separate plan is drawn for each floor.

A floor plan is keyed to specifications and other drawings using symbols. Section lines and references indicate the point at which a cross section is taken for an elevation/section view. Other numbers or letters in circles or hexagons refer to a materials schedule that contains complete descriptions, including any manufacturers' specifications and the quantity of each item.

A plan view is almost always oriented with "project north" at the top of the page. Project north may vary from magnetic north; it's an approximation based on lot lines, streets, and so on. An on-page compass designates north and, where solar orientation is critical, true magnetic north.

Section lines and references indicate where a slice is taken for a section or elevation view. Like an arrow, they point to the direction of the view. The letters and numbers will tell you where to find the referred drawing. The letter or number on the top is the section, while the number on the bottom is the page.

A door is specified by a symbol that's indicated on the legend. The door's direction of swing is shown with an arc.

Dimension lines or stringers specify all dimensions and are notated in feet or inches.

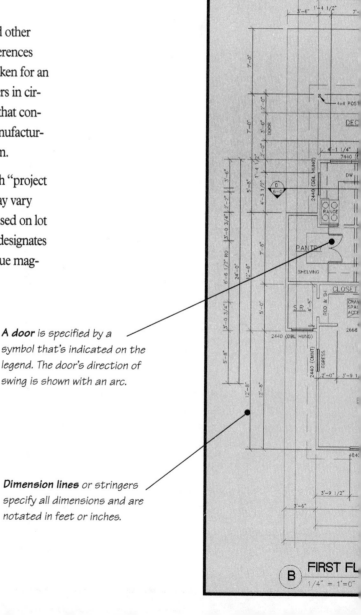

Stairs *are shown as a sequence of treads; an arrow indicates the direction—up for an incline, down for a decline.*

Notes *call out structural requirements.*

Title block *identifies architect*

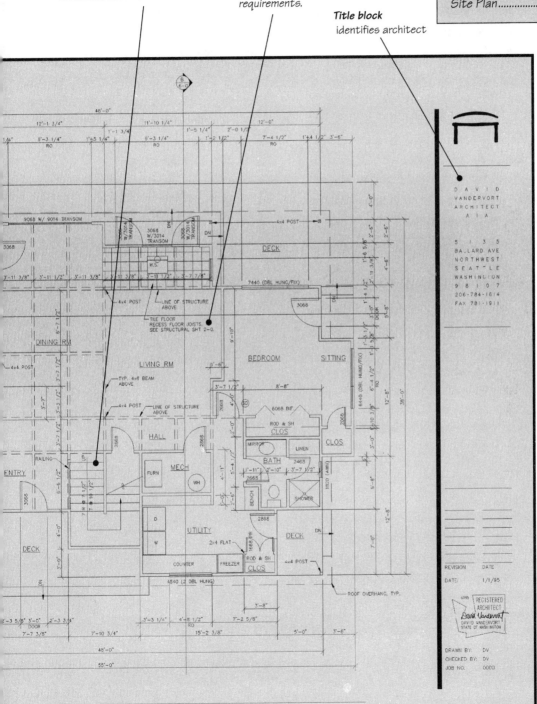

Elevation and section drawings are different from site and floor plans in that they reveal the vertical—not the horizontal— elements of a house. These drawings show walls and roofs from a straight-on perspective. A full set of architectural blueprints contains elevation and section drawings along with floor plans.

An elevation and a section each serves a particular purpose. An elevation shows construction from a full frontal view, with outer coverings, trim, doors, windows, and so on. A section view peels away the coverings, taking a slice through the building at a given point, which is specified on the floor plan, to see how the construction works. Such a view typically is taken through the center of a house to show how various floor levels interrelate.

In a full set of architectural drawings, elevations are given for the front, back, and both sides of the building. These may be labeled Front, Back, Left Side, and Right Side, or, more typically, they may be labeled by compass direction—North, South, and so on. Examining the elevations will give you a better idea of what a house will really look like.

An exterior elevation includes windows, doors, siding, steps, chimneys, roof, and all other details you would see from that view. Interior elevations are drawn for key walls, such as those that are fitted with cabinets, stairs, or similar details. They are also used to show how windows and doors are seen from inside a room. Elevations are labeled with dimensions and materials.

Where very specific dimensions or structural detailing are needed, section views are drawn. Sections are typically taken through the center of a house to show how various floor levels interrelate.

An exterior elevation *shows windows, doors, roof line, and cladding. Standard graphics are used to designate common building materials such as wood siding, brick, and stone. These graphics are indicated on the symbol legend (see page 193). Like floor plans and other architectural drawings, elevations are noted with the scale, building instructions, symbols for specifications, references to other drawings, and so forth.*

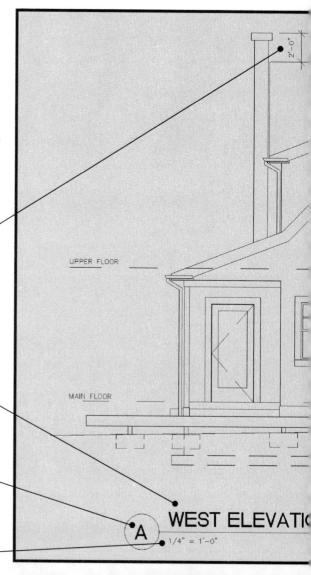

Dimension lines

UPPER FLOOR

2'-0"

Location

MAIN FLOOR

Reference

A

WEST ELEVATI

1/4" = 1'-0"

Scale

A section view slices the house to reveal interior construction details. The location of this slice is called out on the floor plan and may be referenced on other drawings as well. Because section drawings are technical documents needed for construction, they usually include extensive building instructions and detailed dimensions.

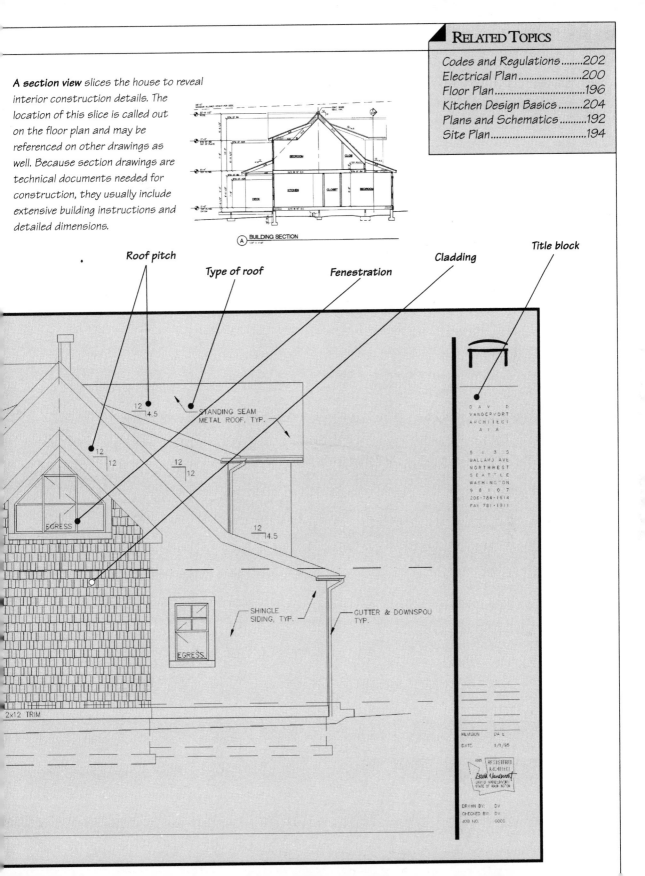

Ⓐ BUILDING SECTION

Roof pitch

Type of roof

Fenestration

Cladding

Title block

12 / 4.5

STANDING SEAM METAL ROOF, TYP.

12 / 12

12 / 12

12 / 4.5

EGRESS

EGRESS

SHINGLE SIDING, TYP.

GUTTER & DOWNSPOUT TYP.

2x12 TRIM

D A V I D
VANDERVORT
ARCHITECT
A I A

5 4 3 5
BALLARD AVE
NORTHWEST
S E A T T L E
WASHINGTON
9 8 1 0 7
206-784-1614
FAX 781-1911

REVISION   DATE
DATE: 1/1/95

DRAWN BY: DV
CHECKED BY: DV
JOB NO.   0000

An electrical plan illustrates a home's electrical lighting, switches, receptacles, phone jacks, doorbells, cable television jacks, and similar electrical devices. It may or may not be included as a separate sheet in a full set of architectural drawings; in many cases, this information is supplied on the main floor plans. A separate electrical plan, however, is a little easier to work with because it isn't cluttered with all the other construction information.

This plan is prepared for two reasons. First, it gives you, the homeowner, a chance to customize the locations of electrical devices, allowing the home to meet your needs. For example, you may want to be able to control bedside lamps from a main switch located at the door or from two three-way switches both by the door and at the side of the bed. The electrical plan provides a basis for dialog between you and the designer.

Second, it gives the electrical contractor the information needed to bid on the job. For this reason, any nonstandard equipment should be called out in a materials schedule that is referenced by the plan.

Be aware that building codes, such as the National Electrical Code®, set basic standards regarding the type of devices and wiring used, as well as appropriate locations. For example, code requires that every usable wall must have an electrical outlet no further than 6 feet from any point along that wall (in most cases, this means outlets are spaced 12 feet apart).

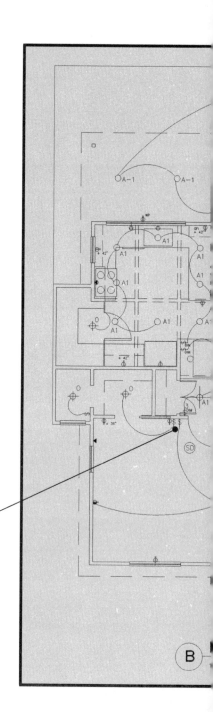

Switches, *also available in several varieties, are designated by symbols that specify single-pole, three-way, four-way, dimmer, or weatherproof models.*

Electrical outlets are designated on an electrical plan by various architectural symbols. A split-wired convenience outlet, like a normal duplex receptacle, has two places to plug in lamps or appliances. One of the two is controlled by a wall switch. A weatherproof outlet is required outdoors. A ground fault interrupter, which shuts off the circuit instantly if there is a short, is required in bathrooms, kitchens, and porches.

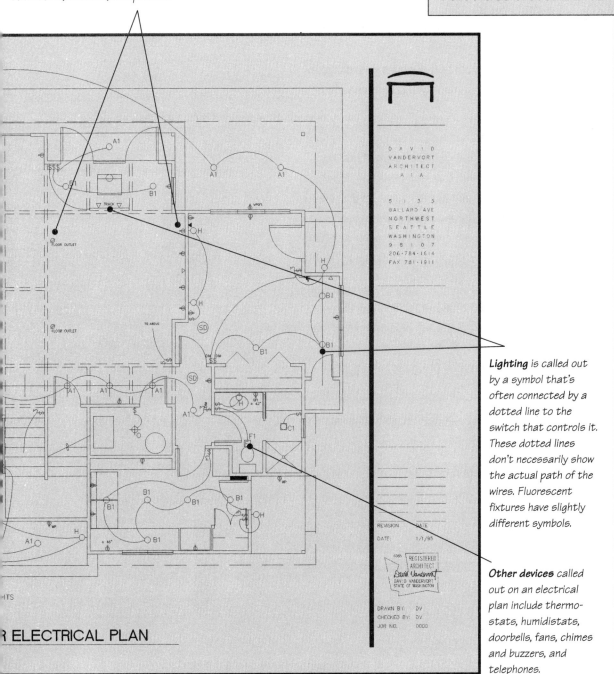

DAVID
VANDERVORT
ARCHITECT
A I A

5 1 3 5
BALLARD AVE
NORTHWEST
SEATTLE
WASHINGTON
9 8 1 0 7
206·784·1614
FAX 781·1911

Lighting is called out by a symbol that's often connected by a dotted line to the switch that controls it. These dotted lines don't necessarily show the actual path of the wires. Fluorescent fixtures have slightly different symbols.

Other devices called out on an electrical plan include thermostats, humidistats, doorbells, fans, chimes and buzzers, and telephones.

R ELECTRICAL PLAN

Home Design Basics

Nearly all houses are built within the guidelines set by building codes and local ordinances meant to ensure the safety and standards of structures for the present and future homeowners. These regulations also come into play when a house is remodeled or when certain types of repairs are done. Before you do any work that involves a house's structure or mechanical systems, check with your local building codes department to see what restrictions may apply. If you don't, you could face fines or legal action.

Building codes, such as the Uniform Building Code, the Basic Building Code, and the Standard Building Code, set forth national standards but are implemented locally. States, cities, and counties may have their own variations on the national codes. All building codes set minimum standards for materials and methods used in construction. They cover foundations, framing, electrical wiring, plumbing, insulation, and more.

Zoning ordinances are local rules that may restrict the type, size, shape, and location of a house or improvements allowed in a neighborhood. They may affect the height of the structure, the percentage of the lot that may be covered by the building, setback (the minimum distance between the

house and property lines) and so on. When a project doesn't fall within the parameters of these regulations, you may seek a variance (an exception).

Other types of restrictions that may affect the improvements on a piece of property are deeds and covenants, which include architectural standards required by the community, easements, and other legal restrictions. These may be written into the title of the property as a condition of ownership. It's important to discover them before you purchase a lot or house.

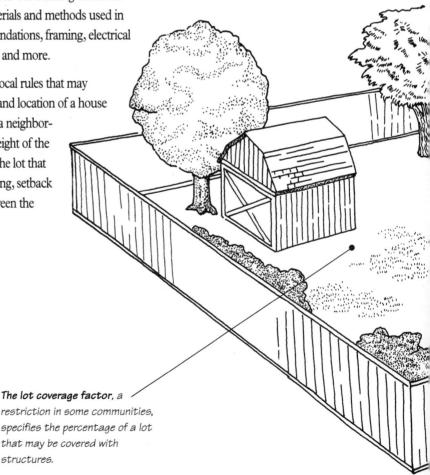

The lot coverage factor, a restriction in some communities, specifies the percentage of a lot that may be covered with structures.

Building codes set minimum standards for the materials used, the overall structure of a house, and the level of workmanship.

Height limits restrict the height of a house, fences, and other structures The total allowable height generally is measured from grade or natural ground level.

Setbacks are zoning restrictions that govern how close to the front, back, and side property lines you may build.

The evolution of the house is nowhere more evident than in the kitchen. Although the kitchen was once a utilitarian workroom, it has become the center of household activity, the hub of both family life and entertaining. As kitchens have grown into this high-profile role, they have gone through many dramatic changes, not only in the appliances they contain but in their basic design. For example, today's kitchens often have adjacent breakfast rooms or counters and open family rooms, and they're frequently designed to accommodate two cooks.

Because the kitchen is the key work area of a home and its layout is critical to successful home design, a few basic considerations are offered here.

You may be familiar with the classic kitchen work triangle. This concept, developed in the 1950s for limited-space housing, set up a basic formula for the placement of three key kitchen appliances: the refrigerator, the sink, and the stove. Because it worked well for the simple, single-cook kitchen, it was adopted in the design of millions of kitchens over many years.

Many of today's kitchen designs break the classic work triangle and are instead allowing for multiple independent work zones. They also incorporate the kitchen into the overall living area.

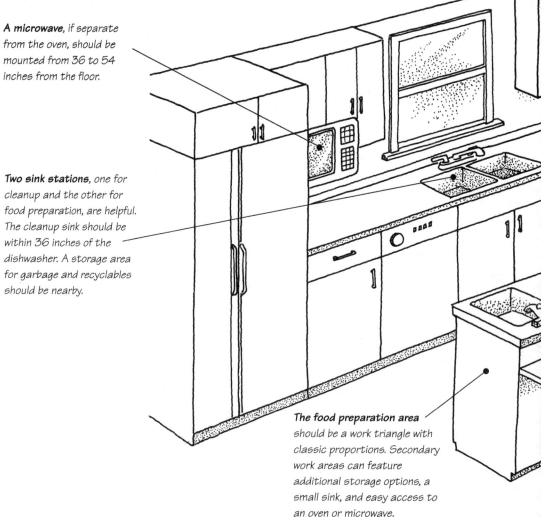

A microwave, if separate from the oven, should be mounted from 36 to 54 inches from the floor.

Two sink stations, one for cleanup and the other for food preparation, are helpful. The cleanup sink should be within 36 inches of the dishwasher. A storage area for garbage and recyclables should be nearby.

The food preparation area should be a work triangle with classic proportions. Secondary work areas can feature additional storage options, a small sink, and easy access to an oven or microwave.

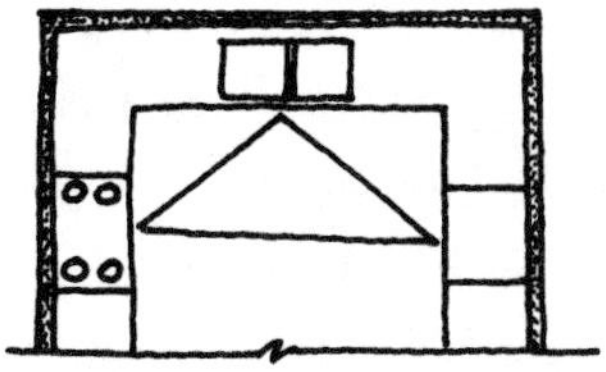

The classic work triangle concept places each appliance at a point on a triangle, then specifies that the total distance of all three sides be less than 26 feet, with no side less than 4 feet. Although it works well for simple, single-cook kitchens, it lacks flexibility.

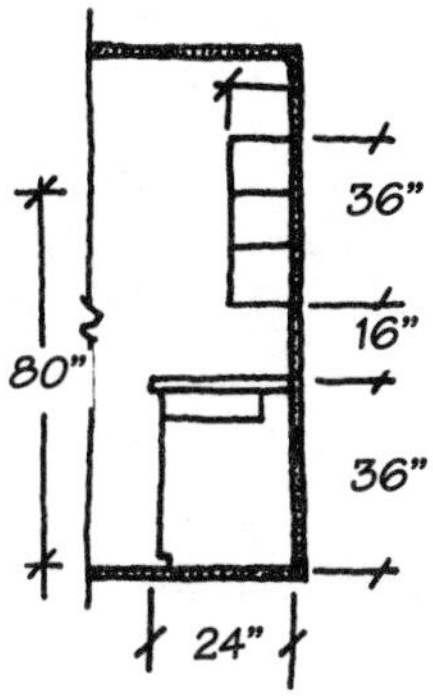

36"

16"

80"

36"

24"

Cabinet heights and dimensions are designed for easy use.

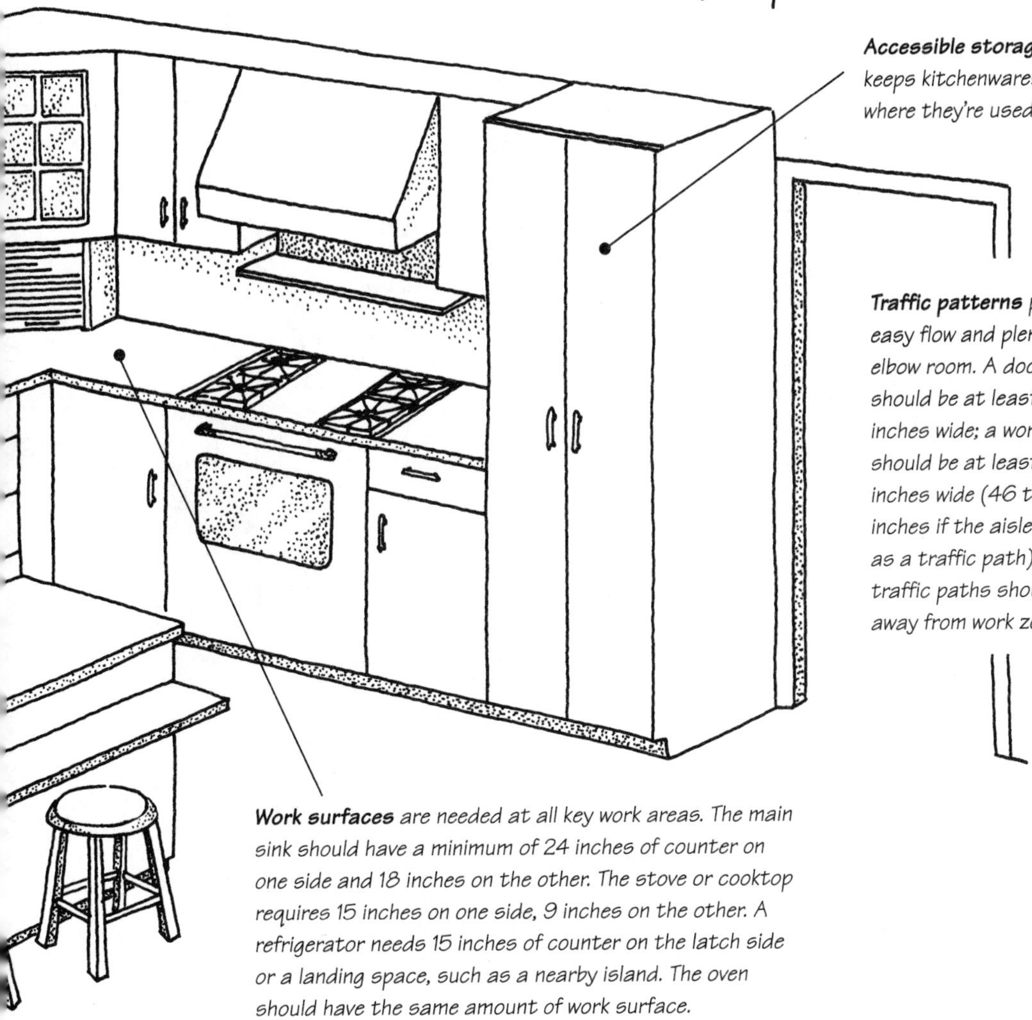

Accessible storage keeps kitchenwares near where they're used.

Traffic patterns provide easy flow and plenty of elbow room. A doorway should be at least 30 inches wide; a work aisle should be at least 42 inches wide (46 to 60 inches if the aisle doubles as a traffic path). Main traffic paths should be away from work zones.

Work surfaces are needed at all key work areas. The main sink should have a minimum of 24 inches of counter on one side and 18 inches on the other. The stove or cooktop requires 15 inches on one side, 9 inches on the other. A refrigerator needs 15 inches of counter on the latch side or a landing space, such as a nearby island. The oven should have the same amount of work surface.

One of the key roles of a house is to provide a safe refuge. Apart from fending off the normal assaults of nature, a house must withstand hurricanes, earthquakes, tornadoes, floods, blizzards, and wildfires. Of course, this isn't always possible, but there are a few steps you can take to reduce losses and increase your family's odds of surviving a disaster. The illustration here highlights key suggestions.

In addition, be sure your house is covered by homeowner's insurance for full replacement value, and find out what your policy doesn't cover. Most policies don't automatically cover earthquake or flood losses, so if you live in an area prone to these disasters, consider additional coverage. Also find out whether your policy will provide for the cost of temporary housing in the event that reconstruction is necessary. Take a complete inventory of your belongings (video documentation is useful).

Be sure everyone in the family knows where to go and what to do during an emergency. Contact a local branch of the American Red Cross for information on emergency planning.

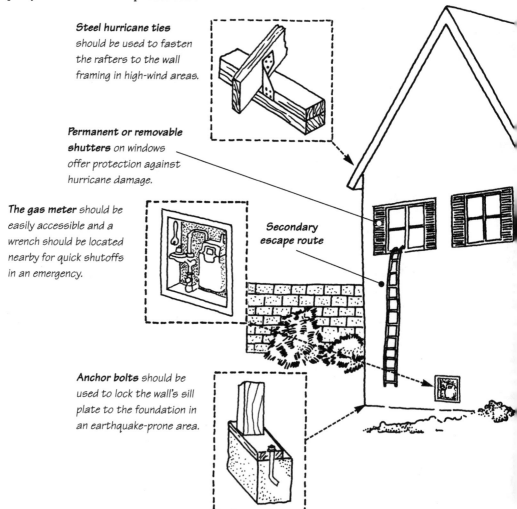

Steel hurricane ties should be used to fasten the rafters to the wall framing in high-wind areas.

Permanent or removable shutters on windows offer protection against hurricane damage.

The gas meter should be easily accessible and a wrench should be located nearby for quick shutoffs in an emergency.

Secondary escape route

Anchor bolts should be used to lock the wall's sill plate to the foundation in an earthquake-prone area.

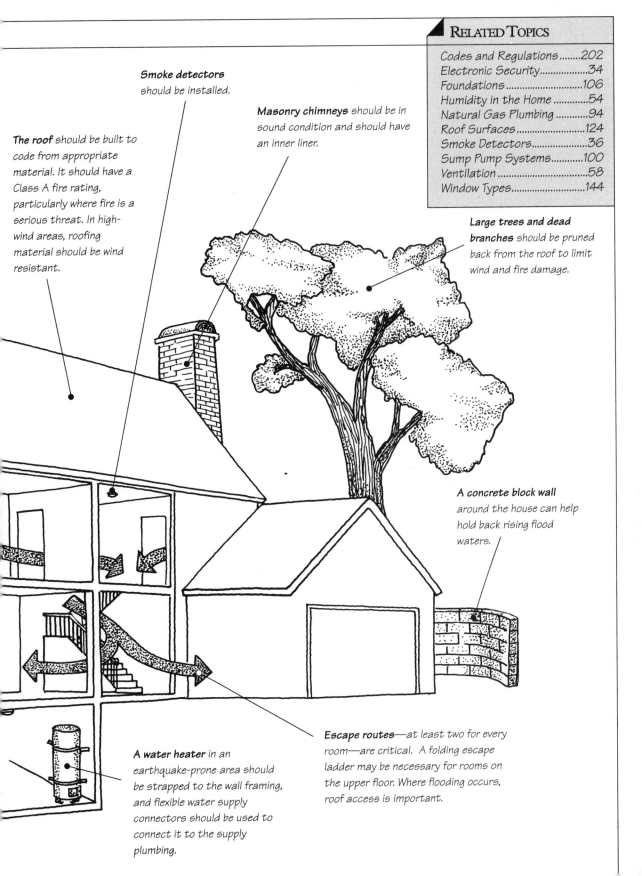

Smoke detectors should be installed.

Masonry chimneys should be in sound condition and should have an inner liner.

The roof should be built to code from appropriate material. It should have a Class A fire rating, particularly where fire is a serious threat. In high-wind areas, roofing material should be wind resistant.

Large trees and dead branches should be pruned back from the roof to limit wind and fire damage.

A concrete block wall around the house can help hold back rising flood waters.

A water heater in an earthquake-prone area should be strapped to the wall framing, and flexible water supply connectors should be used to connect it to the supply plumbing.

Escape routes—at least two for every room—are critical. A folding escape ladder may be necessary for rooms on the upper floor. Where flooding occurs, roof access is important.

Home Tools and Materials

A new car comes with a few essential tools for changing a flat: a jack, a lug wrench, and a temporary spare tire. The idea is that, in a pinch, you can use these to handle a usually minor car emergency. Whether or not you actually do this depends on your confidence in changing a tire and the extent of the emergency.

When you buy a house, a tool kit doesn't come as part of the package, but it's smart to have one on hand for the same reasons. With a basic tool kit, you can take care of minor problems before they become major ones.

In this chapter, you'll find suggestions for a few basic tools, as well as some additional tools for more complex or specialized tasks. You'll also find information on some typical materials and supplies used throughout the house. This should help you on your next visit to the hardware store or home improvement center.

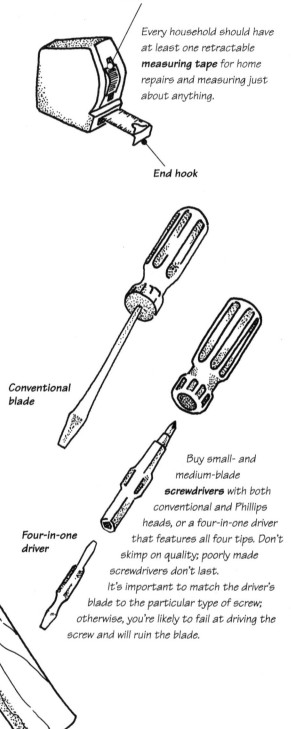

Locking button

*Every household should have at least one retractable **measuring tape** for home repairs and measuring just about anything.*

End hook

Conventional blade

Four-in-one driver

*Buy small- and medium-blade **screwdrivers** with both conventional and Phillips heads, or a four-in-one driver that features all four tips. Don't skimp on quality; poorly made screwdrivers don't last.*

It's important to match the driver's blade to the particular type of screw; otherwise, you're likely to fail at driving the screw and will ruin the blade.

Curved claw

Bell face

*A good **hammer** is essential. In fact, two are ideal: a medium-sized one, such as a 16-ounce curved-claw model, and a second one for small tasks.*

To nail properly, use smooth, even movements. To avoid bending nails, be sure the hammerhead strikes the nailhead squarely. When pulling a nail from wood, slide a block under the hammerhead to protect the surface and improve your leverage.

Related Topics

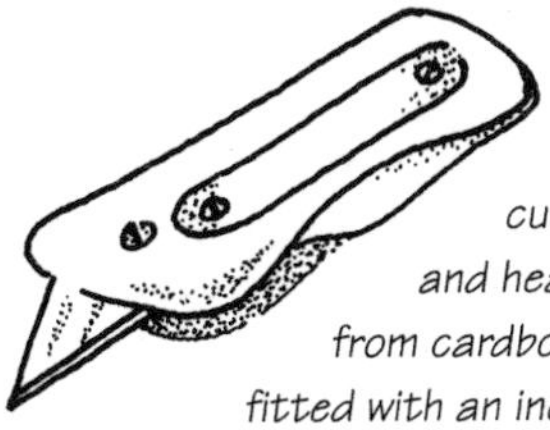

*A **utility knife** can be used for cutting both lightweight and heavy-duty materials—from cardboard to drywall. It's fitted with an inexpensive, razor-sharp, replaceable blade so you don't have to worry about sharpening it.*

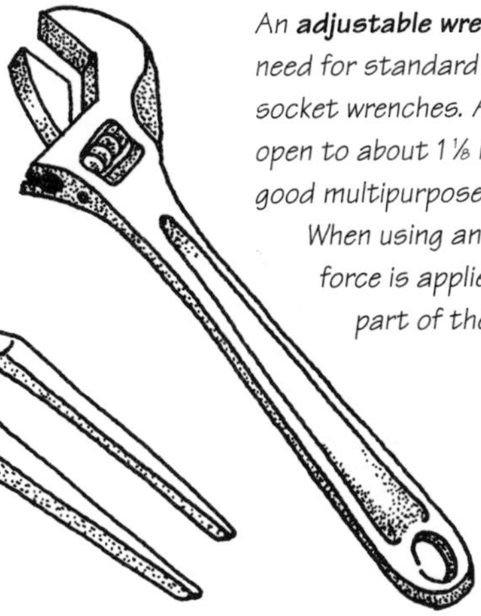

*An **adjustable wrench** eliminates the need for standard box, open-end, and socket wrenches. A 10-inch wrench will open to about 1⅛ inches, making it a good multipurpose tool.*

When using an adjustable wrench, force is applied against the fixed part of the jaws.

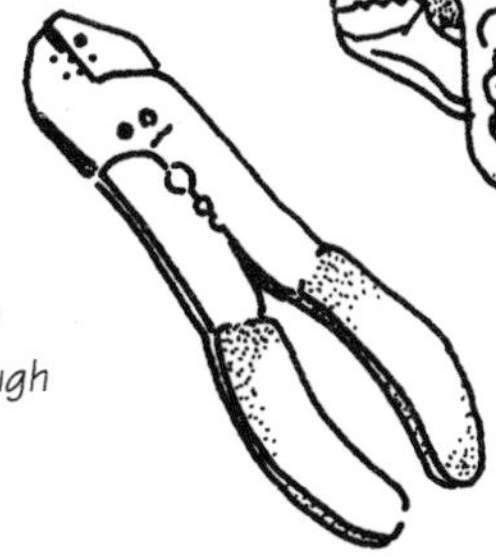

*A small, inexpensive **wire cutter/stripper** is handy for wire connection repairs. The type shown here will both cut and strip the insulation from many different sizes of wire. To strip a wire, carefully cut through the insulation and peel it off.*

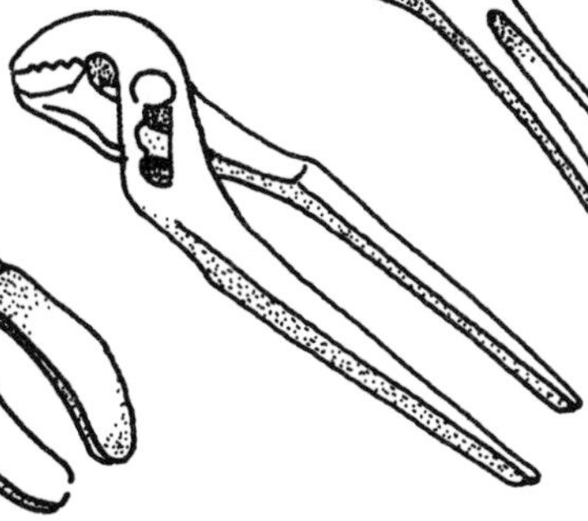

*Adjustable, **rib-joint pliers** are helpful for gripping many things, from sink drain fittings to baby food jar lids.*

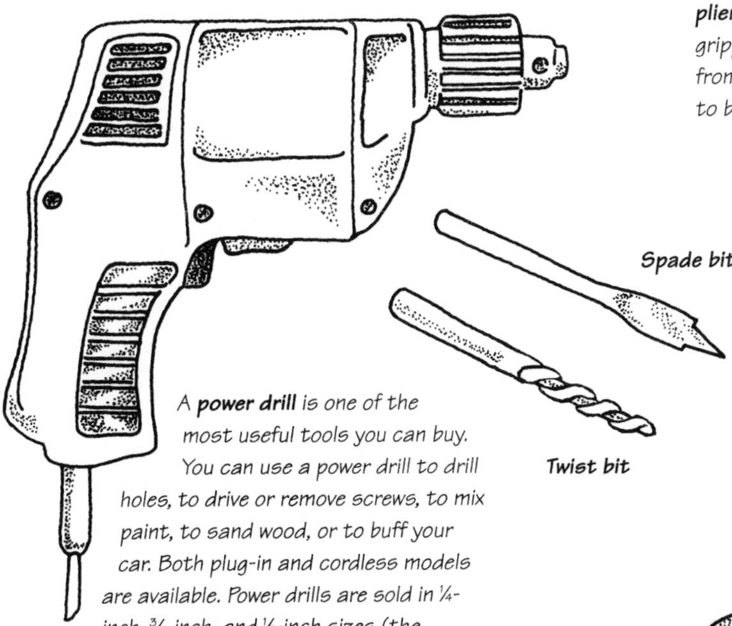

Spade bit

Twist bit

*A **power drill** is one of the most useful tools you can buy. You can use a power drill to drill holes, to drive or remove screws, to mix paint, to sand wood, or to buff your car. Both plug-in and cordless models are available. Power drills are sold in ¼-inch, ⅜-inch, and ½-inch sizes (the diameter of the drill shaft their jaws can hold). Buy a ⅜-inch size, a set of twist bits and spade bits, and screwdriver tips, both Phillips and slotted.*

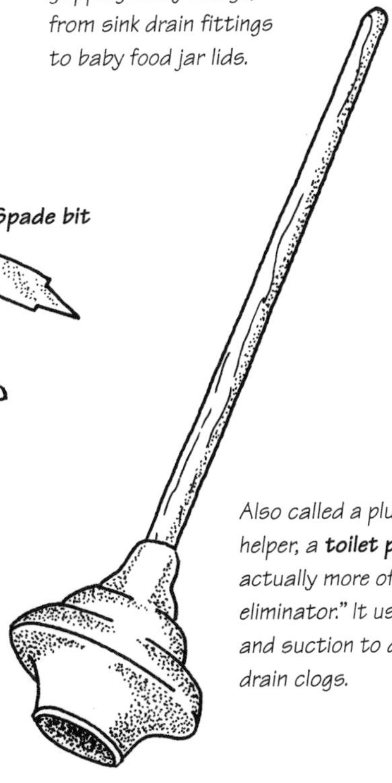

*Also called a plumber's helper, a **toilet plunger** is actually more of a "plumber eliminator." It uses pressure and suction to dislodge drain clogs.*

Home Tools and Materials

If a clearer understanding of the parts, pieces, and systems of your house has encouraged you to try more advanced home repairs and maintenance yourself, you'll need a few more tools than those shown on the previous page. Here are suggestions for additional tools. Of course, you don't need to buy the entire collection all at once; you can wait until the need for each tool actually arises before purchasing it.

A heavy-duty **cold chisel** is used to cut ceramic tile, masonry, and metal. It must be struck with a ball-peen hammer or a mallet, not a claw hammer, and you should wear protective goggles when using it.

Wood chisels are used for some woodworking jobs, such as mortising hinges or locksets into doors. It's best to buy a set of four, from ¼-inch to 1-inch widths.

If you're going to be cutting wood for any project, you'll need a **saw**. Although a power circular saw is best for quickly cutting boards, it's difficult to use if you're a novice. Generally, you can have major cuts made at a lumberyard, then do simpler, finishing work at home with a handsaw. There are two types of handsaws: ripsaws and combination saws. A ripsaw is used to cut boards lengthwise; a combination saw can handle all types of projects, so it's your best choice.

Always cut to the waste side of your cutting line. Start the cut with short backstrokes, then increase to full, smooth strokes. Cut with the blade at approximately a 45° angle to the surface of the wood.

A **nail set** is placed on the head of a finishing or casing nail and tapped with a hammer to set the nailhead below the wood's surface. This technique is used for finish carpentry, such as installing moldings.

Adjustable frame

A **hacksaw** can cut plastic and metal materials, such as pipes and bolts. Its fine-toothed blade fits into an adjustable frame.

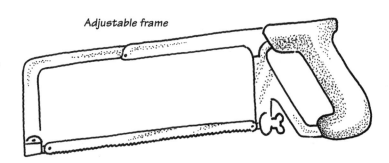

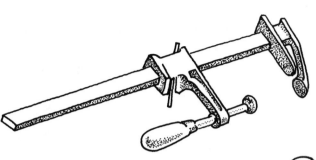

Bar clamps. come in several lengths—up to 6 feet long—but an 18-inch clamp is a good multipurpose tool. Because the jaws can be opened quickly and easily, a bar clamp is helpful for many different jobs.

If you'll be connecting or disconnecting threaded pipes and fittings, you'll need two **pipe wrenches**—one to hold the pipe, the other to turn the fitting.

For jobs that require cutting thin metal—flashing and gutter materials, for instance—**tin snips** are necessary.

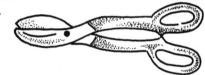

A lightweight **torpedo level** is handy for hanging pictures, setting up bookshelves, leveling washing machines, and other jobs that require finding true level. This type, which may have a magnetic strip along one edge, is small enough to fit conveniently in a toolbox. To check level, be sure the bubble is centered exactly between the two lines on the glass tube.

A flat **pry bar** is necessary for almost any type of tear-out or removal job. Use it to pull nails and pry apart materials.

Sockets

A socket wrench, consisting of a ratchet drive for a range of sockets that fit standard sizes of nuts and bolt heads, is much easier and faster to use than a conventional wrench.

Ratchet drive

Allen wrenches are needed for turning tiny set screws used on some tools and appliances and for assembling some types of furniture. Many different sizes are available; a complete set is relatively inexpensive.

Home **T**ools and **M**aterials

Although many homeowners are reluctant to attempt most home improvement projects, nearly everyone has tried painting at one time or another. Given the right tools and some basic instruction, even those with little experience can usually achieve surprisingly good results.

Some people move on to bigger and better challenges, like applying wall covering such as wallpaper. Although this takes a little more finesse, it, too, is an achievable do-it-yourself project.

If you're interested in taking on your own painting or wallcovering project, you'll find the information here on selecting the appropriate tools helpful.

Wall brush

Sash brush

*It's best to buy **paintbrushes** when you buy the paint. That way, you can find brushes that are appropriate for the job. Natural bristles are best for oil/alkyd-based paint; synthetic bristles may be used for either water-based or oil/alkyd paints. Polyester bristles are preferred for detail work with water-based paints. High-quality brushes have long bristles that splay evenly when you press the brush against your hand.*

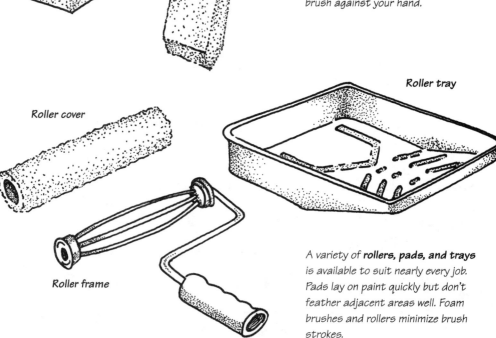

Paint pads

Roller tray

Roller cover

Roller frame

*A variety of **rollers, pads, and trays** is available to suit nearly every job. Pads lay on paint quickly but don't feather adjacent areas well. Foam brushes and rollers minimize brush strokes.*

A refillable **caulking gun** is used to apply fillers, seam sealers, and caulking compounds.

A **smoothing brush**, which is very wide and has a flat profile and short bristles, is used for smoothing wallcovering immediately following application.

Made for applying wallcovering paste, the **pasting brush** is about 6 inches wide and has long, coarse bristles.

Several different kinds of **scrapers** are made for removing paint. Some of these look like putty knives, but they're stiffer. You'll need a wallpaper scraper if you're removing old wallpaper. This tool has a flat, sharp blade and a long handle.

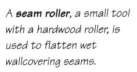

A **seam roller**, a small tool with a hardwood roller, is used to flatten wet wallcovering seams.

A **wire brush** is used to remove flaking paint from wood and rust from metal. Don't use a wire brush on surfaces that can be scratched.

If you plan to do any painting or wallpapering, you'll need a **ladder**. A 6-foot ladder is a good size for most indoor work, and handy for a variety of other tasks. Aluminum ladders are lightweight; wooden ladders tend to be less expensive and sturdier. When using a ladder, be sure it's on a firm, flat surface. Keep your weight centered and don't stand on the top two rungs.

Dollar for dollar, paints and stains can improve the look and durability of a house better than any other home product. They add color and interest to walls, highlight details and features, and most important of all, protect the materials they cover.

Water- or solvent-based? There are two types of house paints and stains: water-based (*latex*) and solvent-based (*oil* or *alkyd*). Water-based paint is thinned with water. Solvent-based paint is thinned with turpentine, a prepared paint thinner, or a similar solvent.

Because solvent-based paints dry to a harder finish and adhere better to new wood, poorly prepared surfaces, and metal, they traditionally have been favored for exterior siding and interior trim, as well as bathroom and kitchen walls, where durability is important. But because the solvents they contain emit noxious fumes, air quality standards have forced the development and use of a variety of water-based alternatives. The better varieties of these water-based finishes outperform their solvent-based counterparts for many uses.

For interior walls and exterior siding, water-based paints and stains are preferred because they are less likely to crack and peel, dry faster, emit less offensive fumes, and are much easier to clean up.

Solvent-based paints are preferred as primers for both solvent- and water-based top coats. They may be applied over old coats of either water- or solvent-based paints and stains.

Paint basics. Paint offers the highest level of protection for both indoor and outdoor surfaces. A paint is composed of pigments for color, a resin or binder for adherence, driers, and a base or carrier (water or solvent). Water-based paints have 100 percent acrylic resins, are at least 30 percent pigment, and contain special, high-quality thickeners. Generally, price is a good measure of quality, since high-quality paints contain greater amounts of better ingredients. Interior paints are usually less expensive than exterior varieties because they can utilize less durable, less expensive pigments and resins.

Paint is sold with varying degrees of luster, from flat to gloss. The luster is determined by the mix of pigment and binder; the more pigment and less binder, the flatter the paint. As a rule, the glossier a paint's finish, the more durable and washable the paint. On the other hand, flat paints do a much better job of hiding surface imperfections. That's why flat paints are usually used for walls and gloss or semigloss enamels highlight the trim. A paint that is termed an enamel is usually very smooth and hard because it has a high proportion of resins.

Formulations are constantly changing. If you're shopping for paint or stains, the best place to get up-to-date information on the right materials for the job you have in mind is a reputable paint dealer.

Exterior stains. When protected by overhangs, some types of wood shingling, such as cedar and redwood, can last a long time. But water, sunlight, and mildew take their toll on the outer surfaces of a house. Constant soaking and drying will cause wood to crack, split, and cup. Ultraviolet rays from the sun will break down wood fibers. Although paint is the most protective and commonly used exterior finish, a number of other finishes are common:

▲ **Clear water repellents.** Where the natural color and pattern of the wood are desired, a clear water-repellent finish is preferable; however, such a stain may darken the wood slightly or give it a damp look. Clear water repellents seal out the damaging effects of rain. Some types also block ultraviolet damage and mildew. Clear, film-forming finishes, such as urethane, varnish, and shellac, are not recommended for exterior surfaces because they peel. Recoating is required every few years.

▲ **Semitransparent stains.** Semitransparent stains contain water repellents and enough pigment to color wood without hiding the wood's natural grain. Such finishes don't form a protective barrier on the wood's surface; instead, they penetrate into the fibers. Semitransparent stains work only on new wood, and they work best on rough-textured wood, where absorption is high.

▲ **Opaque stains.** Opaque, solid-color stains are like thinned paint—they hide the wood grain or previous layers of paint or stain. Unlike semitransparent stains, they form a surface film that, like paint, offers good protection but can peel over time.

▲ **Weathering stains.** Bleaching oils and stains are used on materials such as cedar sidings to give a weathered look and moderate protection. They last about two or three years; a top coating of water repellent every year or two is usually necessary.

Primers. Before top coats of paint are applied, primers are used on many surfaces to ensure a good bond. Raw wood and metal are coated with an alkyd primer; galvanized metal is primed with a special water-based primer. Dry concrete and plaster walls and gypsum wallboard are treated with a latex or PVA (polyvinyl acetate) primer. Knots and pitch pockets in wood are sealed with an alcohol-based primer/sealer.

Either a water- or oil/alkyd-based top coat can go over an oil/alkyd-based primer or paint, but an oil/alkyd-based top coat should not be applied over a water-based primer or paint.

CHOOSING THE RIGHT FINISH

Surface	Recommended Finish
New wood siding	One base coat of water repellent, alkyd primer partially tinted to finish color, acrylic/latex top coat
Exterior trim	One base coat of alkyd primer, two coats of 100 percent acrylic latex
Shingles, shakes, rough-sawn siding	Clear wood preservative with fungicide and mildew retardant in humid areas. Optional finishes: Semitransparent stains
Aluminum or steel	Alkyd primer and 100 percent acrylic top coat
Gypsum wallboard (drywall)	PVA sealer over new drywall and two coats of acrylic latex
New interior trim	Alkyd primer partially tinted to finish color and 100 percent acrylic enamel top coat

Home Tools and Materials

Of all the materials that go into building a typical house, the most prevalent is wood. In one form or another, wood is normally used for the entire skeleton, plus wall, floor, and roof sheathings, finish floors, cabinets and shelves, and doors.

Wood that has been manufactured into cabinets, flooring, and other household materials is discussed under those subject headings throughout this book. Here, you'll find information on lumber and the various wood-based raw materials sold at lumberyards and home improvement centers.

It pays to brush up on basics before buying lumber. With the growing scarcity of wood, you can easily spend two or three dollars per foot for what appears to be a plain board. Knowing basic terminology will help you select the right materials and can save you a bundle.

Softwood and hardwood. Wood is classified as either softwood or hardwood, depending on whether it is from a deciduous tree (hardwood) or a conifer (softwood). Although most hardwoods do tend to be denser and harder than softwoods—oak and maple are much harder than pine—these terms do not refer to the wood's hardness. (Balsa, one of the softest woods, is a hardwood.)

Heartwood and sapwood. The nature of wood differs by the part of a log it's cut from. Heartwood, the older wood at the center of a log, is tighter-grained and resists decay more readily. Sapwood, close to the bark, is more porous.

Species. This is the type of tree the wood is from: oak, Douglas fir, spruce, and so on. Different woods have different qualities. Redwood, cedar, and cypress heartwood, for example, are naturally resistant to decay. That's why these woods are often preferred for outdoor use, such as for decking.

Green, dry, and kiln-dried. When wood is freshly cut, it is called green, or unseasoned. This does not refer to the color. Here, the term *green* means that the wood has a high moisture content (20 percent or higher) because it hasn't been dried yet. Although green wood is fine for some outdoor projects, it will warp, cup, and split as it dries. *Kiln-dried* (KD) lumber has been stacked and dried in a kiln.

Lumber is stamped with a moisture rating. S-GRN means it's green. S-DRY indicates that the material has less than 19 percent moisture. MC-15 means its moisture content is 15 percent or less.

LUMBER SIZING

Nominal Size	Surfaced Size (inches)	Nominal Size	Surfaced Size (inches)
1 x 2	¾ x 1 ½	2 x 6	1 ½ x 5 ½
1 x 3	¾ x 2 ½	2 x 8	1 ½ x 7 ¼
1 x 4	¾ x 3 ½	2 x 10	1 ½ x 9 ¼
1 x 6	¾ x 5 ½	2 x 12	1 ½ x 11 ¼
1 x 8	¾ x 7 ¼	4 x 4	3 ½ x 3 ½
1 x 10	¾ x 9 ¼	4 x 6	3 ½ x 5 ½
1 x 12	¾ x 11 ¼	4 x 8	3 ½ x 7 ¼
2 x 2	1 ½ x 1 ½	4 x 10	3 ½ x 9 ¼
2 x 3	1 ½ x 2 ½	4 x 12	3 ½ x 11 ¼
2 x 4	1 ½ x 3 ½		

Surfaced and rough. Before lumber leaves a mill, it may be dressed so that it is trimmed smooth, or *surfaced*, on two or more sides. Most lumber is surfaced on all four sides (S4S). Unsurfaced lumber is usually referred to as *rough*.

Lumber grading. Lumber is sorted and graded at the mill according to quality. Various grading agencies oversee this process; lumber is stamped with their identifiers. The factors that determine a board's grade include knots and other imperfections. The more numerous the defects, the lower the grade. Because there are several different grading parameters, depending upon the species, it's a good idea to discuss lumber grades with the dealer. You should inspect each board for defects before making a purchase.

Knots

Crook

Checking

Bow

Split

Cupping

Shake

Twist

Wane

Lumber is graded according to the number and type of defects it has. These are some of the possible types.

Plywood. Plywood is made from multiple layers of thin wood veneer, sandwiched, glued, and pressed together with the grain running perpendicular from layer to layer. The resulting panels are extremely strong.

Most plywood panels are 4 by 8 feet; longer panels are available. Common thicknesses range from ¼ to ¾ inch, but you can also buy 1 ⅛-inch-thick panels.

Plywood is manufactured in interior and exterior grades, depending on the glue used. A grade stamp on the plywood should also specify the quality of the face veneers. The letters A through D are used, rating the surfaces from best to worst. A panel marked A-C or A-D is a good choice where only one surface will be visible.

Board foot. This is a unit of measure equal to a piece of wood 1 inch thick, 12 inches long, and 12 inches wide. Lumberyards often quote prices for volume orders based on this unit. When buying individual pieces, you're more likely to be charged by the lineal foot for each piece of lumber.

Sizing. Surfaced lumber actually isn't the same as its nominal size. In other words, a two-by-six is not 2 inches thick and 6 inches wide. After it has been dried and surfaced, it is actually 1 ½ inches by 5 ½ inches. The equivalents to nominal sizes are given on the previous table. Lumber is stocked by most dealers in lengths that range from 6 to 20 feet, normally in even increments.

A variety of nails, screws, bolts, and other fasteners are integral to the construction of houses. Most of these are sold at hardware stores, lumberyards, and home improvement centers; some of the more specialized items are sold at builder's supply outlets.

Nails. Nails, sold by the pound or in 1, 5, and 50-pound boxes, come in different styles and sizes. Nail lengths may be designated by inches, but the term "penny," abbreviated as d, is more common. This term is a carry-over from long ago when it specified the price for a hundred hand-forged nails of a given size.

PENNY EQUIVALENTS	
Designation	**Length**
3d	1 ¼ inch
4d	1 ½ inch
6d	2 inch
7d	2 ¼ inch
8d	2 ½ inch
9d	2 ¾ inch
10d	3 inch
12d	3 ¼ inch
16d	3 ½ inch
20d	4 inch

Most nails are steel, but you can also buy stainless steel, bronze, and aluminum nails for specialty tasks. Galvanized nails, coated with zinc, are meant for rust-resistant use outdoors.

Screws. Screws are stronger than nails and, in most applications, are easily removed. Most are made of zinc-plated steel, but they also are made for special purposes from softer metals, such as brass and aluminum, and may have finishes that are plain, blued, dipped, brass plated, or chrome plated.

Conventional wood screws are measured by length, from ¼ inch to 6 inches, and the size or gauge of the unthreaded shank, from gauges 2 to 24. They have several different types of heads. Before you can drive them, you must drill pilot holes.

Drywall and deck screws have coarse threads along the entire length of their thin shanks, sharp points, and Phillips-type heads; they're designed to be driven with a Phillips screwdriver tip mounted in a power drill or electric screwdriver and generally don't require pilot holes. Lengths range from ¾ inch to 4 inches. Drywall screws have a black coating that isn't rust-proof; deck screws are galvanized for corrosion resistance.

Lag bolts and screw hooks and eyes. These fasteners come in larger sizes than wood screws, with shanks ranging from ¼ inch to ¾ inch in diameter (in $\frac{1}{16}$-inch increments). They're given a zinc coating for rust resistance. Lag bolt heads are meant to be driven with a wrench or a socket wrench. A pilot hole must be drilled and a washer fitted onto the lag bolt before it's driven. Screw hooks and eyes are used to hang various objects.

Bolts. Bolts are threaded to be used with nuts. Made from zinc-plated steel, they provide a strong hold. Many sizes and types are available. Bolts are classified by length, diameter, and number of threads per inch. A nut must match the bolt's thread count.

Wall fasteners. When fastening objects, such as bookshelves or mirrors, to walls, it is ideal to screw through the wall covering into the wall studs or ceiling joists that back the material. Where this isn't possible—between framing members, for instance—wall fasteners can be used as shown. Masonry walls also call for a fastener or anchor that will expand into a drilled hole.

An expanding anchor bolt is inserted in a hole drilled into solid masonry. As the nut is tightened, the anchor expands. Once in the wall, it can't be removed.

A spreading anchor has a sleeve that opens like an umbrella when a bolt is driven into it. Once installed, the bolt can be removed but the anchor is permanent.

A lead shield, inserted in a hole drilled in masonry, receives a screw or bolt that, when tightened, causes the shield to expand in the hole.

A toggle bolt is a two-part fixture consisting of a bolt and spring-loaded "toggle wings" that pop open on the backside of the wall material, providing a sound anchor for tightening the bolt.

Common

Box

Finishing

Casing

Spiral

Ring-shank

Masonry

Roofing

Nails are classified by shank size and type and by the shape of the head, as shown. The main types are common, box, finishing, and casing.

Bolts also are classified by type of head. Stove bolts and machine screws are turned with a screwdriver; hexagon-head and square-head machine bolts are held with a wrench. A carriage bolt head bites into the wood's surface so that the bolt won't turn when a nut is tightened. A stove bolt is turned with a screwdriver.

Hex   Square   Stove
        Carriage

Lag bolt   Screw eye

Screw hook

Lag bolts and screw hooks and eyes have many different household uses. Lag bolts feature heavy, partly threaded shanks. Screw hooks and eyes come in various sizes, from tiny cup hooks to very large utility hooks that can support heavy objects.

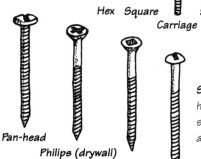

Pan-head

Philips (drywall)

Square-drive

Round-head

Screws are classified by type of head, each requiring a specific screwdriver tip: standard, Phillips, and square-drive.